Tsunami!

By Richard Martin Stern

Tsunami

Richard

Martin Stern

W·W·NORTON & COMPANY

New York · London

Published simultaneously in Canada by Penguin Books Canada Ltd.,
2801 John Street, Markham, Ontario L3R 1B4.
Printed in the United States of America.

The text of this book is composed in Times Roman,
with display type set in Inverserif Heavy Italic.
Composition and manufacturing by The Haddon Craftsmen, Inc.
Book design by Jacques Chazaud.

First Edition

Library of Congress Cataloging-in-Publication Data

Stern, Richard Martin, 1915–
Tsunami!

I. Title.
PS3569.T394T78 1988 813'.54 87–35017

ISBN 0-393-02529-2

W. W. Norton & Company, Inc., 500 Fifth Avenue, New York, N. Y. 10110
W. W. Norton & Company Ltd., 37 Great Russell Street, London WC1B 3NU

1 2 3 4 5 6 7 8 9 0

For D. A. S. with love
always

Author's Note

This is a work of fiction, and since it is not in any sense a *roman à clef,* it does not portray, nor is it intended to portray, any actual person, living or dead. If the characters seem real, I am flattered, because they are purely creatures of invention.

Encino Beach is also a locale of my own invention, one which years ago I used as the setting for a number of short stories, novelettes and serials in the old *Saturday Evening Post.* It does bear some resemblance to a real area, but I have taken liberties as seemed necessary.

Conventional wisdom has it that this area of Southern California, having a broad continental shelf, is *probably* immune to severe tsunami wave damage. I repeat, this is a work of fiction, not of prediction.

In the gathering of the background information and material that I used in my own way in the novel, I am indebted to numbers of persons beginning with a geology professor, name now long forgotten, who over fifty years ago introduced me to the details of the Krakatoa explosion of 1883 and first aroused my interest in the tsunami phenomena.

More recently I am indebted to several anonymous members of the Los Alamos National Scientific Laboratory staff who supplied me with information concerning our own thermonuclear tests out in the Pacific before the treaty signed by the USSR, Great Britain and the United States banned such tests; and to William G. Van Dorn of the Scripps Institution of Oceanography, most especially for his splendid book *Oceanography and Seamanship,* from which I have drawn much useful information and lore.

I am indebted also to: Carl Brandt, my literary agent, always the stout critic, staff and support; to Eric Swenson of W. W. Norton and Angela Plowden-Warlaw of Reader's Digest Condensed Books for their comments and suggestions; and to Barley Alison of Secker & Warburg, my British publishers, whose enthusiasms both in person and in transatlantic correspondence are always a spur.

Santa Fe, New Mexico

Tsunami!

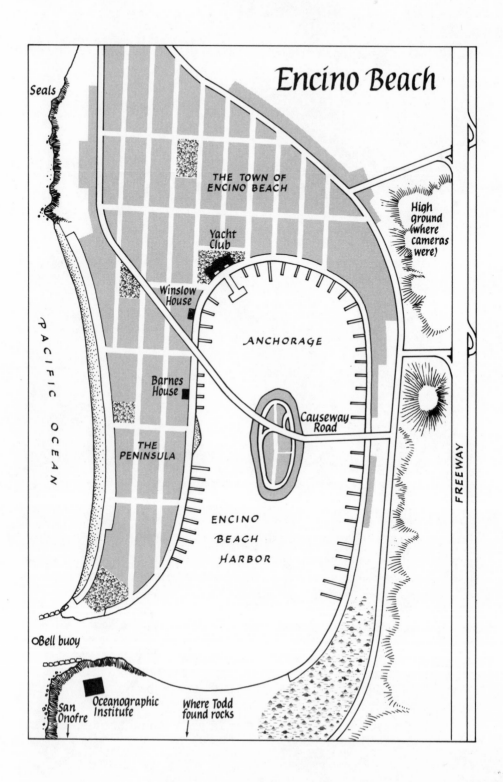

Prologue

Even before they reached the seven-thousand-foot depth, the steadily decreasing sunlight had disappeared altogether, and outside the small portholes there was only total blackness.

The water-temperature gauge showed merely minor fluctuations in its inexorable drop, which would eventually reach near freezing in their descent; and the pressures on the tiny submarine's hull would continue to build to an ultimate of approximately one-and-one-half tons per square inch, ample force to flatten the hulls of lesser vessels like so many beer cans.

The cramped and dimly lighted interior was filled with instrumentation and controls, condemning the two men to limited movements, which after a dive of several hours would be almost unbearably confining, with muscle spasms, cramps, becoming the norm, impossible to relieve by stretching.

Henry Larson, biologist, like Pete in tee shirt, jeans and sneakers, unshaven and wearing headphones, said, "Your second time down, right? I've pretty well lost count, but it's still a little different from a trip to the corner grocery store."

"A bit," Pete said—Peter Wayne Williamson, Ph.D., geophysicist, senior fellow at the Encino Beach, California, Oceanographic Institute. He was experiencing the same sensations as diving the first dive, he thought: not of claustrophobia, nor yet of leaving the real world behind, because these were in a way associated with the moment in scuba diving when the water closed above you, all too familiar.

But he was conscious that his pulse rate had risen, he knew that his blood pressure would have increased and, most markedly, he was aware of a heightened sense of alertness, of hearing, sight and touch as if an internal switch had been thrown the moment the water had risen above the portholes and the sky had disappeared, suddenly stepping up his total range of acuity.

"Three thousand meters," Henry said. "Still not much to see yet, but we might as well have some light anyway." He flipped a switch, and instantly the external floodlights turned the blackness beyond the portholes into a monochromatic world in which unidentified things moved without pattern.

Pete watched the scene without comment.

"Shark," Henry said. "See him? Big fellow. Fascinating swimmers." The sleek vision was almost instantly gone beyond the floodlight's range into the surrounding gloom.

"Geology's your bag, no?" Henry said then. He smiled, mocking himself. "But, then, they all come together, don't they? My father used to tell me that when he was going to school, chemistry and physics and biology and zoology and all the rest were separate, distinct disciplines. Hard to believe, isn't it?"

The man was merely making conversation, Pete thought. Why? To put him at ease? Or maybe even himself? He glanced at the depth gauge. "Four thousand meters," he said, and did the multiplication in his head: about thirteen thousand feet, and steadily descending.

"There," Henry said suddenly. "See it? The escarpment?"

"I see it."

Pete had been watching the dimly defined bulk of the submerged cliff coming into view for some time. They were descending into a massive canyon near the nineteenth parallel of the South Pacific, wide enough and deep enough to contain the Grand Canyon as a minor wrinkle, but still only a tiny part of the largest geological feature on earth, a submerged mountain range and rift system over forty thousand miles in length and in places six miles deep, extending into and through all four oceans of the world.

And of all of that, Pete was thinking, man has seen for himself only forty miles or so, which was why they were making this dive, the seventh of the expedition's planned fifteen-dive series funded by the Department of Defense and drawing upon the scientists of all of the nation's four oceanographic institutes—Woods Hole, Lamont, Scripps and Encino Beach. It was all part of the continuing efforts to unlock the secrets of the earth's origins and to understand undersea behavior of the oceans and ocean currents.

In a way it was like looking up at a clear night sky and seeing a few million of the thousands of billions of stars contained in the universe, and it produced a sense almost of infinity. But my view is more limited, Pete thought, because I am really interested in only one thing.

"I'm curious," Henry said. "I know the official poop, but I get the impression you're not just along for the joyride. Are you looking for something special?"

"Just rock. I'm a geologist, remember?"

"Geophysicist. Geologists hunt for oil and minerals."

"Some of us look at the oceans, too. Land *and* water."

The tiny submarine gave a sudden lurch, righting itself quickly with apparent ease. The feeling brought a faint queasiness to Pete's stomach. "The currents are funny sometimes," Henry said. "Thermal layers mixing? Out of my field. I'm interested in beasties."

"All kinds of possible causes," Pete said. "Too many to speculate." Maybe yes, maybe no; but this was neither the time nor the place for discussion.

He was staring fixedly at the bulk of the canyon wall, still too dim to be seen clearly, while at the same time he brought into focus in his almost photographic memory the way it had looked the last time he had seen it nineteen months ago. For long moments he held his breath as he looked, and then let it out with an inaudible sigh. Yes, damn it, there were changes, as he had anticipated!

Special, precision, wide-angle cameras to take before-and-after pictures would have been infinitely better, of course, but the cost of the equipment would have been prohibitive even if space in the tiny, crowded interior had been available; and the cameras the tiny submarine was equipped with, designed only to take close-up photos, were of no use at all for his purposes. So I do the best I can, Pete told himself, and probably no one will believe me anyway.

Almost fifteen thousand feet, and there, yes, was the broad ledge Pete remembered, curving off into the murky distance beyond the range of the floodlights. He studied it carefully, too, searching for the telltale changes.

"There is animal life in these depths," Henry said, "even though when you think about it, it's hard to believe, considering the enormous pressures and the scarcity of food, so the visible concentration of living matter is diffuse. But down on the bottom, now, even though the pressures are much greater, so is the food supply, and there is visible life galore. You'll see."

Pete wished the man would stop mouthing facts Pete knew as well as he did.

On the bottom of this great chasm, as Pete had seen before, was indeed another world of huge blood-red worms within forests of white tubes that looked as if they were made of plastic; of great clams related to, but far different from, those found in shallow mud flats on the earth's surface; of jets of water warmed by the earth's interior heat spewing dark clouds of mineral matter as from factory chimneys; of plant and animal food in far greater concentration than in surface waters; of crablike creatures able to withstand the enormous pressures of the depths and unable to survive in less; and, most important to Pete, of areas both seen and photographed where molten magma, the stuff of the earth's interior, oozed out through widening cracks in the sea floor to cool like taffy into strange formations, building more of the surface crust similar to the landmasses upon which man dwells.

He was quite familiar with all this, and with the demonstrable facts that vast tectonic plates, sections of the earth's crust, some of which in a manner of speaking bore entire continents upon their backs, were forever in motion, separating, colliding, altering seemingly without pattern the physical world we live in.

When they reached the bottom of the trench, he and Henry would busy themselves with the multitude of tasks assigned to this dive—manning the sampling, measuring, observing and gathering facilities crowded into this tiny craft. There were cameras, and the external claw which could be maneuvered to collect samples of rock or of living matter; and there were the registering dials and recording instruments to be read, and their information to be relayed via the electronic umbilical cord to the mother ship on the surface. All of this Pete would be involved in, in a sense earning his way, as he had on the previous dive nineteen months before.

But his interests right now were on none of this, but, rather, on the looming mass of the canyon walls that on either side came closer as they descended into the gigantic V-shaped abyss.

"Approaching nine thousand meters," Henry said. "A fair piece down, no?"

A little farther beneath the ocean's surface, Pete thought, than the summit of Mount Everest was above it, and yet still some thousands of feet above the deepest of the mountain range and rift system's areas. He was silent, his eyes still fixed upon the canyon walls, measuring against memory these fresh visual data, digesting them and storing them in his mind for later consideration, thought and speculation.

But already the uneasiness had begun, at last based on more than purely statistical suspicion.

❦

Astonishingly in retrospect, it began as a day very much like any other, with the first indications of a smog cloud already blurring the sharp outline of the ridge separating the Valley from the Los Angeles Basin itself.

Dan Garfield had the car radio tuned to the classical FM station now playing quietly in stereo a new recording of Mozart's Piano Concerto No. 19, Murray Perahia soloist, flowing, effortless music that once upon a time Garfield would have scorned as old-fashioned, out of step with the modern world. He had worn long hair then, too, he sometimes remembered these days, and had even tried a scraggly beard, which itched, and he had been convinced that no one in the world could match his young intellectual capabilities.

But you changed your tastes and your opinions as you found your way through your twenties and thirties—or you had damn well better adjust, as he occasionally had cause to think watching some who did not—and you were no longer the same person at forty-two that you had been at twenty, even though there were times when it seemed that the metamorphosis had been so effortless as to feel unreal.

The guard at the Garfield Associates electronics plant gate gave him an automatic quasi-military salute and did not even glance at the ID Garfield conscientiously held up as he drove through the raised barrier, up the hedge-lined road straight to the central building, where he parked in the slot that bore his name.

The guard at the front door said, "Good morning, Mr. Garfield," and the phrase was repeated by the receptionist inside, by two men just stepping out of the elevator and by the executive suite receptionist on the third floor. Garfield had a smile, a nod and a "good morning" for each.

The always efficient Helen was waiting in his inner office with her usual smile and inevitable greeting. Then immediately down to business, reading from the ever-present notebook.

"Baker, the Plant Three manager, would like to see you at your convenience. I have set the appointment tentatively at ten-thirty." One raised eyebrow asked the question her voice did not.

"Right," Garfield said, and wondered what bee was in Baker's bonnet now. Never mind. The man was easily dealt with.

"At nine-thirty," Helen said, "there is the engineering staff meeting. If you wish to attend." Again the raised eyebrow.

"Keep it open."

"At eleven o'clock there will be a conference call from Washington, DOD priority, and the chairman of the Armed Services Committee will be on the call as well."

Garfield took his time. "They're still pushing? They know our
. . . views. They're . . . dreaming." And I've damn well made that
plain, he thought, but did not say aloud. "What else?"

Helen's voice was toneless. "Mr. Case and Mr. Carmichael
would like to see you at nine o'clock. Mr. Case called. He said it was
urgent." No raised eyebrow this time.

"It frequently is," Garfield said. "Urgent, I mean. Never mind.
I'll see them, of course." He glanced at his watch. "Fifteen minutes.
Mail to see?"

"On your desk," Helen said, and turned away. At the door she
paused and turned back. "Your luncheon date with Miss Anderson
is noon, you remember. Angelo's. I have booked your usual table."

All quite normal so far.

Paul Case and Walker Carmichael arrived precisely as the digital clock on Garfield's desk registered 9:00. The punctuality, Garfield
thought, would have been Paul's doing, his facts-and-figures mental-
ity demanding precision. Walker, the salesman, marched to a less
regulated drumbeat. "Paul," he said, "Walker, good morning. Sit
down, please." He watched Case close the door carefully and take
his seat with his usual neat movements. Carmichael plumped into an
overstuffed chair and looked uneasy. Garfield waited.

Case said slowly, carefully, articulating with great clarity, "The
Atlas offer is still on the table, Dan."

"We've already discussed that."

Carmichael cleared his throat. "They've sweetened the pot. By
six and a half percent." He emphasized the figures.

"Which works out for each of us," Case said, "counting stock
and stock options to very close to—"

"I'm not even interested in the figures," Garfield said. "They're
meaningless. We built this place from nothing, and each of us is
already taking out more than he can ever spend—"

"The figures," Case said, "do not even include continuing royalties on your personal patents, Dan. You would be an enormously
wealthy man. Enormously. We all would, as far as that goes."

The trick, he had long ago learned, was never to show your
temper or even your impatience. The politician's or debater's smile

and quiet logic were the tools of persuasion. And if persuasion failed, there was always at last resort a show of the authority that had become habitual over the years. "We're all three still young," Garfield said. "And we're still growing. Our reputation, which is precisely what Atlas wants to buy, guarantees that we will continue to grow. And prosper. We—"

Carmichael, the salesman, said, "How much is enough, Dan? There's a big, wide, wonderful world out there, and I for one want to enjoy it. All of it." He seemed to hesitate.

"Go on, Walker," Garfield said. "Spell it out."

Indecision was plain, struggling with the salesman's confidence. Indecision, and perhaps trepidation, too? The office was still.

"Okay," Carmichael said at last, decision made. "I'm tired of the place. I want out. No more sales pitches, no more flying trips, no more haggling and arguing with gourd-headed bureaucrats and congressmen, no more service headaches . . ." The words ran down. "That's the bottom line, Dan."

He could recognize and face finality when he saw it, another of the strengths he had somehow acquired along the way. And he could make decisions on the spot. "All right," Garfield said. "If you've made up your mind, Walker—"

"I have."

"—then Paul and I can buy you out. Our partnership agreement provides for that. We—"

Paul Case cleared his throat with an astonishingly loud sound, almost a bark. "Uh," he said, "negative, Dan." And again the office was suddenly still, an almost deafening silence. "We have had competent legal advice, and there will be no difficulties—"

"Except me," Garfield said, at last letting the authority show. But he did manage to conceal the temper. "I won't go along, period. And I won't even bother to repeat my reasons."

Paul Case took off his glasses and looked at them. From his breast pocket he took a folded, clean handkerchief and in the silence began to polish the lenses automatically. He looked up at last. "You have no say, Dan," he said then, enunciating each word with clarity. "You are president and CEO, and we have always deferred to your judgment, which up to now has been infallible. But the partnership agreement still obtains. We have had legal verification of that. And in this instance, you are outvoted. We have instructed our attorneys to notify Atlas that its tender is accepted, and transfer of ownership will go forward."

Case stood up then, straight and as tall as he could manage. "I believe there is nothing more to be said." He was gone, and the door closed gently.

Carmichael heaved himself out of the large chair. "Sorry about this, Dan," he said, but his voice lacked its hearty quality. "But their offer was too good to turn down." Some of the heartiness returned. "You're going to be rolling in it, boy, absolutely rolling, your continuing royalties plus what each of us is getting." He shook his head and produced a smile. "Gotrocks Garfield. That's you. Better try to get used to it."

As simple, as unexpected and as devastating as that.

❧

"This is purely informal," the assistant secretary said, looking around the table, "a seminar-type discussion, or"—he produced a quick smile—"as I believe our Madison Avenue friends call it, a brainstorming session." The smile faded. "The indications are that the French are planning another nuclear test in the South Pacific. What are we to make of that?"

The DOD (Department of Defense) man said, "So what else is new? They've been doing it for years. It's a nuisance, but they give warning in the area, and the South Pacific is so damned big. . . ." He shook his head. "No big deal. They'll kill some fish, is all."

The scientific adviser said, "Unless—" And then he stopped and shook his head. "Too many variables, an equation full of unknowns. Will this be another fission test? Or is there a possibility of fusion?"

The assistant secretary said, "At present unclear. Is it important?"

"The difference," the scientific adviser said, "is between kilotons—that is to say, thousands of tons—and megatons, millions of tons. Of TNT, that is. The difference can be almost qualitative rather than merely quantitive, a difference of kind rather than just degree."

"It's still the hell of a big ocean," the DOD man said.

The scientific adviser smiled. "Agreed."

"And we have no way of stopping it, anyway," an undersecretary said. "We've exhausted all diplomatic channels."

The assistant secretary was looking at the scientific adviser. "Give us a worst-case scenario."

Still smiling, "Insufficient data," the scientific adviser said.

"Give it a wild guess. What could possibly be the worst result?" The assistant secretary hesitated. "Are you thinking . . . tidal waves?"

"Tsunami is the proper word," the scientific adviser said. "Caused by some kind of seismic disturbance, an earthquake, volcanic explosion, that kind of thing. They can be . . . devastating. And their extent can be almost unbelievable."

"An example?"

"In 1960," the scientific adviser said, "an earthquake on the coast of Chile of magnitude in excess of seven-point-five on the Richter scale sent out tsunami that crossed the entire Pacific Ocean. On the way, they, the so-called tidal waves, devastated two square miles of downtown Hilo in Hawaii, modern buildings of reinforced concrete destroyed, and then continued their course to cause some three hundred and fifty million dollars in damages in the harbors of Honshu and Hokkaido in Japan, a total distance in excess of ten thousand miles, the waves traveling at speeds in excess of four hundred and fifty miles per hour."

He looked around at them all, smiling again. "The Japanese have records going back to the tenth century of earthquakes and tsunami generated by them, some of which are reputed to have killed as many as a hundred thousand people. The records are . . . interesting."

"And," the DOD man said, "you're thinking that a test in the South Pacific, even a fusion test, hydrogen bomb device, could set off that kind of thing? Poppycock! We ran tests ourselves and nothing happened."

The scientific adviser disliked arguments or even theoretical discussions with laymen. They rarely led to anything but confusion. "No doubt you're right," he said. "I was just giving examples."

Part I

For the first time in his adult life that he could remember, Dan
Garfield felt over his depth, not merely uncertain, but totally ignorant and unable to cope with the situation in which he found himself.
Helpless was the word that sounded in his mind like a drumbeat of
doom.

"To sum up," the lawyer said, "the partnership agreement is
valid and your partners are within their rights to overrule your
wishes. You could, of course, initiate a lawsuit to prevent the sale of
your company, but in my opinion it would be a futile gesture."

Foolish was what he meant, Garfield thought, and found the
word apt to describe himself and his predicament. And this was
worst of all because he had always prided himself on his logic and
his knowledge of facts in governing his actions and his life. A smart
fellow, Dan Garfield, clear-sighted, prescient, suddenly and without
warning blind-sided, as they said in football, by two men he had

always considered completely under his domination and control. The shock still stunned him. *Humiliation* was also the word. He watched as in a nightmare as negotiations proceeded.

The Atlas people with their Fortune 500 standing and their multibillion-dollar balance sheet were polite, even affable, but their tone held a hint of condescension. Hawkins, the Atlas CEO, flew out from New York in one of the corporate jets for the final hour of the closing and even had a few words alone with Garfield.

"A nice little company you've built up here," Hawkins said. "It will fit admirably into our scheme of things. If you choose to stay on in your present position, with semiautonomy understood, we'll be pleased to have you aboard."

He actually used the nautical word, ludicrous as it sounded, Garfield noted, and without even a hint of jocularity. But Garfield was in no mood for even a smile. Stay on, in effect as a flunky, which was what "semiautonomy" would work out to mean, after being from the start in total and absolute control? Never. "I think not," he said as calmly as he could.

"Suit yourself," Hawkins said as if he could not have cared less whether Garfield stayed or not. He glanced at his Rolex. "Time to go. I'm due in Dallas." He held out his hand. "Nice to meet you." His grip was firm, confident, assured—and impersonal.

The Atlas chief counsel said, "You are about to become an enormously wealthy man, Mr. Garfield. Congratulations." Was there envy in his tone? "No doubt you have plans?"

"I'm going to blow myself to a new pair of sneakers," Garfield said. "My old ones are worn through."

Everybody assumed that the sale was his idea, and the admiration expressed for his business acumen merely made matters worse. I am a sham, he told himself, but could not bring himself to tell anyone else, not even Maude Anderson, especially Maude. He had had his chance, and not taken it, that first day at lunch at Angelo's.

She had worn—he could see it now—a dress of a particular shade of blue that accentuated the tone of her eyes and the even, glowing tan her skin never seemed to lose. "You're preoccupied," she said, and smiled. "But, then, you usually are—except sometimes when I do think I get your whole attention. As you get mine." The smile spread. "But that's not in public."

Usually he enjoyed vague references to their intimacy, but today it made him uncomfortable. Everything was suddenly changed. "You've been away," he said. "I've missed you. Good trip?"

"Old friends. Tahoe. Some water-skiing, much talk, a job offer." The suddenness of her smile always startled him as it transformed her face and lighted her eyes. "I like it here in the L.A. area better," she said. "And if I sell a house or two every now and again, I have all I need." The smile disappeared. "You *are* preoccupied, Dan. What is it?"

"Hunger. Shall we order?" And so the moment had passed and not returned.

Running into Tom Winslow was sheer chance, on the street almost immediately following the Atlas closing. Tom's physician's eyes did not miss much. "You look," he said, "as if somebody just stole your candy."

"I lost my taste for sweets years ago."

"Then you're not sleeping well." The tone was light, but there was an undercurrent of seriousness, too. "And from what I read in the financial pages, I don't wonder. Big negotiations. High finance." His eyes had not left Dan's face. "Clara tells me there is even a piece about you in *Time* making you out as a genius."

He was beginning to feel that he was playing a part in a script over which he had no control. "They usually manage to skew the facts," he said. "If they said that, they're a hundred and eighty degrees wrong."

Tom glanced at his watch. "How about a cup of coffee? My next patient isn't due for a half hour"

They sat in a booth in relative seclusion. "We go back how long?" Tom said. "Twenty years?"

Almost exactly. Garfield had been a young Ph.D. in electronics and Tom had just been finishing his hospital residency in internal medicine when they met. "About that," Garfield said.

"You had big ideas and I was going to cure the world's illnesses. Your ideas succeeded spectacularly"—Tom smiled suddenly—"and I haven't even made a dent in all the bellyaches and ulcers and hypertensions man is prey to." He was still studying Garfield with his internist's eye, and his tone was almost casual. "Clara's opening the house down at the beach. She and Lucy are moving down for the summer. I'll get down mostly on weekends." And with no change of tone he added, "Why don't you go down for a little rest and keep them company? Frankly, boy, you look as if you could use a change." His tone was serious.

Garfield wore a wry smile, turned inwards, mocking his own thoughts. "It shows?" Trying to make it light.

"It does." Tom stood up abruptly. "Be right back," he said, and was gone, walking purposefully. He was back in a matter of minutes, smiling as he slid again into his seat. "All set," he said. "Clara's delighted. She's looking forward to having a man around the house."

"Now, wait a minute. Maybe after she's settled in, a weekend when you go down, that kind of thing. But not just . . . dumping me in her lap like this when she's busy. She—"

"I told you. She's delighted, looking forward to having you there. And I'd say you need it bad even if I don't know why." Tom paused. "Give me one good reason against."

There was the trouble. He didn't have any reason against. Change, any change, would be an improvement, distraction from his bitter thoughts. And he knew Encino Beach and its sun and its surf and its laid-back style, no hurry for much of anything. He sat silent, tempted but reluctant.

"You can change light bulbs," Tom said, "and put that electronics expertise to work fixing the toaster. It's kaput." He finished his coffee at a gulp and stood up again. "From what I read, you can afford the check." He waited briefly, but there was no answer. "I told Clara you'd be down this afternoon," he said. "If you don't appear, she'll start worrying." He was smiling again. "See you, boy." He was gone.

❀

Once Encino Beach was just another seacoast harbor town south of Los Angeles, with a commercial fishing fleet, a boatbuilding yard, a single yacht club and scattered cottages owned by visitors who enjoyed sailing, then not yet popular as a sport in the Southern California area, or who owned small power cruisers, usually with deepwater fishing gear aboard.

The harbor was natural and protected against storms by the low, narrow peninsula. Later stone jetties were added, extending the natural channel for further protection.

In town there was a restaurant and a bowling alley with a good-sized ballroom which in time became a focal point for Los Angeles youth on school and college vacations, sufficiently popular that peripatetic big-name bands of the era were attracted for one- or two-night stands between big-city engagements.

After World War II, as Southern California exploded in population and money became plentiful, larger and more expensive houses were built in all areas fronting on or near the harbor. Thirty- by-ninety-foot waterfront lots (no building allowed within eighteen inches, of the property line) quickly changed ownership, and houses twenty-seven feet wide eventually began to fetch prices in the six- and seven-figure range.

On holidays and summer weekends the broad beach on the ocean side of the peninsula, running northwest-southeast, was filled with visitors who romped in the breakers or sunned themselves, while serious surfers transported their boards to San Onofre or Malibu, where by quirks of underwater topography, the incoming swells, feeling the shallow water drag unevenly, piled up surf of sometimes ferocious, even terrifying size, and a surfer cutting diagonally across the breaking wave front might disappear beneath the curl and sometimes emerge triumphantly, still balanced, crouching on his board as he rode into shallower, calmer water.

When the freeway came, it bypassed Encino Beach well inland on higher ground, leaving the old, overburdened, coast highway at near sea level to carry the traffic, with only a handful of crowded roads leading from it away from the ocean to higher ground.

Wall-to-wall people, Peter Williamson liked to describe it, and the phrase was apt. More and more, Encino Beach had become a year-round residential area, a Los Angeles bedroom community, where, during rush hours, commuting traffic moved bumper to bumper almost by fits and starts.

෨

His Honor, Jimmy Silva, mayor of Encino Beach, was an insurance man by trade, native son, product of three generations of local
commercial fishermen. In his youth he had distinguished himself by
taking on and thoroughly whipping in a bloody fistfight the bully
bodyguard of one of the number of early postwar film stars who kept
oversized power cruisers in slips in Encino Beach largely for party
and tax purposes.

Now in his fifties, Silva was getting thick around the middle,
something he attempted to conceal by wearing wildly patterned
aloha shirts, their short sleeves amply displaying his hairy, brawny
forearms.

He knew all the longtime locals and a good share of the regular
visitors. He had known Joe Hines, Encino Beach harbormaster, since
youth. Joe Hines sat in his office now, the door to the reception room
closed.

"Too many people," Joe Hines was saying, "too many boats, too
damn much money floating around in the whole country, if you ask
me." Hines was tall and lean and weathered, once a prized crewman
for big ocean-racing sailing yachts.

"More people," Jimmy said, "more money. Simple as that. You
got to catch up."

Joe was not to be diverted from his subject. "Not an empty
slip or an empty mooring in the whole damn harbor. Anywhere
up and down the coast, comes to that. You want to buy a boat,
first thing you better think is where'n hell you're going to keep
it."

"We're going to help solve that," His Honor said, and took
rolled architect's drawings from a shelf beside his desk. "Have a look
here."

The first drawing was a plan sketch of multiple houses, complete with swimming pools, each house fronting on a canal with
its own slip and moored sail or power yacht. Joe studied the plan
carefully.

"Neat, huh?" His Honor said.

Joe's eyes were still on the sketch. "And just where in hell are you figuring to put this?"

"Over in the back bay where you and I used to go clamming on those mud flats."

Joe looked up then. "Dredge her out?"

"Dredge her out and build her up, solid landfill. If we had big tides to contend with now, we might have problems." The mayor shook his head. "But we don't. A few feet, is all."

"You in real estate now? I can't keep up with you. Says *In*surance on the door."

"Just spreading my bets," His Honor said. His grin was complacent. "I rub elbows with some of these city operators. I listen. All you're interested in is boats."

Joe Hines was studying the sketch again, his lips moving as he counted the number of houses shown. He said at last, "Over fifty. That's going to take a lot of dredging and filling." He looked at the mayor. "And a whole hell of a lot of money." The statement asked a question.

"Simple," His Honor said. "Bond issue. They're big now, municipal bonds, tax-free income, what they call tax shelter. All that money you were talking about has to be put somewhere."

Joe Hines sighed and stood up. "All I got to say is we already got too many boats in this harbor, and too many of them owned by piss-to-windward landlubbers who don't know how to handle them. If we ever had to get all those boats out to sea—"

"Now just why in hell would we have to get all the boats out to sea? Tell me that."

"Dunno," Joe Hines said. "But what happened up at Crescent City when those tidal waves hit back in '64—"

"This isn't Crescent City, goddamn it," Jimmy Silva said. "This here is Encino Beach, and we got the peninsula and the breakwater and those fancy new jetties you howled about building that cost an arm and a leg—" He stopped, breathing hard. "What's got into you, anyway? That Crescent City thing was more than twenty years ago!"

Joe Hines glanced again at the drawings. He looked as if he wanted to spit. "This is what you call progress?"

"That's the word," His Honor said.

ଷ

Dan Garfield turned off the coast highway and drove slowly
along Encino Beach's main street, which here at its beginning offered
a stunning view of the harbor, the bay flat and shining in the late-
afternoon sun, the houses cheek by jowl lining the shore, the thousands of pleasure boats riding on their moorings or resting in their
slips. The moored sailboats, Garfield noted, all pointed up the bay,
their deep keels responding uniformly to the outgoing tidal current.
The high-sided cabin cruisers were relatively unaffected, pointing
whichever way errant wind currents swung them. The inexorable
laws of physics, neat, predictable, determined their behavior. Physics, science in general were a world unlike that of humans and one
in which Garfield had always felt at home. By comparison, the
unpleasant memories of that closing, Hawkins's attitude of condescension, the totally unexpected behavior of Paul Case and Walker
Carmichael—all of this was to him incomprehensible and aberrant,
abiding by no rules but those of self-indulgence. Somehow, some
way, he was going to retaliate. Just how, he did not yet know.

Well, down here at Encino Beach maybe he could relax, re-
charge his exhausted batteries and somehow figure out how to regain
the identity he could not help feeling that he had lost. Face it, he told
himself, all you are now is rich. And that in no way compensated for
lack of . . . stature in his own eyes and in the eyes of others.

It was in this frame of mind that he drove slowly down the
familiar streets to the Winslow house.

Clara was in the kitchen, in cutoff jeans, sneakers and a short-
sleeved blouse, already showing the first faint coloring of what would
be a summer tan. She had always been a stunning woman, Garfield
thought, and the years—she was now just forty—had, if anything,
increased her attractiveness with a calmness and an unmistakable quality of quiet confidence that had been unformed in the early
years. Her smile seemed to light up the entire room. "Welcome,
stranger!" she said. "I could hardly believe it when Tom said you
were coming." Her kiss was warm with the intimacy of long friend-
ship.

"You are good to take me in." Words were banal and totally inadequate. He was already beginning to relax.

"And Lucy is in a complete tizzy. You represent glamour."

"Tinsel, nothing more." The feeling was again strong that he was playing a strange part, speaking lines that lacked conviction, masking the truth. "I'm simply one of the unemployed."

"Good. Then Lucy and I can monopolize you." Her eyes went beyond him. "Here she is now."

Garfield turned, stared and spoke the first word that did not seem to have been scripted. "Migod!" he said, and meant it.

Lucy was now sixteen, and Garfield had known her since she was a baby, but not like this, suddenly blossomed into rounded womanly curves that filled her scant bikini, the awkwardness of adolescence entirely gone. He shook his head in slow wonder, conscious of Clara's amused smile. "I didn't quite expect this," he said.

"Big deal," Lucy said. "It happens to all of us." And then, suddenly shy, added: "Hi. We haven't seen you in a long time." The shyness deepened, and a faint blush appeared. "You're . . . famous now. And rich."

And what did one say to that? Garfield hoped that his smile showed no embarrassment.

Clara said, "You know where your room is, Dan. And you'll have time for a drink before dinner." Temporary release.

There was a visitor in the kitchen when Garfield returned after unpacking his bag. "Pete Williamson," Clara said. "Pete's our next-door neighbor."

A middle-sized, muscular, deeply tanned man in swim trunks, a tee shirt and ragged sneakers, wearing at least a full day's growth of whiskers. His handshake was firm, and his smile friendly. "Welcome to the beach."

"Pete," Lucy said, "is an oceanographer at the Encino Beach Oceanographic Institute. He's just back from the bottom of the ocean way out in the South Pacific. He brought me some coral."

"Don't give away everything, Princess. Our affair is just between us, remember?" Amused affection was plain.

Clara said, "Why don't you two take drinks out on the porch and leave Lucy and me to produce some dinner? You'll stay, Pete?"

"With pleasure."

The two men sat on the porch in the fading light, looking out over the bay, the boats, the houses jammed together. "It grows on you," Pete said. "The place, and the life."

"I've known it for quite a while."

Pete nodded. "But knowing it and living in it are two different things. From what I read, you've been too busy for this relaxed life."

True. And also uncomfortably close to the bone. Garfield changed the subject. "The bottom of the ocean, Lucy said. Hyperbole?"

Pete had a quick grin. "Not exactly. Minisub, diving. Near the equator out in that big damned Pacific, on the bottom at a bit over nine thousand meters."

"Thirty thousand feet or so," Garfield said, and looked at the man with fresh interest. "One of the trenches? Doing what, if it isn't a secret?"

"Pursuing a pet theory. Long story." Pete waved one hand in a vague gesture. "An unpopular theory in some circles." Again the quick grin. "Many circles, including my own hierarchy." He was silent for a few moments, staring out at the bay, the grin gone. "Oceanographers, most scientists, I guess, tend to be . . . conservative."

"And you're rocking the boat, making waves?"

"Something like that."

Garfield sipped his drink, his eyes on the bay, his thoughts running close to home, to his own experience. "A lot of people say something can't be done or it isn't so," he said. "Even when you show them the facts, they won't accept them."

"You sound as if you've been there."

"Once or twice." And very recently, he thought. "I think I'd like to hear your long story—if you're willing to tell it, that is."

"It's pretty far-out. And what data I have are . . . sketchy."

"I'd still like to hear it."

Pete hesitated and then produced the quick grin again. "Done," he said. "It'll be a pleasure to talk to somebody new. How about a walk tomorrow, over on the ocean side, say, about noon?"

"I can't think of anything I'd like better," Garfield said, and suddenly realized that he meant it.

2

Lucy was in the kitchen when Garfield came from his room the next morning. "Mom's gone up to town on errands," Lucy said. "I'm coping. What do you like for breakfast? Fruit juice? Omelet? Bacon?"

"Sounds elegant." It was hard to take his eyes from the girl's young, blooming beauty. "I can't get over the change in you," Garfield said, "even though it was, as you said, inevitable."

"I'm trying to get used to it, too." The shy smile had appeared. "It isn't always easy the way some people stare at me."

"I can't blame them."

Lucy changed the subject. "Juice is in the refrigerator. I'll whomp up the rest." She busied herself at the stove, her movements quick and deft. "I read that story about you in *Time*." Her face was turned from him, so he could not see her expression. "They say you're a genius."

"I'm a fraud." Strangely, he found no pain in the saying.

"Some fraud, raking in all that loot. How does cheese omelet grab you?"

"Wonderful."

"You and Pete hit it off, didn't you? He's a nice guy, maybe a little flaky in some ways, but real nice."

Garfield sipped his juice. "How, flaky?"

"Oh, he talks to seals, and gulls, and there's this moray eel out in the rocks of the point—you don't mess with moray eels, you know?"

"I know."

"Well, Pete says this one's getting to know him. He blows bubbles at him and makes noises almost like conversation, and when I say, 'Hey! He doesn't know you, Pete!' Pete just says, 'How do you know that?' and grins in the way he has. It's . . . weird." In the silence she turned from the stove to study Garfield's face carefully; a tiny frown formed between her eyebrows. "What're you thinking?"

Garfield was smiling. "That maybe there's more to Pete Williamson than shows on the surface."

Lucy turned back to her cooking. "I used to be scared of you, did you know that? Funny, now I'm not anymore."

Garfield felt as if he had just been knighted.

He helped with the dishes after breakfast. That chore done, "You'll be okay?" Lucy said. "I mean, Mom said to see you don't feel left out."

"I'm just fine. I'm going to the library, some reading to do. And then I'll meet Pete over on the ocean side of the peninsula. Does all that fit?"

"Right on. I've got things to do, too."

The smiling local librarian said, "Dr. Peter Williamson? But, of course. We have all his published monographs and papers. Was there anything in particular?"

"I'd like to look through all of them," Garfield said, "if you please."

It was quarter to twelve when he returned the papers, thanked the librarian and set out for his meeting. For the first time in many days the bitter memories of recent events were not impinging on his consciousness. Instead, he found himself thinking eagerly of this talk with Pete Williamson. There were many questions in his mind.

Pete, clean-shaven and dressed in faded jeans, tee shirt and the same ragged sneakers, was waiting on a bench facing the ocean, watching the lines of swells as they marched in, slowed as they felt the bottom drag, grew in height to become white-topped and then broke upon the sands in endless procession. Their regularity, Garfield thought as he sat down on the bench, was almost hypnotic in its effect. "Good morning," he said, and waited quietly.

Pete said, "You still want to hear my . . . far-out theories?"

"Very much."

Pete nodded. "Okay." He was silent for a moment, obviously gathering his thoughts. "July twenty-fifth, 1963—ring any bells?"

Garfield closed his eyes. "Twenty-four years ago. I was eighteen, just finished my junior year at Cal Tech." He opened his eyes then and smiled. "I had managed to grow a straggly beard and I walked around with a portentous expression and I was convinced that nobody on earth was as smart as I was." He shook his head. "The date has no connotations. Unless it had to do with electronics, I wouldn't even have noticed what was happening. My head was in the clouds."

Pete nodded as if he had expected no other answer. "The U.S., Russia and Britain signed a treaty," he said, "banning all nuclear testing except underground."

Garfield said, "Oh." He paused contemplatively. "I'm beginning to see the light. Go on."

"Only those three were signatories," Pete said. "France, for instance, has never felt bound by the treaty."

"Hence their continuing testing in the South Pacific?"

"You catch on quick."

"I spent the morning in the library," Garfield said, "but I'm not sure I see the connection."

Pete nodded again. "Without the data, you wouldn't or couldn't." He picked up a handful of sand and toyed with it as he put his thoughts in order. Abruptly he dusted his hands clean and faced Dan.

"The French sometimes don't listen very carefully. Before the treaty was signed, we had people, geophysicists and others at Los Alamos, plotting and predicting the possible underwater effects of the testing we were planning. Big stuff. What could or would be the effect of exploding devices in the, say, multimegaton range? That kind of thing, also down in the South Pacific. When the treaty was signed, all that research stopped, but the collected and projected data were still available. You're with me so far?"

Garfield was silent. He merely nodded.

"When the French started testing," Pete said, "we warned them of some of the predicted results. As I said, sometimes they don't listen very good, and as a result, one of their land sites they figured was safe is now eight feet underwater. So are the buildings they had put up."

Garfield thought about it in the way he had—total concentration, everything else wiped from his mind, factors both known and unknown set in order to form equations which could or could not be solved, results examined from all sides.

He said at last, "I think I'm seeing at least the direction you're going, but—" He shook his head. "Maybe it's best if you start at the beginning. I don't want to assume knowledge I don't have." That kind of behavior was for pompous fools. "I'll listen."

"Right," was Pete's only comment. "A quick once-over." And, with a broad gesture at the shining ocean that lay before them: "The Pacific, seventy million square miles of it, one-third of the earth's surface, the biggest and deepest of all the oceans. Those swells"—he gestured at the endless rows marching in past the bell buoy that bowed to their rhythm and tolled their number—"have come maybe five, six thousand miles in lines that are usually so straight that hundreds of years ago in the South Pacific Polynesians used to navigate their sailing canoes, the big ones, hundreds of miles from island to island just by steering at given angles to the lines of swells." He paused. "So the ocean is predictable, no? Only it isn't. Not by a long shot."

The man was good, Garfield thought briefly as he listened. He knew his subject and was able to explain it—within the scientific community a rare ability indeed, as he knew well.

"Counterclockwise from the top," Pete said now, and gestured, describing a circle as he spoke, "Alaska and Russian Kamchatka to the north; Indonesia, Philippines, Japan to the west; Australia, New Zealand, Antarctica to the south; and to the east the coasts of South, Central and North America: that more or less defines the Pacific Basin. Ringed with volcanoes *and* fracture zones with more volcanoes like Kilauea in Hawaii dotted here and there, and more fracture zones on the sea bottom out in the middle where it's deepest. Called the 'Ring of Fire,' the whole area. With reason. It's in flux, the whole damned thing. You probably read all that at the library, but let me put it in perspective."

Garfield nodded again in silence.

"As an example," Pete said, "the entire cordillera, the mountain chain that runs from Alaska to the tip of South America, all of it, is geologically young and in a sense still being formed. Which is why we get things like that mud slide in Colombia that killed twenty-five, thirty thousand people; the Mexico earthquake a few years back; the Mount St. Helens eruption; Mont Pelée in Martinique, which blew up and wiped out the city of St.-Pierre, another thirty thousand people; the San Andreas fault here that one day will go into action. And on the other side of the ocean, Krakatoa, which exploded back in 1883 with the loudest bang ever heard by man and killed nobody knows how many. These are just a few examples, and they're all part of the same thing—the Ring of Fire."

"I gathered that in the library," Garfield said, "and in papers of yours I read that it's your judgment that a large movement is due in one of those mid-Pacific fracture zones, maybe overdue, and a different kind of movement."

"Call me Cassandra." Pete Williamson spread his hands helplessly. "I can't prove it. Nobody can. But—" He shrugged.

Garfield waited, impassive.

"I've gone back as far as any reports or even folktales go concerning my particular mid-Pacific fracture zone, which is down where I made that dive," Peter said. "I've pushed all available information around into various patterns and shapes. I've had an old chum up at Cal Tech set up computer models, taken them apart and put them back together again." He spread his hands once more. "We simply don't *know* enough about what's happening in the deeps to predict with any assurance or accuracy what's going to happen. Or when."

Garfield said thoughtfully, "The French are still testing, no?"

"You don't need a diagram, do you?" Pete said. "That's why I wangled a ride on this last dive, which was in the same area where I dove nineteen months ago. In the meantime, we've had seismic disturbances in that area of the South Pacific almost smack on the equator. It's a restless planet we live on. Its crust is always moving, twitching like a horse's skin in fly time. But I wanted to see for myself if I could detect any changes in nineteen months right there." He paused.

"All I have is visual evidence," Pete said at last, "but there *have* been changes, seismic changes. And according to my data, the seismic activity correlates with the known underwater testing the French have carried out." He paused again. "So what do we have? Guesswork, sure. But—" He sat silent, watching Garfield's face.

"I think I see it," Garfield said, "but go on."

Pete drew a deep breath. "Ever see what an avalanche can do? A big one, even on a stable mountainside? There's the result of one in Austria up in the Brenner Pass, I remember seeing. It's almost a half mile wide and close to a mile long. Trees, rocks, the surface structure itself are gouged out as if by a giant bulldozer. Wet, unstable, spring snow up near the top of the mountain began to slide and gathered material, and momentum, as it went. And it *could* have been started, and maybe even was, by as minor a disturbance as a gunshot, or even a yodel or a sharp whistle."

"And you think an underwater explosion could trigger the same kind of thing?" Garfield said.

Pete was well into his subject now. "That entire trench, as you called it last night is a fracture zone. I could see cracks that run along a broad ledge at about the forty-five-hundred-meter depth. How far those cracks extend I don't know; our lights reached only so far. But I see no reason to believe that the cracks are localized, and the ledge does extend for a hundred miles or so. It *may* all be unstable like the wet snow on the mountaintop, ready to go. And then?" He was silent.

"You're talking tsunami," Garfield said slowly, and nodded. "I thought that might be it. What the newspapers call tidal waves, and aren't. Ocean waves caused by seismic movement—an earthquake, a volcanic explosion, whatever—waves that can travel up to six hundred miles an hour for great distances, waves of enormous energy involving millions of tons of water. They slow when they reach shallow water and begin to build like these breakers here, but tsunami can reach, and have reached, heights of one hundred, two hundred feet and may even have wiped out the entire Minoan civilization on the island of Crete in the Med in ancient times. That's what you're talking about, isn't it?"

Pete said slowly, "In one morning you did a lot of reading."

"Yes. I'm good at that. And I remember what I read. A quick study."

He said it, Pete noticed, without pretension or any special emphasis, almost as if he were saying, "Yes, I'm left-handed. I was born that way."

Pete said, "Not all seismic disturbances, even underwater ones, cause tsunami. There has to be vertical movement which causes displacement in the underwater mass, big movement of big mass, a disturbance producing maybe seven-point-five and up on the Richter scale on the seismographs."

Garfield said, "Isn't that exactly what you're talking about if that ledge does extend a hundred miles or so and if it is unstable its entire length? An underwater avalanche of that magnitude would displace an enormous amount of water mass, wouldn't it?"

"Yeah." Pete was silent, staring out to sea again. "So you see how far-out I am? Just because of what I've researched, deduced and been able to check only visually, almost casually, as we descended?" He scooped up a second handful of sand, looked at it and then tossed the entire handful away in one violent motion before he turned to look at Garfield again.

Garfield ignored him and stared at the ocean for a long time, scarcely aware of, but vaguely hearing almost as accompaniment to his thoughts, the gentle thunder of the breakers on the white beach, a continuous timpani beat beneath and behind the sounds of the wind and the cries of gulls wheeling and swooping as they followed a school of fish just offshore.

Sailboats from the harbor were out, a few sailing off the wind, their multicolored spinnakers set and drawing, filled in voluptuous curves in the ocean breeze. A peaceful scene.

He turned to Pete again at last. "And what," he said, "would be the results of all this—*if* it were to happen—a huge underwater avalanche in your unstable area triggered by, say, another underwater explosion, the avalanche producing a Richter-scale magnitude reading of maybe eight or even higher?"

"Why," Peter said, "the International Tsunami Warning Commission headquartered in Hawaii would go into action, collecting data from reporting stations all around the Pacific Basin. They'd pinpoint the epicenter, the surface directly above the center of the disturbance. If tsunami were generated, and they most likely would be, their speed through the water from the epicenter, and their wavelength—the distance between crests of the swells—would be converted into predicted arrival times at various shore locations, along with approximate . . . strength." He smiled almost sadly. "But about all there would be to do when you got the warning would be to put to sea if you had a boat or head for high ground if you were on land." He spread his hands.

"Put to sea?"

"The swells," Pete said, "maybe traveling at four hundred and fifty miles an hour, would be only two or maybe three feet high. At sea you wouldn't even notice one passing under your hull. It's when they reach shallow water and start to build, and all the water, maybe a hundred miles of it before the next crest, hundreds of millions of tons of water would build the slowing swell into a wave, like those breakers out there, but big, big, big and powerful beyond imagining. That's what would do the damage."

"How far away?"

Pete blew out his breath in a soundless whistle. "You want an example? Okay. Probably the best is that 1960 earthquake on the coast of Chile, way down in South America, that produced tsunami that traveled over five thousand miles in just under fifteen hours to destroy part of downtown Hilo, Hawaii—*destroy,* not just flood— and the waves kept right on going for another five thousand miles—

that's ten thousand miles total—to tear up harbor installations in Honshu and Hokkaido, Japan, causing some three hundred and fifty million dollars in damage. Hawaii, especially Hilo, and the Japanese islands because of their coastal configurations are particularly vulnerable. The Japanese have records of tsunami disasters going back to the tenth century. As a matter of fact, the word itself is Japanese; it means 'large waves in harbor.' "

He smiled sadly again. "In 1703 a single series of tsunami waves are thought to have killed a hundred thousand people in a bay on the Sanriku coast of Japan. Fun, huh?"

Garfield said, "And here? Right here?"

"We have a wide continental shelf," Pete said, "that's the shallow part before the bottom drops off into really deep water, and that should protect us pretty well."

"Should?"

"Oh, hell," Pete said in sudden, helpless exasperation, "we're not dealing with certainties. This kind of thing isn't like your electronic circuitry because no matter how complex that may be, you know precisely what will happen. We don't. We *think* we know. There *could* be factors, I suppose, that would tend to make us less than immune to—"

"Such as?"

Pete blew out his breath again in that soundless whistle. "You really bore in, don't you? Okay. Waves have periodicity. See those swells out there? They're almost as regular as clockbeats. We could have a storm, a big one, pushing shore water levels well above normal, *and* a spring tide—that's the highest tide of the month—at the same time, and *if* a tsunami swell coincided *exactly* with the periodicity of the storm waves, you'd get an amplification of forces— you know about these things as well as I do."

"Wave reinforcement," Garfield said. He nodded. "What you're saying is that there's no telling what might happen. Isn't that it?"

Pete's voice was suddenly soft, angry. *"If* it all worked out that way," he said, "worst possible case, then what even one big, destructive tsunami wave would do on this low-lying California coast, all prosperous and fat and happy, with wall-to-wall people and cars and houses and boats in the harbor all jammed together—" He shook his head. "It doesn't bear thinking about."

Everything that had been said had led up to this moment and this inevitable conclusion, as, right from the start, Garfield had been reasonably certain it would.

"You're wrong, you know," he said. He spoke in a conversational tone, but the words carried the authority of incontrovertible fact. "It *demands* thinking about."

Pete was silent for a long time, staring fixedly out to sea. Garfield wondered if he was seeing anything besides his thoughts. "Okay," Pete said at last, in a different, almost angry voice. He turned to look at Garfield. "You knew right from the beginning you'd make that point, didn't you?" The flat muscles of his cheeks worked almost rhythmically. "You throw responsibility at me when all I have is a wild theory based on some questionable data. You're the big-picture man, looking ahead and seeing possibilities. That piece in *Time* about you emphasized your . . . vision. I—" He stopped and spread his hands.

As he had with Walker Carmichael, Garfield said, "Go on, spell it out. You resent me, no?"

Pete nodded. "I do. Because you're dead right and I'm just an oceanographer, not a mover and shaker. Sure, I have ideas, but that's all they amount to, ideas. And what the hell is there to do about it, anyway?"

Garfield shook his head in an almost imperceptible negating gesture. "I don't know yet," he said. "But you make a convincing case, and if it stands up to scrutiny, then you can't just ignore it."

"*I* can't?"

"Neither can I, as far as that goes." He was committing himself, he thought, and that had not been his purpose—or had it? All his life he had made up his mind quickly, analyzing and digesting facts and possibilities and setting his course accordingly. The success of Garfield Associates had been based almost solely on that capacity of his to see ahead with clarity and act without hesitation. So where was the difference here? "It's not my field," he said, "as you know. But facts are facts and logic is logic regardless of the subject matter."

Again Pete was silent, looking once more out to sea as if the answers to his dilemma were rolling in with the far-traveled swells. Again he looked at Garfield, and the resentful anger was no longer visible. "My ideas," he said, "run directly counter to conventional wisdom. Southern California has never to anyone's knowledge had tsunami damage, probably because of that wide continental shelf. Places like Hilo and Japan, Chile and perhaps parts of Central America are far more likely to be . . . devastated *if* my theories are correct."

"But in your worst-possible scenario," Garfield said, "we *could* possibly have trouble here as well."

Pete nodded. "That's how I see it. So what do we do about it?"

"We scrutinize your data first."

"We?"

"You have that computer printout. Let me study it. I'm not exactly a stranger to data analysis, and you can provide the technical expertise I lack."

"You have it all laid out, don't you?" Pete said, and some of the resentful anger had returned. "First verification. Then what?"

"We decide what can be done. And do it."

Pete shook his head in gathering wonder. A wry grin slowly replaced the angry look. "Boy, howdy!" he said. "You are something else! The man with all the answers." But there was no longer resentment behind the words. Instead, what he felt was a sense of relief that at last he was no longer alone with his dark, hidden thoughts.

"We'll see," Garfield said. "Maybe I'm just the man with the questions."

3

Maude Anderson read the *Time* story too, with its detailed account of the sale of Garfield Associates to Atlas Telecommunications and its praise for Garfield's apparently calculated reluctance, which resulted in a far higher price than originally offered. The story seemed to cheer David for getting the better of the bargain with the giant Goliath.

Then she thought back to that last lunch with Dan, whom she had neither seen nor heard from since, and sat for a long time staring out the window of her Westwood apartment, her thoughts ranging from happiness for Dan to puzzlement over his long silence and confusion concerning her own feelings.

She had no real claim on him, she told herself sternly. Their relationship had been without conditions, an adult association between a man and a woman, no more than that, which was precisely the way she had wanted it. For reasons.

Lunches at places like Angelo's; seats in a box at the Hollywood Bowl; that weekend flight, first-class, to Hawaii, the Big Island, and the suite at the Mauna Kea Hotel—such activities as those, yes, but no deep *personal* involvement, because she had learned her lesson in that direction, and after a divorce it had taken months, no, years, to regain her sense of *wholeness,* and she was not about to jeopardize it again even with someone she liked as much as Dan Garfield.

But why had Dan suddenly dropped out of her life? Because he was now no longer merely well-off but, if the *Time* piece was to be believed, wealthy almost beyond comprehension? If that was it, she could not escape a feeling of resentment.

She was a direct, straightforward person, and her immediate impulse was to pick up the phone and demand an explanation, an impulse she quickly stifled. She had never pursued a man in her life, and she was not about to start now. She remembered a friend saying of an acquaintance they had in common who had recently married, "She ran from him—until she caught him." And she remembered, too, her somewhat scornful amusement at the concept. Under no circumstances would she put herself in a similar position, particularly in view of Dan's present circumstances. What was the term that was once used to describe women who behaved like that: gold diggers?

So Dan could call or not, as he chose, and that was an end to it.

But when Jack and Betsy Barnes at a party one night said that they were opening their Encino Beach house for the summer and why didn't she come down for a week or so as relief from the rat race, she did not hesitate. "Love to," she said, and reflected that in the face of what could not be sheer coincidence but somehow had to have been *ordained,* there was neither point nor heroism in resistance.

❧

Pete went back to his office at the oceanographic institute that afternoon after delivering the computer printout to Garfield. On his way he stopped by habit at the seismograph room for a look at the revolving cylinder on which the mechanical pen traced a continuous line. There were the usual squiggles and minor, sharp irregularities; the line was never entirely smooth because somewhere, at some magnitude, the earth's crust was being disturbed and the vibrations from those disturbances traveled through and around the earth in varying types of shock waves that registered on the seismograph. As he had told Dan, ours was a restless planet.

This afternoon Pete stared at the revolving cylinder with new eyes, and lines from *The Rubaiyat* occurred to him as he watched the inked line drawing its patterns:

"The Moving Finger writes; and, having writ,/ Moves on: nor all your Piety nor Wit/ Shall lure it back to cancel half a Line./ Nor all your Tears wash out a Word of it."

His original resentment began to rise again, overpowering the relief. Damn that Dan Garfield anyway, he thought. He felt tricked, maneuvered by relentless logic into admitting aloud what all along had been in the back of his mind, but comfortably quiescent, ever since he had studied that broad ledge on the cliff wall during the tiny submarine's descent. Now, thanks to Garfield, he had to face both facts and implications.

He walked along the hall to his office and plumped down in his desk chair to stare at the huge wall map of the Pacific Ocean. *There,* in the vastness of the ocean, only a little north of the equator, was where he had made both dives; he had marked the location carefully with a small *x.* The large-scale wall map, of course, told him nothing except relative location, but he had detailed bottom charts—the results of innumerable soundings made accurate by modern technology to a matter of feet and even centimeters.

The ledge was there; the charts corroborated that. And it did extend for almost 100 miles, about 160 kilometers. How much of it was as apparently unstable as the tiny portion he had been able to study so briefly, he could not say; soundings did not show that. But there was no reason to suppose that most or all of it was not. So?

So, face it, he told himself, the worst-case scenario Dan had maneuvered him into describing *was* possible, no? Yes, damn it; it was. And there was another possibility he had not even mentioned, and it could make the situation far worse.

Tropical disturbances sometimes turned into full-fledged hurricanes. And *usually* in the Northern Hemisphere. Pacific hurricanes tended to swing southward. But hurricanes, like grizzly bears, were totally unpredictable. They made their own decisions, and occasionally one would choose to turn rogue and swing north.

It had happened. If memory served, it was in 1939 that the fringe of a hurricane had caught this low-lying California coast, and waves had swept across the Encino Beach peninsula and into the harbor. Encino Beach was not wall-to-wall people then, and damage had not been great.

But suppose, just suppose, instead of a mere storm, a *hurricane* fringe were to coincide with tsunami waves emanating from that *x* marked on the wall map and speeding in all directions, as ripples spread in a pool. What would be the result then?

Sheer, utter and total disaster. Nothing less.

ॐ

Jack and Betsy Barnes were in their late thirties, attractive, gregarious, wealthy, not in the sense of old-family money, but instead on the basis of Jack's high six-figure earnings and shrewd real estate investments.

They owned a mortgaged home in Brentwood, a waterfront house in Encino Beach and a half share of a condo at Big Bear which they used during the skiing season. At Encino Beach they kept a fifty-foot Grand Banks power cruiser on a mooring at the yacht club. They both drove BMW automobiles.

They knew Maude Anderson through her real estate dealings. They were taking the sun, drinks at hand, on the deck overlooking the bay when Maude arrived for her planned visit.

"Looking good, babe," Jack said as he kissed her lightly in welcome. "Take off the clothes, get comfortable and join us. I'll build you a drink."

But it was Betsy later, in private, who broached the real subject.

"Your man's down here. You knew that, of course. That's really why you came down, isn't it? Don't answer that." Her mind rarely stayed on one subject long. "New swimsuit?" She nodded. "The 'modest' look, which is anything but. I've always thought one-piece could be far sexier than bikinis. All they do is display." And again the change of pace. "We're going out to dinner, hon. A new place Jack found."

Maude nodded, feeling vaguely shamed seeing herself through another's eyes, somehow cheapened. "I'll change," she said.

The new place was called Harbor Haven, and it featured, as Jack put it, "either blackened—that is, charred—seafood or beef grilled over mesquite-wood fire. They're the 'in' things this week. God only knows what next week's will be."

In essence, Maude was thinking, Jack was expressing precisely what non-Southern Californians considered the basic criticism of the area: its constant change. She had heard it up at Tahoe from San Francisco friends; she had heard it in the East long before she ever came to L.A. *Impermanence* was the word, and since her thoughts were running in that direction, she wondered if the word applied to Dan Garfield as well.

"Pensive, aren't we, hon?" Betsy said. "Have you heard from glamour boy at all since he won the jackpot?"

Maude smiled without answering.

"If and when you see him," Jack said, "you might tell him that I've got a couple of propositions that could interest him. He has to put all that money somewhere."

Betsy said, "You promised to lay off business while Maude's here."

"Just a word and a hint. Waiter!"

Garfield's name surfaced again later in the meal. "I heard he's staying with the Winslows," Betsy said. "Old friends. I was on the Arts Festival Committee last year with Clara Winslow, so we could ask them over for drinks or something."

Maude felt naked, exposed, and merely shook her head in silence.

"Don't try to rush it, huh?" Betsy said, and nodded. "Probably you're right. Let's wait a couple of days and see what happens. If he catches sight of you in the swimsuit—" She shook her head and smiled. "I noticed lover boy here perked up when you came out on the deck in it."

"And I," Jack said, "do not impress easily."

Betsy was still smiling. "Since when?"

Maybe coming down here at all was a mistake, Maude thought, but it was too late now to reconsider. "I like this blackened fish," she said, and managed to smile.

❧

The assistant secretary had the scientific adviser alone in his office. "Off the record," the assistant secretary said, "we've tried a little pressure, but our Gallic friends have told us reasonably politely to attend to our own problems, say, in the Persian Gulf and in Korea and down in Central America, and leave them alone to work out their own experiments. In a word, they intend to go ahead with their underwater testing. Suggestions?"

"I've given it some thought," the scientific adviser said. "There's a man, an oceanographer out on the Coast at the Encino Beach Oceanographic Institute who's written a paper. Fellow named Williamson. Well thought of, if maybe a little far-out. I might fly out there and have a talk with him. His ideas could give us ammunition."

The assistant secretary leaned back in his chair and studied the ceiling for a time in silence. He sat up straight then and faced his visitor. "You do think there's danger?"

"I don't know enough to have an opinion—yet. Will the next test be fission or fusion? If it's fusion, how sure are they of their megaton range? At the start we were only guessing with our hydrogen bomb. Then there's a lot more data that could be pertinent—time, weather, tides, bottom configuration and solidity—" He spread his hands. "Not a simple equation."

"And really none of our business when it comes to that," the assistant secretary said. "Unless something bad happens, that is. Then Congress will want to know why we didn't foresee it." He pushed back his chair and stood up, holding out his hand. "Thanks for coming in. After you've talked with Williamson, be back in touch, okay? To be honest, I don't know what good it will do, but at least we can make an effort if we think it justified."

⁊

Garfield sat on the porch facing, but oblivious to, the shining bay, its perimeter of houses, its thousands of boats. The stack of computer printout sheets Pete had given him was on his lap, and a yellow pad and pencil were on the table at his elbow. Staring but unseeing, he tried to analyze his thoughts.

There was a measure of regret at what he had let himself in for, the analysis of data in a field that was unfamiliar to him. And that would be followed inevitably by the necessity to express opinions on which decisions could and would be based and even probably the making of some of the decisions themselves.

On the face of it the situation was ridiculous and yet, in a curious way he did not even try to analyze, as natural and inevitable and right as almost all the big turning points in his life had been—except one, the Garfield Associates sale, which he still resented deeply.

Once, early in their association and after a somewhat heated discussion of policy, Garfield had overheard Walker Carmichael saying to Paul Case, "Face it, Dan's a take-charge guy. He isn't happy unless he's calling the shots. So let him."

Garfield had never thought of himself in that way, and yet, when he pondered it, he had to admit that almost inevitably he ended up as the man out front, setting both the direction and the pace. Well, somebody had to.

And so it was here with Pete Williamson, who had seen the problem his theories posed and chosen to ignore it when it simply *could not be ignored.* All he, Garfield, had done was point out that basic truth, and now here he was in a sense holding the baby. Nor was it in him to try to walk away.

So there we are, he told himself, and settled down to study the computer printout, all other considerations automatically fading into nothingness as his mind focused clearly on the facts and figures.

It was there that Clara found him when she returned from her errands in town. She settled quietly into a nearby chair and watched him, smiling, as he read and pondered, reread and took notes on the yellow pad, at times closing his eyes in deep concentration and showing, by the satisfied expression on his face when he opened them, that the problem, whatever it had been, had been solved and he could proceed. For long minutes he was oblivious of her presence.

She said at last, "I think a little relaxation, Dan. This is supposed to be a rest, you know."

His head came up, and he blinked several times as if coming out of a deep sleep. His smile was sheepish. "Sorry," he said. "I didn't—"

"Of course, you didn't realize I was here. I understood that. It was flattering. It meant you felt at ease with me and weren't disturbed."

"I always have felt at ease with you."

"I know that, too."

"You're a lovely woman, Clara." It was what he had long felt and never managed to say.

She was smiling again. "Let's not talk about me. Let's talk about Maude Anderson. She's down here, you know. Or did you?"

"Maude?" He shook his head. "I didn't."

"She's staying with some people I know. I ran into her at market." Her eyes studied him as her husband's had, the same look of appraisal and puzzlement. "What's troubling you, Dan? Tom said he didn't know, but it was obvious that something was. And on the face of it, things could not have gone better for you."

"Long story."

Clara waited, but there was no explanation forthcoming. "I've never seen you running away from something before, Dan. What is it? Maude?"

"No." And yet, in a sense, Maude was part of the problem because she was associated with his old life as head of Garfield Associates. Down here with Pete and Clara and Lucy there were no reminders bringing back memories to trouble him.

"Is it yourself, Dan? That's the one person you can't run from, you know." Clara stood up then, and her hand brushed his cheek gently. "If I can help, let me know. Please." She was gone, inside the house.

Garfield looked again at the numbers and symbols of the print-out. They had suddenly become almost meaningless.

❦

The Hansens, Olaf and Lydia, lived next door to Pete Williamson, on the other side from the Winslows, amid a welter of books, charts, Coast and Geodetic Survey publications, ship models, scuba-diving gear, Eskimo walrus-tusk carvings, soapstone sculptures and transient guests who sometimes overflowed into Pete's house.

Olaf Hansen was a retired professor of history from either the University of Kansas or Kansas State; Pete could never remember which. What was more to the point was that Olaf had endured more than forty years in academia in a geographical location just about as far from the sea as one could get in the United States and had loathed every minute of it. There was salt water in Olaf's Nordic blood, and the day he retired from his university post, he walked down the path to the already loaded car where Lydia waited, got in and headed for the salt air of Encino Beach as a newly hatched duckling heads for the nearest water. He never saw Kansas again.

He was a small man in his late sixties, with a shock of gray hair, usually two or three days' growth of white whiskers and bright eyes as blue as deep water on a sparkling day. Lydia was his female counterpart, slim, trim, wiry and quick in her movements. They had two sons, academics both.

"They were born to be farmers," Olaf had told Pete once. "When they see acres of wheat or corn, they inhale deeply in ecstasy. They think the sea is for fish."

The Hansens owned a thirty-five-foot motor sailer into which they had poured their life savings and all of the affection the two landlocked sons no longer required. Over Lydia's objections, Olaf had named the boat after her, and the identical names sometimes caused confusion.

"I'm taking Lydia to Mexico, down the Baja," could mean that Olaf was flying to Mexico with his wife, sailing the boat alone or, more likely, taking to the sea with both of his beloved Lydias.

The houseguests came in all shapes, sizes and assorted backgrounds. All had two things in common: a love of the sea and the deepwater sailor's indifference to cramped quarters and lack of privacy. Pete found some of them fascinating.

There was, for example, the Ivy League astronomer, a Nobel laureate, who, in the anonymity of Encino Beach during his occasional visits, was constantly barefoot and unshaven and who sunbathed nude in the Hansens' tiny enclosed backyard while conducting astronomy seminars for anyone who cared to attend.

There was the green-eyed titled English girl named Daphne who had gone aboard *Lydia* one night in La Paz and sailed with the Hansens the next morning without bothering to return to her hotel for her clothing and other possessions. Among other things she and Olaf found a common interest in the implications of Stonehenge and whether the computer analysis that purported to have solved the mysteries of that circle of stones was, or was not, to be taken at face value.

There was the advertising executive from Chicago who had turned his back on what he called the rat race and now earned a precarious living crewing on Encino Beach boats that set out on extended cruises, destinations not important. "Beats racing inland lake scows by a mile," he said. "Even Superior is comprehensible, finite. The Pacific is not, and one lifetime isn't enough to see it all."

It was to Olaf and Lydia that Pete talked one evening some days after that beachside conversation with Dan.

"Dan Garfield," he told them, "is like the radar they have in the military. He locks on to something with a kind of monomaniacal tunnel vision. I'm just beginning to see that right from the start he steered our conversation. His mind was already made up."

Pete was uncomfortably aware that his mood and his thoughts had switched 180 degrees since he had sat in his office and stared gloomily at the wall map. It was the enormousness of the possibilities now out in the open for the first time that troubled him, he told himself.

"You have talked since," Lydia said. "Is he beginning to have doubts, too, about the seriousness of the situation?"

Yes, we've talked, Pete thought, and while in one sense I still resent him, I'll have to admit that my anger has turned to admiration, and most of my early resentment to acceptance of what is. It was strange that he could admit all this even to himself.

"I don't think he has doubts. That isn't a mind he has; it's some kind of computer, and computers don't worry about things. In two days he's found more in that computer analysis than I could have found in a year, if ever. And none of it changes his thinking a bit."

"The movers and shakers, in the current phrase," Olaf said, "have always been convinced of their own rectitude. That's a truism." The bright blue eyes studied Pete carefully. "You *think* he's right, but you hesitate to take the final step of commitment, isn't that about it? But after all, it's your research, your observations and your knowledge of possibilities he's relying on." He shook his head. "And I don't believe you intended any of it to be taken lightly. Did you?"

"You're pinning me down," Pete said, "making it sound as if I want to have it both ways: I want to be right and take some credit for it, but I don't want to be blamed if I'm wrong, no?" He thought about it in silence for a few moments, aware that both Lydia and Olaf watched him, waiting patiently. He said at last, "Oh, hell, I suppose you're right." He was angry with himself. "Make up your mind, Williamson!"

Olaf said, "I have only a layman's knowledge in this direction and little more than a passing acquaintance with the word *tsunami.* Assuming that your research, your observations and the possibilities you have explained are all correct in predicting something more than the likelihood of trouble, how serious could this be?"

Pete spread his hands and said, "Whoosh! How big is catastrophe?"

Lydia and Olaf watched him in silence.

"In Hilo, Hawaii, in 1960," Pete said, "entire buildings of steel and reinforced concrete were driven through one another in an area of two square miles and left in a tangled mess of wreckage by a single tsunami wave estimated to have been only thirty-five feet high. A wave that size and that strength would sweep across the peninsula here without even slowing. It would wipe out these waterfront houses and probably smash into kindling whatever boats were in the harbor. I wake up sweating when I dream about it."

Lydia said, "Where is safety?"

"Inland on high ground," Pete said, "or at sea, beyond the ten-fathom line, say, a few miles beyond." He looked at both faces. "Out there you'd only have storm seas to contend with, which could be more than enough, but nothing like what could happen ashore."

Daphne, the green-eyed titled English girl, had come into the room unnoticed. She said now, "You're speaking of tsunami? In his mature years my great-uncle Bertie commanded a ship of some sort, a battle cruiser, I believe, and he had tall tales to tell of his midshipman days down around Java and Sumatra when Krakatoa was fussing about." She smiled at Olaf and Lydia. "I think, chaps, that we would do well to keep *Lydia* stocked with food and fueled up against possibilities. It could be a long stint at sea."

Lydia said, "Once the danger was past, we could come back inside, couldn't we?" She looked at Pete.

Daphne said, "I doubt there would be anything left to come back to." She, too, looked at Pete. "Would there be?"

Pete hesitated. "In the scenario we're talking about, no," he said.

There was silence. It was Olaf who said at last, "Given that your assessments are correct, what do you propose to do about it?"

"Do?" Daphne said. "Damn all. What is there to do, burn incense and pray?"

"I believe," Olaf said at last, "that I begin to perceive your dilemma. In most battles, surrender is possible, and the shooting stops. Nature, however, knows no code of chivalry. She is relentless." He smiled wryly. "And yet we have the audacity to believe ourselves well in charge of things. Amusing, isn't it?"

4

The Encino Beach City Council was mostly, but not entirely, hand-picked by His Honor Jimmy Silva. If Jimmy openly backed a candidate, that candidate was as good as elected. If Jimmy kept hands off, the election could go whichever way the electorate happened to decide.

"Let's not be greedy," Jimmy had been known to say to a few intimates. "A majority is all we want; otherwise it looks phony."

He had his majority, four of the seven members. The remaining three were, as Jimmy had foreseen, well-off residents who practiced their professions—architecture, medicine and the law, respectively—in Los Angeles. To a man they were amateur ecologists and members of the Sierra Club. At times, in Jimmy's estimation although he never said so, they were also a pain in the ass that had to be put up with.

In closed session the Council members heard Jimmy's explanation of the marina he had in mind for the back bay mud flats. They listened in polite silence until he was finished, at which time he waved his pointer to indicate that the floor was open. "Questions?" he said.

Brown, the lawyer among the minority, said, "That's shorebird habitat."

"Yep," Jimmy said. "Sure is. So it's birds against people, and I'm on the people side. Besides—" he paused for emphasis—"besides, there's that bird sanctuary only two, three miles up the coast and a little inland, same kind of brackish water and mud flats and no boats or people to disturb nesting."

The lawyer nodded, acknowledging the point. His objection, he had to admit, had been automatic.

The architect said, "Who's going to do the designs?"

"Big L.A. firm." Jimmy named it. "And they'll want advice— consultation, they call it—with somebody who knows the beach area. I gave them your name. I hope that was okay." From the satisfied look on the architect's face, Jimmy thought, there would be no opposition from that direction. Strange, how much so little could accomplish.

It was for the surgeon, an orthopod with considerable personal estate planning financial knowledge, to bring up the matter of funding.

"Glad you asked that," Jimmy said. "I went to Merrill Lynch in town. They're your brokers, too, I hear." He watched the surgeon nod. "Bright young guy," Jimmy said. "Told me all about bond issues for municipal improvements. Tax-free income. Shelters, they call them. He worked up a little proposal for me, and I had copies made. I'll pass them around." He did. "Take them home, take your time and see what you think. Me, I don't see any holes in it. All we need is to put it on the ballot."

"Only one more question," the lawyer said. "Assuming this goes ahead, who arranges acquisition of the land from the city and sells the houses. In other words, who makes the money? You?"

"*In*surance is my thing," Jimmy said. "I'm no real estate guy. And the way we have it set up—structured is how the Merrill Lynch guy calls it—the city doesn't sell the land; it leases it. It's a municipal project, and sure, we pay commissions, but that's all. We also collect lease money, and we add to our tax base by land improvement."

"I'll have to hand it to you," Brown said. "You make some of the L.A. developers look like amateurs the way you put the package together before we even saw it."

"I haven't committed us to a thing," Jimmy said, and spread his big hands to show that he had nothing to conceal. He looked around at the seven faces and saw no further questions or objections. He said to the City Council president, a member of the handpicked majority, "If you got nothing else, Zeke, maybe you want to adjourn. It's getting late."

"Meeting adjourned," Zeke said. They were his first words since opening the session.

The next day Jimmy had a visitor, Maude's host. "Jack Barnes. You don't know me, Mr. Silva," Jack said, "but—"

"Barnes, John T.," Jimmy said. "A Grand Banks fifty-footer. Yacht club member. Waterfront house off Onyx. Real estate, aren't you? Sit down."

Jack sat down and mentally revised his game plan, along with his opinion of ex-fishermen. "I've heard about your planned development over in the back bay."

"Word gets around, doesn't it?" Jimmy said. He showed no annoyance; he had expected talk.

"I've also heard," Jack said, "that you're going to lease, not sell the land." He nodded approval. "That's smart. How long will the leases run?"

"Not decided yet," Jimmy said. "What do you think would be the right length?"

Jack thought about it. "Twenty-five years is too short when you're talking about houses in the half million range. On the other hand, while ninety-nine years may be all right for the land the Empire State Building sits on in New York City, it could sound a little awkward here." He was silent.

Jimmy said, "If you was to be selling the houses, what would be a good lease span to make your sales pitch easiest?"

Jack thought about it. "Maybe forty years. To the people who'll be in the market for the houses, forty years is more time than they'll figure they have to enjoy it. We're talking about 2026 or '27, and who knows if anybody will be around then?"

"You think good," Jimmy said. "Is that why you're here? You're interested in being the one to handle the house sales?"

"The thought had entered my mind."

"Your name was one of those that kept turning up," Jimmy said, and left it there.

Jack Barnes took a deep breath. He hoped he had figured it right. "Of course," he said, "it would seem only fair that whoever thought this up in the first place and then went to a lot of work putting it together ought to get some benefit, don't you think?"

"You're talking about me." Jimmy's voice was expressionless.

"I sort of thought I might be."

"I'm an elected official, and I'm doing this for the good of Encino Beach."

Jack nodded gravely. "Of course. But you have put in a lot of your own time, maybe taken time from your insurance business, sacrificed business deals you might have followed up."

Jimmy looked at the far wall and sighed. "There is that, now that you mention it. In that sense, it's cost me money working to put this all together." He looked again at Jack and waited.

"And so," Jack said, "I think you ought to derive some benefit. Say a little something from each house sold. Maybe a half point of the commission?"

Jimmy took his time. He said at last, "I think maybe we can do business, Mr. Barnes."

"Call me Jack."

"My name's Jimmy."

❧

A knock on the door awakened Pete the morning after his talk with Olaf and Lydia, and in pajama bottoms he went to answer it. Daphne was there, in cutoff jeans, barefoot and wearing a short-sleeved blouse that showed her slim, strong, tanned arms to advantage. She made no comment on Pete's pajamas as she walked in and sat down. "I missed part of that conversation last night, Peter," she said. "May I have a résumé, please?"

He had been over the ground twice quite thoroughly recently,

Pete thought, first with Garfield and last night with Olaf and Lydia. The sequence of explanation was well established in his mind, and he went through the fact of the treaty, the continued French nuclear testing and the correlation of the tests with the geologic changes he had seen during his two dives with almost practiced ease.

Daphne sat quiet, listening, watching Pete's face as he talked, her green eyes bright with interest. And when he finished, "I was somehow under the impression," she said, "that seismic disturbances, as you call them, could not be predicted."

"Maybe yes, maybe no. You want some coffee? Because I do."

"Delighted." Daphne stood up. "Show me whatever mechanism you have to make it, and then go do whatever you do to prepare yourself for the day." She raised one peremptory hand. "No apologies. I was uninvited." She smiled quickly. "Pajama bottoms, whiskers and tousled hair become you, Peter. Unfortunately, most men first thing in the morning are nothing short of repugnant."

They sat at the small table in the tiny kitchen. Daphne nodded approvingly. "Like a galley, a place for everything and everything in its place, shipshape and Bristol fashion." She leaned her chin on her hands, her elbows propped on the table. "Now tell me. What does 'maybe yes, maybe no' mean?"

"There are small indications, warnings," Pete said, "if you can read them. In the 1964 Alaska earthquake, the brown bears on Kodiak Island, the largest carnivores in the world, with no natural enemies, left their winter dens two weeks early, which just happened to be the day before the quake. And although bears are hungry after their winter of fasting and near hibernation, these bears didn't hang around looking for food. They took off away from the quake area at speed."

Daphne smiled. "Cunning chaps, no?"

"And if we had had inclinometers in place, they would have registered slight changes in the gradients of some slopes, and magnetometers would probably have registered earth magnetic field changes. Water levels in reservoirs and wells would have shown changes. Probably domestic farm animals would have shown signs of panic." Pete spread his hands. "The Chinese have come up with evidence of all kinds of abnormal animal behavior just before big seismic disturbances. The pieces are there, if we can put them together."

"But on the sea bottom," Daphne said, "you don't have bears or domestic farm animals to tip you off."

Pete studied the girl. She had been listening *and* absorbing what he said; that was obvious. *And* thinking. He had not paid too much attention to her up to now, and he wondered why. Beautiful *and* bright—the two words passed through his mind. "True," he said. "What I have, all that I have for sure, is a collection of data going back some hundreds of years. You can look at it and go crazy trying to put it into a pattern." Those green eyes watched him steadily, and that was disconcerting; but her expression was *open,* and it was obvious that she was withholding judgment until she heard him out.

"Last night," he said, "I was still feeling somewhat teed off at Garfield. He's so damn sure of himself. In only a few days, starting almost from scratch, he's about as far into this whole thing as I am after two or three years."

"But he had all your thinking and knowledge to begin with, didn't he?"

"More or less. But he's getting things out of that computer printout that I didn't even know were there."

Daphne looked contemplative. "And what does he propose now?"

"We haven't talked yet. He's not quite ready."

Again Daphne was thoughtful. She said at last, "Tell me, Peter, what do you think will happen? If anything?"

"All I have is a gut feeling."

"That's what I would like to hear about."

"I think we're in for it. Sooner, rather than later. Something on the order of the scenario we talked about last night."

"Batten down the hatches?" Daphne said. "Shorten sail.? Stand by for heavy squalls?"

Pete nodded. "All of that. And more."

Daphne studied him in silence for long moments. She said at last. "You know, you are quite a chap, Peter. I just hadn't realized it before."

❦

Pete had another visitor that morning in his office at the institute. It was the scientific adviser out from Washington. "Harry Saunders," the scientific adviser said, and presented his official card. "Ignore the title. They have me handy just to remind them of whatever basic science they took once and long ago forgot. Do you have a few minutes?"

He sat down, and his eye caught the large Pacific chart on the wall and the small x marked in the middle of its vastness. "That's your spot, isn't it?" he said, pointing. "I checked coordinates. I hear some call that bit of the big formation Williamson's Trench."

"The feeling is," Pete said, "that I'm so hipped on it I can't think of anything else."

Saunders smiled. "I've heard rumors. And I've read several of your papers. I'd like to hear it firsthand, if you have the time."

For the second time that day, and the fourth time in recent days, Pete went over his theory that underwater nuclear testing was causing geologic changes along the broad ledge he had observed and that the result was likely to be an underwater avalanche of devastating proportions.

Saunders listened quietly, without comment, and, when Pete was done, asked quietly, "Of sufficient magnitude to cause tsunami?"

"That's my estimate."

Saunders looked contemplative. "Nasty things, tsunami," he said. "Hawaii and Japan, of course, are always at risk when a large disturbance occurs almost anywhere in the Pacific basin. As are other spots in the Far East and places along the South American coast. And in 1964, of course, following the quake near Anchorage in the Denali fault system, Crescent City on the coast of northern California was pretty well damaged." He watched Pete and seemed to be waiting for comment.

Saunders had done his homework, Pete thought, but, then, that was no more than was to be expected from a scientist of Saunders's quality. Pete had heard of him, a topflight physicist on leave from MIT to serve a hitch in Washington. "But," Pete said, "I imagine what you're really concerned about are military establishments out in the Pacific, yes?"

Saunders nodded, pleased by the question and the quick intelligence that had prompted it. "Of course. Pearl Harbor, Subic Bay, others less well known. With ships or aircraft the solutions are simple: The ships put to sea and the aircraft fly to safer places once the tsunami alarm is sounded. Shore installations and troop concentrations present greater problems." He paused, studying Pete's face. "Do I gather that you are thinking of other danger points as well?"

It was a good opportunity, Pete thought, to lay out Garfield's thesis of local danger, which he now shared, for a disinterested opinion. "As a matter of fact," he said, "we are. Right here, among other places."

Saunders's reaction was what he had anticipated, faintly raised eyebrows and a questioning look. "I hadn't known," Saunders said, "that Southern California was prone to this kind of—threat."

"Normally, because of the continental shelf, it isn't. But a worst-case scenario shows a different picture. If you're interested."

"I am, indeed."

It was, Pete admitted, a long shot, requiring the concatenation of a heavy storm, even perhaps a hurricane fringe, high spring tides and the tsunami waves of considerable magnitude. "But," he finished, "we're convinced it could happen."

Saunders was smiling now. "Murphy's Law," he said, "whatever bad can happen will." He nodded. "You make a strong case." And for long moments he was silent, obviously deep in thought. He said at last, "You use the word *we?* Other geophysicists share your view?"

"Negative," Pete said. "Just one other person so far, and he's not in . . . the field. Fellow named Garfield, Dan Garfield." With some surprise he watched Saunders's expression change. "You know him?"

"I've met him. We sat on a board together a year or two back. A very good man, indeed. And he is . . . convinced? May I ask how he came into it?"

Just one of those things, Pete explained, almost a chance meeting, a casual remark on his part about his far-out theory. "He picked right up on it and wanted to know more."

Saunders was silent again for a little time. "And he is now scrutinizing your data, you say?"

Pete nodded.

Saunders stood up. He was smiling again as he held out his hand. "Luck," he said, "turns up in the oddest places and times. I'd very much like to know Garfield's conclusions when he has drawn them. The phone number on that card will reach me." His handshake was firm, cordial. "I appreciate your time," he said, "as well as your information. You will call?"

"That," Pete said, "goes without saying. I think we're going to need any help we can get."

"I shouldn't be surprised." Saunders's smile was gone. "Bad news is not easily accepted. In any quarter."

☙

Garfield put down the computer printout sheets and his pencil and leaned back in his chair to stare out at the bay and the moored boats. It was morning, and the breeze was just beginning to freshen, stirring the flat water of the harbor, swinging the high-sided cabin cruisers on their moorings until they tugged gently at their lines as if anxious to pull free. A sleek sailboat under power came down the channel past the yacht club, made a slow turn around the moored fleet and headed for the harbor entrance and the open ocean.

Garfield watched it idly, two disparate thoughts struggling for dominance in his mind. The first concerned the computer data he had been through. The second was Maude Anderson and, as far as that went since Clara had made him look at the situation with different eyes, himself.

He glanced at the stacked computer sheets and smiled faintly. They were the easy, familiar problem, the kind he had faced countless times before. With them only logic was required in order to reach a conclusion.

With the other problem, Maude and himself, he was dealing with human intangibles, and the familiar tools of mathematics were of absolutely no use. I know things, he thought, not people, and immediately found himself examining that concept and fitting it to other applications than those of the present.

Had he understood people better, he wondered, might he not have foreseen what he had come to think of as Walker Carmichael's and Paul Case's treachery? Foreseen it and headed it off? Had there been indications of their unhappiness which he had ignored until it was too late? He had thought that everything was running smoothly, and obviously he had been dead wrong. The Atlas offer he had considered merely a minor temptation which he could brush aside almost contemptuously with logic, reason. He had been wrong because logic and reason did not seem to apply to people, only to things.

So, all right, he told himself, it *was* my fault. So? Did that lessen the pain and the bitterness? Not a whit. Then forget it; was that not the logical course to take? But logic not only failed when applied to others but was just as useless when he tried to apply it to himself. He could not forget the forced sale of Garfield Associates which Carmichael, Case and he had built from nothing into the sturdy company it had become. And because the ideas on which the company had been founded and had succeeded had been *his* ideas, neither could he forgive.

All of which took him a long way from his original problem, which was Maude. He glanced again at the stack of computer sheets. That at least, he thought, he could deal with, and should. The other, intangible thinking could wait. He heaved himself out of the chair and went into Tom Winslow's study to the telephone.

Pete was in his office at the oceanographic institute. "I've been through the printout," Garfield said.

"And?" Was there a smile in Pete's voice?

"And I think we'd better have a talk. About a number of things."

There was a short silence. "I'll come over," Pete said. His tone had changed. "That's me you see coming in the door."

5

Garfield had the computer printout sheets neatly stacked and his handwritten notes in order when Pete arrived. Thoughts of Maude Anderson still nagged at him, but he put them aside and concentrated on the business at hand.

Pete said, "Before we get into this, I had a visitor yesterday. I thought you'd be interested." He held out the scientific adviser's card as he sat down.

Garfield looked at it in silence for a few moments. Then: "Harry Saunders is interested?" He watched Pete's nod. "Then," Garfield said, "maybe that changes things a little. Maybe a considerable amount." He did not bother to explain what he meant.

"And there's one other thing," Pete said. "The minisub's been diving again in the same location where I went down. I don't like it."

Garfield watched him in silence, expressionless.

"Too much could happen along that ledge," Pete said. "We

don't know what it might take to trigger an underwater avalanche. And if the sub were on the bottom when it happened, it wouldn't have a chance."

"You went down."

"All I had then was curiosity and maybe a vague suspicion of what I'd find."

"And now you're convinced of the danger?"

Pete thought of Daphne watching him with her green eyes as she waited for him to tell about his gut reaction. "I'm convinced," Pete said. He nodded toward the pile of printout sheets. "Are you?"

"Almost. Say on the order of eighty percent."

"So what do we do now?"

Garfield sat quiet for a few moments before he reached out and patted the pile of sheets. "These are good as far as they go, but they don't go far enough. Hear me out. I know the Cal Tech people, and I know the computer capabilities they have. This was a favor to you, you said. Fine. What we need is a far deeper analysis, adding in, among other things, your interpretation of the changes you saw during your second dive, correlated with the known dates and data of the underwater nuclear testing."

Pete pursed his lips in a silent whistle. "Shall we throw in the moon and a few stars while we're wishing? You're talking about big-time stuff, a complicated program and time on one of those supercomputer monsters."

Garfield indicated the card Pete had given him. "Harry Saunders could be the key. That's why I said he might make a difference. He's smart. He'll see the need."

"He asked me to call him," Pete said. His voice was doubtful. Then he brightened perceptibly. "You'll talk to him? He said you'd met."

"And worked a bit together." Garfield nodded. "I'll talk to him, of course, and explain our problem."

Still, Pete hesitated. "One more thing. On a different level." He seemed slightly uncomfortable. "I'm attached to the oceanographic institute. I have a lot of leeway, but I am supposed to keep in some kind of touch, at least let them know from time to time what direction I'm working in. Howard Boggs—"

"Who's he?"

"My boss. The director. He kind of likes to know what's going on."

In for a penny, in for a pound, Garfield was thinking; he had already gone this far, and the only sensible course was to go the whole distance. "Then we'll tell him," he said. "We'll tell him that the institute is about to receive a special grant to further your research."

Pete blinked. "You'll tell him that?"

"I don't think he'll argue," Garfield said. "I've yet to know a department of a university that can't use more funds. You'll set up a meeting?"

Pete stood up. "As soon as I get back to my office." He glanced at Saunders's card on the table. "You'd better keep that." He started for the house and then stopped and turned to face Garfield again. "Who arranges these things, anyway?" he said. "You of all people turning up just when I needed somebody to talk to, just when I was back from the equator and that dive?"

Garfield produced one of his rare smiles. "I don't know the answer."

"Probably there isn't one," Pete said, "but it makes you wonder. See you." He was gone.

Garfield looked at the stack of printout sheets and at Saunders's card. Pete was right to wonder, he told himself, because sometimes things did have a way of dovetailing, almost as if they had been planned.

He, too, stood up then. He had been sitting too long. A walk would be a good idea. This matter with Pete had been decided. Now it was time he took a long look at the other matter, Maude. And again he had the feeling that he was going to be a whole lot less sure of himself in that direction. There was also the matter of manners; he was, after all, a houseguest.

He found Clara on her knees in the dirt area behind the house, setting out plants in a minuscule garden plot, patting them carefully into place. She looked up when Garfield appeared, smiled and held up her grubby hands for his inspection. "I ought to wear gloves, but I've never been able to work in them the way some can."

"I used to like getting my hands dirty just fussing with things."
Garfield found himself smiling in memory. "Once when I was a kid,
I took the family TV apart and had it in pieces when my father came
home and wanted to watch a ball game." He shook his head, smiling
still. "There was hell to pay."

Clara patted the last plant into place. "In all the time we've
known each other," she said, "I don't think I've ever heard you speak
of either your father or your mother." Her eyes were on his face as
she stood up and rubbed some of the dirt from her hands. "Most
people do sooner or later." A statement, but it asked a question.

They walked together into the house. "Not much to tell," Garfield said. "Mother died of cancer when I was not quite sixteen."

Clara walked to the sink and began to scrub at her hands. Her
back was to him. "You were at school?"

"Finishing my freshman year at Cal Tech."

Younger than Lucy is now, Clara thought, and already a year
in college, and his mother gone—just like that. "I'm sorry," she said.
"But maybe boys don't need mothers as much at that age." She
turned from the sink and began drying her hands with the kitchen
towel. "And your father?"

"He had a reserve commission in the army. He volunteered for
Vietnam. I don't think he could face things without her—my
mother. His name is on that wall in Washington."

Clara blinked and went on drying her fingers. "How old were
you then?"

"Almost eighteen. I was all right. I had a scholarship. No
money problems. I wasn't used to much. Besides, I was all wrapped
up in my studies and experiments." He made a small gesture of
dismissal. "I haven't been much of a houseguest," he said. "Sorry
about that."

"Pete's been monopolizing you." Clara was smiling. "You're
not a guest, Dan. You're family. You know that."

"I was thinking maybe a walk."

"Am I included?"

"Definitely."

The sea breeze was brisk now, and boats filled the lower basin
of the harbor, heading for the ocean, multicolored sails set in the

bright sunlight. Garfield and Clara walked slowly along the narrow strip of sand at the bay's edge, watching the sight.

Clara said suddenly, unexpectedly, "Your mother and your father, Dan—no other family?"

"I think there are some cousins in the East somewhere. I've never met them."

" 'The Cat That Walked by Himself'? Kipling's story. I think it goes on, 'and all places were alike to him.' " She glanced up at Garfield's face. "The end of it, I think," she said, "is, 'He goes out to the Wet Wild Woods or up the Wet Wild Trees or on the Wet Wild Roofs, waving his wild tail and walking by his wild lone.' Did you ever read the *Just So Stories*?"

He had not, nor as far as he could remember until this moment had he ever heard of them. "I guess I missed quite a few things. I had funny ideas about what was important."

"Girls?"

"Not until later. I stayed in the academic womb until I was twenty-two. By then I had a Ph.D. and some big ideas. And I met a young medico, Tom, and decided to come out into the real world."

"With enormous success."

"I'm beginning to question that."

Clara glanced up at his face again, was about to speak and then changed her mind and said nothing. They walked on, across the peninsula to the ocean side.

It was Garfield who broke their silence. "You asked me a question the other day," he said. "It was about Maude."

For the second time Clara was about to speak and changed her mind.

Garfield glanced at her curiously. "No comment?"

"When did you see her last, Dan?"

The day the roof fell in, he thought, and again the bitterness returned in full flood. "Over a month ago."

"You were seeing her fairly regularly, weren't you? That was my impression."

"Yes."

"Then, don't you see, the inevitable question: What happened? I think she is wondering, too."

"I lost my faith." He had not even realized that the concept was in his mind, and the words seemed to slip out of their own accord, but once spoken, they brought a strange measure of relief.

"In her?" Clara was frowning now.

"In myself." There, he thought, it was out in the open, and he was not sure whether he was glad or sorry.

Clara had stopped walking and was studying him carefully. "There's a bench," she said. "Let's sit down, Dan. You've . . . shaken me. No, don't apologize. It's just that coming from you, it was so . . . unexpected."

It was the same bench on which he and Pete had sat for their long talk, Garfield realized. What looked to be the same endless swells were marching in and breaking on the sand just as they had been that day, but now he, Dan Garfield, was no longer the same person. What had changed he had no idea.

"Do you want to tell me about it, Dan?"

He thought about it and nodded slowly. "Strangely enough, I think I do." Another surprise. For the first time in a long time, he realized, he no longer felt that he was speaking lines that seemed to have been scripted by someone else but was speaking his own mind. "You're easy to talk to," he said.

"We've been friends a long time." Clara hesitated. "And you don't have many friends, do you?"

He had not really thought of it before, but it was true. Acquaintances, yes, a myriad of those. And colleagues, associates. But friends?

"I guess not." He could smile faintly. " 'The Cat That Walked by Himself'?"

"I think maybe something like that. That's pretty hard, Dan." Clara was silent for a few moments, staring out to sea. "Something's been bothering you, and I haven't had a clue because everything seemed to have gone so *right* for you." She turned to look at him then.

"Wrong." Once begun, the words came out in a flood. "I didn't negotiate the sale of Garfield Associates. I lost it. Or maybe it's better to say it was taken away from me. By a company that will probably suck its reputation dry, and milk it for all it's worth, and two partners I ought to have been able to control. In fact, I was confident I had them under control. My fault." He recounted the talk that morning in his office when Carmichael and Case had . . . revolted.

"And you've been brooding about it ever since?" Clara's voice was gentle.

"It's not something you forget." He produced a wry smile. "All I am now is rich. That's pretty funny, isn't it?"

"No. Sad. Is that why there's no room for Maude?"

"I hadn't thought of it that way."

"Maybe you'd better, Dan."

He studied her face. "Explain that."

"I don't think you've lost your . . . faith. I think you've just lost some of the superficial confidence that went with the . . . position you were in, head of a successful company, someone of guaranteed stature in your world. But you haven't changed, Dan. You're still the same person you were six weeks ago. I've watched you with Pete. You're sure of yourself, just as you always have been."

He could smile and mean it, suddenly more relaxed than in a long time. "Insufferable is what you mean."

"No. Never that. Confident of your abilities. With ample reason." She touched his arm gently. "You haven't lost anything except the . . . trappings of success, and they don't really count."

"A good pep talk." He was smiling still.

Clara shook her head emphatically. "I'm only speaking the truth. I don't think you've ever seen yourself as others see you, as Tom and I have seen you all these years. You don't need . . . position to establish yourself as a person. You stand out all by yourself in any group." She stood up from the bench with decision. "Enough for now." She was smiling, too. "You'll work it out. Shall we go on with our walk?"

The sun was bright, highlighting the scattered, fluffy cumulus clouds that dotted the horizon. And the fresh breeze from the sea was refreshing. Garfield was constantly aware of the slow timpani beat of the surf that seemed as in a symphony to hint of a coming change of tempo, perhaps a climax of some sort—fanciful thought. He smiled at Clara with sudden, open fondness. "Tom and Lucy are lucky to have you," he said.

"I'm lucky to have them. I'm a very lucky person, Dan."

"I've always had the conceit that we make our own luck, largely anyway."

"I think that's true. And you've made yours." And then, with no change of tone: "Lucy is smitten with you. I hope you realize that."

He had not, and the statement came to him with something of a shock. "I'm badly miscast."

"On the contrary, you're role-perfect for the teenage idol—older, but not out of reach; attractive and faintly mysterious—"

"Wait a minute."

"To her you are mysterious, because you come from a grown-up world of business enterprise she knows nothing about, and you don't talk much about yourself." Clara smiled suddenly. "You're also rich. And then there was that *Time* article."

"Pure puffery. I glanced through it. About all they had right was the spelling of my name. I told you, I didn't arrange that sale. I tried to prevent it and failed."

"Appearances are what count. And you came out of it the apparent winner." Again her hand touched his arm. "So accept it, Dan. Everyone else does."

They walked in silence and after a time turned inland again to the bay. More boats were out now, both sail and power, and the harbor was a moving panorama of shapes and colors. "Tom will be down this weekend," Clara said. "He'll come Friday unless something turns up."

"You'll be glad to see him."

Clara's smile was wistful. "Yes. We don't have much time together. But I want him to see you, too, and changed, Dan. He was worried. As I have been." For the third time her hand touched his arm with gentle pressure. "Will you see Maude, talk to her? For me? Please. It will be better for you both."

His smile was wry. "I've been trying to think what we might talk about."

Clara's smile was brilliant. "You'll think of something. I'm sure of it." She had stopped walking. "Do it, Dan. She's staying with the Barnes's in that brown shingle house." She pointed. "I'll leave you now." She was gone, walking quickly.

Garfield stood indecisive, looking at the house Clara had pointed out. She had tricked him, led him here, he thought, but, oddly, although he disliked being maneuvered he felt no sense of resentment. He started slowly toward the house, indecisive still, suddenly feeling exposed, foolish and awkward, like a young boy approaching his first date, wondering what he would find to say if some stranger answered his knock.

He was spared that confrontation because Maude was outside, on the narrow stretch of sand between the walk and the water, sunning herself. Her eyes were closed, and for an uncertain moment Garfield stood silent, looking down at her.

She wore the brief one-piece swimsuit both Betsy and Jack Barnes had remarked. Its color was that of the dress she had worn at that last lunch, and it clung to her body with fidelity, intimately following each lovely curve of hip, waist and breast. Garfield was unaware that Maude's eyes had opened and that she was watching him quietly.

"Do I pass inspection?" she said, and her voice caught him momentarily off-balance.

He gathered his composure. "You always have, with or without clothes."

Maude hesitated. "Am I blushing?"

"Not that I can see."

"Good." Suddenly she was smiling. "Long time, Dan."

"Yes."

"Sit down. The sand is soft." She watched him lower himself to sit facing her. "You've been busy," Maude said. "I read about it."

"Something like that." He was still uncertain, not at all in command of the situation and finding conversation difficult.

"I saw Clara Winslow at the market."

"She told me." And she sent me here to see you, he thought, feeling very much like a boy following his mother's directions.

"You're a celebrity," Maude said. "Is that why you're down here, as . . . escape?" She sat up suddenly, shaking her head in annoyance at herself. "Strike that. It was a nosy question. Are you staying long?"

"It . . . depends." He was thinking of Pete and of Pete's boss,

Howard Boggs, and Harry Saunders, by now almost certainly back in Washington and reachable by phone.

"You're preoccupied again," Maude said. She was smiling, her face suddenly transformed as it sometimes was. "Just as you were the last time I saw you. Am I the cause?" Her smile was fond. "Don't answer that. It's good to see you, Dan. I've missed you. That's hardly the ladylike thing to say—is it?—but it's true. I've missed you, and I wondered why I didn't see you. But you've been busy, and maybe that explains it."

"Not entirely." It was the honest answer, and he wondered where he went from that point. He would think of something, Clara had said. Well, he didn't think of anything that could be said aloud. This was Maude, not Clara, and there was a vast difference in his reaction to each. "I had a lot of thinking to do. I still have." He heaved himself to a squatting position and straightened slowly. "How long will you be here?"

Her smile had faded. Now it reappeared, full-blown. "It . . . depends."

He watched her yet a moment more in silence, trying to make up his mind. He said at last, "Let's see how it works out."

"Yes," Maude said slowly, "let's see." She watched him as he walked away. Tears were very close.

6

The office of J. Howard Boggs, the director of the Encino Beach Oceanographic Institute, was just down the hall from Pete's office, and Boggs was waiting for them the next morning. He rose to shake hands. "I'm very pleased to meet you, Mr. Garfield. I've heard and read a good deal about you. Dr. Williamson, Pete, tells me you're interested in his research."

"His research and his theories. I've seen his computer printouts, and I'd like to know more about it."

Pete, watching, thought that Boggs's eyes turned shrewd, the eyes of a man calculating odds at a gaming table. "We have a number of very interesting and important projects aside from his—" Boggs began.

"I'm sure. But at the moment I'm interested in what Pete is doing, and if I were to make a grant, I'd reserve the right to limit its application to that."

Boggs thought about it. "I'm not sure we could accept . . . dictation. We pride ourselves on academic freedom and independence—" He stopped. "You smile. May I ask why?"

"I've dealt with academia before," Garfield said. "Funded research is not uncommon, and frequently the direction of that research is stipulated by the donor. I think your university president, whom I know, by the way, would see it like that, but if you'd prefer, I'll ask him." His thoughts were running smoothly, jumping well in advance, as they had been accustomed to jumping during all those years running Garfield Associates, anticipating each move and countermove in order to achieve the end he wanted.

Pete, watching in silence, saw no reaction in Bogg's face beyond a blink of mild surprise as if he had not expected resistance. "I don't think that will be necessary," Boggs said. He was smiling no longer. "May I ask what size grant you had in mind?"

"One hundred thousand dollars. More, if it is required to carry the research as far as Pete and I think necessary."

Pete opened his mouth and shut it again in silence. We do not fool around, he told himself. He looked at Boggs again and waited.

"We could certainly use the money," Boggs said. "But to assign that much to a single narrow field of research—"

"There may be considerable expense involved. Travel, for example."

Boggs glanced at Pete, disapproval plain. He said, "We tend to frown on . . . outright, selfish solicitation by—"

"There was no solicitation," Garfield said. "The idea was entirely mine. As I said, I've studied the computer printouts, and I think they're going in an interesting direction, but I don't believe they've gone quite far enough."

"With all due respect, you are not an oceanographer, Mr. Garfield. You—"

"But I do know a considerable amount about data analysis and computer capabilities, with due respect, perhaps even more than you do, Dr. Boggs. And as far as selfishness is concerned, doesn't any successful research done under university auspices redound to the university's credit?"

Boggs was clearly on the defensive now. "What you want—" he began.

"To put it plainly," Garfield said, "what I want for my grant is for Pete's research data to be analyzed as thoroughly as is possible under his and my direction, and—"

"How will you accomplish that?"

"I'll arrange it. It will cost the university nothing beyond Pete's time."

Boggs swallowed hard. "And then?"

"Then we'll see which direction we want to go from that point."

"But—"

Garfield held up his hand. "Let me finish, please. When we have accomplished all that we think necessary, whatever funds remain will be turned over to your general fund to support other research." He watched Boggs for a long time in silence, his face showing nothing. "Do we have a deal, Doctor?"

Boggs got out his handkerchief and wiped his forehead. Slowly he nodded. "I see no objections. In your phrase, a deal, Mr. Garfield."

Pete and Garfield walked in silence down the hall to Pete's office. Pete plumped down in his desk chair and shook his head slowly. "That," he said, "was quite a show. You don't pull your punches, do you? And Howard is no pushover."

"I had all the cards."

"Even so." Pete smiled in admiration. "So now what?"

"I'll try Harry Saunders in Washington."

"Here?"

Garfield was still thinking in the old, familiar way, clearly, with certainty and without hesitation or doubt. "I think not. We want that in private."

Pete stood up. "Okay. But first—" He walked to the door and closed it, walked to the window and drew the heavy curtains, shutting out all daylight. "I want to show you something I've kept to watch every now and again just to remind me what I'm thinking and talking about. A bit of movie film, amateur stuff."

He already had the screen set up and a loaded movie projector on a table. In the dimness of the darkened room he moved to them, flipped a switch, and the film began. "Here we go," he said.

The picture that appeared showed a broad channel and on one side rising green hills, "Pure luck," Pete said. "This is one of those Aleutian towns nobody ever heard of with an unpronounceable name, too out of the way and too small to make the news. An amateur photographer took these, a good camera on a tripod with a zoom lens, from up behind the town. He wanted film of a pretty little harbor and a quaint town with the tide coming in." He was silent for a few moments as the projector whirred on, showing the flat water, no breath of breeze to disturb its surface. "This," Pete said, "is what he got. Watch!"

Garfield stared unbelievingly as the water level suddenly began to drop precisely as the level of water in a basin drops when the drain plug is removed. "You said the *in*coming tide!"

"Yep. Only it wasn't."

Mud flats that had been hidden began to appear as if the ground itself were rising. Still, eerily, the surface of the inlet channel's water remained almost undisturbed, only small ripples appearing around the higher ground portions as they became exposed.

"This was the warning," Pete said. "Textbook stuff; you can almost hear the sucking sound the outgoing water would make. The photographer didn't understand, but he had the wit to keep his camera rolling. Now, watch!"

The bottom of the channel was showing, almost all water drained away. Rocks long hidden appeared, along with bottom debris, some of it encrusted and unrecognizable, but here broken and twisted metal parts—of what, Garfield could only guess—and there an entire boat frame, its naked ribs gaping obscenely.

And then, without warning and with unbelievable swiftness, the water began to rise again, covering the channel bottom, the rocks, the debris, the mud flats, filling the inlet to its normal depth, and above, flooding the banks and rising still.

At its edges the water was beginning to churn and froth, and out in the center of the inlet whirlpools appeared, currents moving swiftly.

"Here it comes!" Pete said.

It was an incoming ocean swell, filling the camera's frame from side to side, rising, building, channeling its force into the inlet's mouth. As it swept up-channel, it grew in height, higher and higher, seemingly without end, retaining still its smooth shape. The lack of sound increased the feeling of unreality.

Garfield found that he was holding his breath, waiting for the swell to topple of its own weight as breakers do on the beach, but instead, it continued to grow, to swell into a monstrous, smooth, shiny entity charging up-channel directly at the camera's lens.

"Too much water behind it and within it for it to break," Pete said. "There's no real point of reference, but at this stage it's about thirty feet high and still growing. I've worked it out after watching the film God only knows how many times. Now watch as it comes out of the channel into the harbor area. There's ample room, and it ought to diminish and spread out, but it doesn't."

Freed of the channel's constraint, able to spread its energy, the monster swell nonetheless retained its full shape and size, and as the photographer adroitly adjusted the zoom lens to show the greater area, the swell undiminished, if anything still growing in height, continued to fill the camera's frame from side to side.

There was only one boat in the harbor, Garfield saw now, a trawler at anchor, one man on its deck. Onshore there was a single dock and a shedlike building outside which men were standing, their backs to the camera, staring out to sea.

"Keep your eye on that trawler," Pete said. His voice was carefully expressionless, but beneath it was an obvious sense of rising excitement. "And watch those men on the dock."

The swell reached the anchored trawler first. So smoothly and easily that the motion seemed almost gentle, the swell lifted the boat, higher and higher until the anchor line was clearly visible for a moment before it parted and whipped through the air like a thing alive. Still, the trawler remained upright, continuing to rise to the very crest of the swell, where it hung, balanced, as the mass of water bore down upon the dock and the startled men outside the shed.

They hesitated only a moment longer, looking upward to face

the monster, their bodies stiffened in fright. Then, as one man, they turned and fled in panic along the dock toward the shore.

"There are seven of them," Pete's voice said, expressionless still. "Now there are six, four, two and then one. And there he goes."

The men simply disappeared. One moment they were visible, racing toward the camera, the swell looming huge behind them. The next moment they were gone, and the smooth surface of the gigantic swell, undisturbed, still carrying the trawler on its crest, swept over the dock and onto the shore.

"I've taken measurements," Pete said, "comparing the swell to the men in size. At this point I'd put its height at about fifty feet. But with the entire inlet full of water behind it, you can only guess at its force."

The picture on the screen died suddenly, and only light showed from the projector. The sound of the film end slapping against the metal as it continued to turn seemed overloud in what, Garfield thought, ought to have been a funereal hush.

Pete switched off the camera. "That," he said, "is a tsunami wave. The film ran out, and the photographer didn't even notice. Can't say I blame him.

"That trawler, by the way," Pete went on, smiling now as one does in the face of the nearly incredible, "ended a mile and a half up into town. It must have been carried over half a dozen buildings to the place where it was finally put down." He shook his head in wonder. "There were two men aboard. They weren't even scratched."

Garfield was still staring at the blank screen. He said slowly, "I've imagined what one of the waves would be like, but—" He shook his head as if stunned and looked at Pete. "Between imagining and seeing—" Again the head shake.

"Yeah." Pete was busy rewinding the film. "That's why I run that every so often, just to remind myself exactly what we're dealing with." He straightened from the projector. "We'll scare the hell out of some people when we get around to talking about what we think might happen right here. You realize that?"

"I've thought about it." Garfield's voice was quiet. "Do you see an alternative?"

"That," Pete said, "is the worst of it. There is none." He made a short, sharp, angry gesture of dismissal as he walked to the window and threw open the curtains. Daylight filled the office. "Now shall we go see if Saunders will give us a hand?"

Driving back to the Winslow house, Pete seemed compelled to talk. Garfield listened in silence, unable to shake the picture of that gigantic tsunami swell, smooth, swift and inexorable, driven by incalculable energy and weight of moving water toward the harbor and the town, relentless as the plague of the Middle Ages that had wiped out a third of Europe's population.

"The first thing you think of," Pete was saying, "is some kind of defense. But there is no defense except being on high ground or at sea when the tsunami pass in the form of harmless, low swells, their crests hundreds of miles apart.

"We know a great deal about tsunami," Pete went on, "but we don't know the two most important things. We know that their speed is a function of the water depth in which they travel. The average depth of the Pacific is about sixteen thousand feet. Tsunami waves over water of that depth travel on the order of five hundred mph; over thirty-thousand-foot depth of water, their speed is more than a hundred mph greater, on the order of six hundred and seventy-five mph, jet plane speed. At those speeds the swells are two feet, maybe three feet high, rarely more. A ship at sea won't even notice them, particularly since their crests' being hundreds of miles apart means that a swell will pass only every hour or so.

"But," Pete said, "as each swell reaches shallower water, it begins to slow because of the drag of the bottom, and it loses a half of its speed, then three-quarters and more, and all that water behind it begins to pile up, millions of tons of it, maybe hundreds of millions of tons. And then you can get something such as we saw on the film."

Again Garfield could see that moving water sweeping toward the camera, almost, it had seemed, threatening to sweep into the office where they sat.

"But the two things we don't know," Pete was saying, "are when the tsunami will be generated and how to cope with them after they are formed and are on their way." He glanced at Garfield's face.

"Do you think the computer analysis you have in mind might give us a clue to the first—the *when,* the matter of prediction?"

"Maybe."

"The second, what to do if Murphy's Law applies and we get all the wrong factors of heavy storm and spring tides at the same time—that is something else again."

"We'll work on that," Garfield said, his voice definite, *"when* we see where we stand. There is no point in raising fears before we're sure of our ground." He paused and smiled suddenly, mocking his thoughts. "Or as sure as we can be."

Clara was not at the Winslow house when they arrived, but Lucy was, curled up on a settee with a copy of *Vogue.* "Hi," she said, and was on her feet all in one long, smooth, effortless motion, the magazine forgotten. "What's doing?" And she added without seeming to take a breath, "They say the surf's up at Onofre." She looked at Garfield. "You a surfer?"

It was impossible not to smile at her enthusiasm. "Not since I was your age. Or younger. I'm an old man, honey."

"Pooey! Pete surfs. Lots do, even older than you."

Pete said, "We've got business, Princess. Sorry." He started to follow Garfield toward Tom Winslow's study. Lucy's voice stopped him.

"Todd's looking for you," Lucy said. "You know, Todd Wilson. They just got down for the summer, Todd, Tina and Mrs. Wilson." She wore a curious, puzzled expression. "He, Todd, talks about you as Dr. Williamson now. I asked him why when he's always called you Pete like the rest of us, and he just looked kind of funny and shook his head."

"What did he want?"

"He wouldn't tell me."

"Male chauvinist pigs," Pete said. "That's what we all are."

"You know what? You're right." Lucy stuck out her tongue as the study door closed.

Garfield was already dialing the number on Saunder's card. He gave his name to the answering female voice, and in only moments Saunders came on the line. "Dan. How are things? I read about your . . . coup with Atlas. Congratulations."

Appearances were what counted Clara had said, and here Garfield was seeing the ironic truth of it. It was, he supposed, something he was just going to have to live with. "I'm with Pete Williamson," he said.

"You've gone over his computer printout?"

"Carefully."

"And?" The voice was sharp with interest. "I have reasons for asking."

Garfield smiled faintly. "I can guess at them." He saw immediately, as Pete had seen before him, how the far-flung military installations in the Pacific could be helped in their preparations if prior knowledge of a tsunami warning were possible. "I told Pete I was on the order of eighty percent convinced that there's an imminent danger. We want to dig deeper. With your help, one of your big mainframe computers."

"You think—" Saunders began, and stopped. "Of course, you do or you wouldn't be asking." There was a short silence. "Give me fifteen, twenty minutes," he said then. "Stay by the phone. What's your number?" He listened. "Got it." His tone changed. "It's good to know you're in on this, Dan. Frankly, there aren't too many whose word I'd take without going over the data myself. Somebody'll call shortly. Good to talk to you." The line went dead.

Garfield hung up and leaned back in the chair. "A few minutes," he told Pete.

"I heard." There was a new note almost of awe in Pete's voice. "You have clout."

"They have an interest, just as we do. That's all it is."

The telephone call came in a little less than fifteen minutes. "Mr. Dan Garfield? My name is Robinson, Bert Robinson. I was told to call you."

"You're the computer man?"

"That's me."

"I have considerable data, some questions and an expert to fill in any gaps," Garfield said. "What we're after are probabilities, a wide range of probabilities."

"Sounds interesting."

"Where?" Garfield said. "And when?" With the phone tucked

between cheek and shoulder, he began to write quickly on his yellow pad. And when he was done: "Two o'clock tomorrow. We'll be there."

"I'll be waiting."

He hung up. He sat for a moment in silence before he gathered himself and smiled at Pete. "We're on our way," he said. His face showed nothing. "Pasadena."

Pete nodded. "We'll allow two hours to make sure we're on time." He got up from his chair. "Now I can take the princess surfing with a clear conscience. Want to come?"

"You know," Garfield said, "I think I do." He felt almost eager.

7

Again in the cramped and dimly lighted interior of the minisubmarine two men sat in their respective chairs while the daylight disappeared as they descended. The indicator on the depth gauge rose steadily. And as during Pete's dive, Henry Larson, biologist, in tee shirt, jeans and sneakers, unshaven and wearing headphones, watched through his small porthole as the darkness outside deepened.

"Three thousand meters," he said, and threw the switch that turned on the outside floodlights, bringing a monochromatic world into clear view.

The second man, whose name was Vanden, watched through his porthole in fascination. "We're *inside* the aquarium," he said in a tone of wonder. "I hadn't really thought of it that way before." It was his first dive. "Giant squid over yonder, see him? Sperm whale fodder." He smiled. "How would you like to tangle with one of those?"

"No, thanks. Even the little ones they serve in restaurants can be tough enough." Larson glanced at the depth gauge. "Four thousand. There's the escarpment. See it?"

Vanden was silent for some moments, studying the sheer cliff walls. "Oversized Grand Canyon," he said, and smiled. "You run a spectacular trip, I must say."

"Wait till you see the bottom. You've seen films and still photos, but the actual thing is something else. I never get used to it."

They sat silent for a little time, watching the changing scene. A hammerhead shark appeared suddenly, hung motionless, staring at them with its widely spaced eyes, and then in a flash disappeared. A school of small fish, swimming as one, executed a swift, cartwheeling mass pirouette and was quickly gone. Dim shapes in the edge of the lighted area appeared and vanished like shadows. . . .

"Forty-five hundred meters," Larson said. "There's that broad ledge that runs for a hundred kilometers and more. It—" His voice stopped suddenly, and for long moments he was silent. He said at last, "Never noticed that before. The ledge looked as if it were hardly attached to the cliff wall. Cracks. I wonder what caused those."

"Five thousand meters," Vanden said. The ledge was no longer in view. "What's drifting down like autumn leaves? Not animal life. What is it?" He peered more closely through the porthole. "Falling rock," he said. "Little pieces, must be flaking off the wall. That the way it always is?"

"I've never seen it before," Larson said. "Must be currents flaking it loose. Six thousand meters. Time to start getting ready for the bottom. We've got a lot to do on this dive."

❦

Pete, Lucy and Garfield drove down to San Onofre in Pete's open car, Pete's and Lucy's surfboards in the rear. Once San Onofre had been a deserted beach, part of the large Camp Pendleton marine base, known only to serious surfers and frequented by them with tacit USMC permission.

It is now a state beach, complete with lined parking areas, posted regulations and paved one-way roads. But the surfing beach is unchanged, an open, shallowly curved cove, on the order of a half mile between its extended, low headlands. The endless swells, marching in, slow as they obey the drag of the bottom and, feeling the effect of the submarine ridge that bisects the cove, slow first in the center, and enter the cove in concave lines, directing their energy inward and building as they slow to produce surf that arguably provides the best surfing in North America.

"Changed since I was last here," Garfield said as they walked from the car. His eyes were on the twin containment domes of the Southern California Edison Company's nuclear reactor complex that almost dominates the scene. From the domes enormous steel tower structures march across the rolling hills, carrying heavy electrical cables to feed the Southern California power grid.

"I knew the reactor was here, of course," Garfield said, "but I hadn't realized it was quite as close to sea level." He looked meaningfully at Pete.

"Yeah," Pete said. "Something to think about. How long is shutdown time?"

Lucy said, "What in the world are you two talking about? We came here to surf, didn't we?" She smiled shyly at Garfield. "You going to? Or are you just going to watch?"

"Today I'm strictly a spectator." Garfield was in swim trunks, feeling very much out of place with his white skin among all the tanned bodies. "And in not very long I'm going to cover up as well before I fry to a crisp."

"Prudent," Pete said. "Come on, Princess."

Garfield sat on the sand. It was twenty years and more, he thought, since he had been part of this kind of beach scene. And there were changes to remind him how out of date his memories were.

Once, he remembered, there had been ferocious competition and antagonism between those who rode the old, heavy surfboards with their curved contours and their great maneuverability.

In heavy surf, it was said then, light boards were a menace because if a surfer wiped out, his light board could dive beneath the breaking wave, "sound" and, by its natural buoyancy, shoot suddenly to the surface, its momentum carrying it sometimes eight or ten feet into the air, a projectile that could shatter the jaw of some other unlucky surfer.

But all of the boards now, he saw, were the light, fiber glass variety, and the technique of riding them had advanced so far that it looked almost easy.

He watched a swell, larger than the rest, begin to slow and build as it curved inward. Surfers on their boards, alert now, kneeling, began to paddle furiously with both hands to match the growing swell's momentum. One by one, as they felt the surging power beneath them take hold, they sprang to their feet, to stand obliquely, arms spread for balance as they began their run toward shore.

He watched Pete shift his weight and steer his board diagonally across the face of the curling breaker. Lucy followed immediately, her slim, curved body gracefully balanced, arms spread as a ballet dancer's. She was partially crouched and smiling, as by her diagonal course she traveled a greater distance, at a greater speed within the time the wave rolled in to flatten itself on the shore.

She stepped off the board as it almost scraped bottom, caught it up in both hands and paused for only a moment to look in his direction and wave. Garfield waved back, feeling his own smile beginning as he caught the contagion of the girl's expression.

The smile faded as he turned to look again at the twin domes of the nuclear reactor, so close to sea level, so potentially . . . vulnerable, he thought, if Pete's worst-case scenario were to happen.

Murphy's Law, he found himself thinking—whatever bad can happen will—and this happy, healthy, carefree scene could be converted almost at once into . . . tragic catastrophe.

ॐ

They arrived back at the Winslow house in late afternoon. Lucy, sitting between Pete and Garfield, said, "Next time you'll try it?" She spoke to Garfield, and her eyes watched his face almost anxiously.

"We'll see," Garfield said. He was remembering one of the surfers who had not quite maintained his balance as he tried to cut across the face of a curling wave. The surfer had teetered desperately on one foot for only a moment, arms flailing, trying to regain control before he wiped out, cartwheeling to disappear in the breaker, and the free fiber glass board, sounding briefly, by its buoyancy reappeared and shot skyward four or five feet before it, too, fell into the turbulence and began to tumble side over side and end over end in the foaming white water. The surfer's head bobbed up behind the breaker as he began the lonely swim toward shore. "I'll make a fool of myself for sure," Garfield said, smiling, "but it wouldn't be the first time." He was thinking of Case and Carmichael again, and it occurred to him that he hadn't thought of them in some time.

Todd Wilson came out of the back door of the house as they drove in, a sizable young man with shaggy, sun-streaked blond hair and a body fitted muscularly into faded swim trunks. He nodded to Lucy. To Pete, he said, "Hi, Dr. Williamson. I wanted to talk to you." And he added, suddenly unsure of himself, "If that's okay, I mean."

"Why," Pete said as he got out of the car, "I think I can put up with it. This is Daniel Garfield, Todd Wilson."

The boy's eyes widened. "I've read about you. I mean, I guess everybody has."

"I hope not," Garfield said easily. He could smile.

And Pete said, "What's on your mind, Todd?"

The boy took a deep breath. "I'm majoring in geology at college, and, well, on a kind of field trip, you know, looking at this and that, just sort of poking around." He pointed toward the low hills inland. "Back in there. Maybe seven, eight miles on the LaPorte land. We had permission. We—"

"You found what?" Pete said.

"Rocks. Big ones. I couldn't lift a couple of them."

"Outcroppings?"

"No." The boy's headshake was emphatic. "Loose. Just scattered around. But the funny thing is—" He stopped and shook his head. "I know it sounds far-out, but they were the same kind of rock the point is composed of, igneous, isn't it?"

Pete nodded.

"And the exposed rock around there, where we found these boulders, I mean, the underlying rock is all sedimentary, sandstone, I think." He took a deep breath. "So how could boulders that size get up there from the shore?"

"Interesting point," Pete said, and there was no mockery at all in his voice.

"They weren't there to build anything," Todd said. "And who'd go to all the trouble of hauling them up there—it would take heavy equipment—just for the fun of it?"

Pete nodded. "As I said, an interesting point." He was silent for a moment, conscious that Garfield watched him. "Seven, eight miles from shore, you said?"

Todd said, "You know that side gate on the west side of the LaPorte property?" He watched Pete nod. "Well, it was beyond that because that's where we went in, and we turned inland, north, and walked maybe a couple miles up that old stream bed. The rocks were part buried, but they were loose, just dirt around them like they'd been there a long time."

"I imagine they had," Pete said. He glanced at Garfield. "Interesting," he said again.

Todd was suddenly ill at ease. "Maybe it doesn't mean a thing," he said, "but, well, I thought it was kind of . . . strange, you know? And—"

"Very strange," Pete said.

The boy relaxed again. "Would you like to see them? It wouldn't take long."

"I would indeed." Pete looked again at Garfield. "Coming?"

Lucy, lips pressed tightly together, watched the three men get into Pete's car and drive off. She walked into the house and slammed the door.

The rocks were there, as Todd had said, boulder size, one or two of them weighing, Pete estimated, two hundred pounds or more. And unlike the shore formations from which they undoubtedly came, they bore no sharp edges or points.

"What's smoothed them out is called exfoliation," Pete explained almost automatically while his mind wandered. "A combination of water erosion when this dry arroyo is filled as they sometimes are, or rain, and temperature changes from the sun's heat of the day and nighttime cooling, tends after a long time to flake off the sharp edges." He patted the largest of the rocks almost hesitantly.

"But where did they come from?" Todd said. "I'd say the shore, but that doesn't make sense, does it?"

"Maybe," Pete said. He stared at the rocks in silence for a long time and then looked around, estimating distance from the shore and height above sea level. He shook his head in slow wonder and looked at the boy. "You're a surfer. You know waves. What kind of wave would it take to bring these rocks up here?"

"You're kidding!"

Garfield watched in silence.

Pete smiled without amusement. "Maybe not. How would you like to try to ride a wave that big? *If* one ever appeared?"

Todd looked again at the rocks. He shook his head. "A wave big enough to move these would—why, it would go right across the peninsula as if the land weren't even there. It would wipe out Encino Beach, *total* it! You *are* kidding, aren't you?"

"Not kidding," Pete said, "just . . . speculating on wholly insufficient data. But such waves are possible. They're called tsunami, and I'll tell you about them on the way back."

Later, sitting alone with Garfield on the Winslow porch, looking out over the bay, Pete said, "Anomaly, turning up without warning, the accidental find of a kid who was curious." He shook his head. "It happens. You know the Lascaux caves story? Magnificent Paleolithic cave paintings in France, discovered entirely by accident by a kid, chasing his dog, I think, in 1940. Gone all those centuries without being found. We've got something of the same kind of thing here. Possible—I emphasize *possible*—indication, if not proof, that at some time this coast *was* hit with tsunami. At least offhand I can't *think* of any other explanation for those rocks. Can you?"

Garfield shook his head. He was thinking again of that monster tsunami wave sweeping toward the camera. "Scary, isn't it?" he said.

❦

Bert Robinson, the computer man in Pasadena, wore a beard and longish hair, with jeans, a tee shirt and worn jogging shoes. He studied Pete's typed data, the computer printout pages and then the pages of Garfield's handwritten notes. When he finished, he looked at them both and smiled, showing white teeth through the thicket of black beard.

"I'm tempted to ask if you're kidding," he said, "but under the circumstances, I know damn well you aren't. We don't play games on my big baby. Time on it is too important." The smile disappeared. "In these typed data, you have facts that aren't facts at all, but folktales going back hundreds of years. You want those taken into consideration?"

Garfield was obviously in charge. "Definitely yes. And weighted against what we know are facts going back into the early seventeenth century."

Robinson nodded. "Got it. And time probability is what you're aiming at, no?"

Both men nodded.

"We give the Japanese data full credence?"

Pete said, "We do. They even gave the phenomenon the name tsunami, which means 'large waves in harbor.' Their earthquake records go way back, and we know, for example, that in 869 there was a tsunami in Japan that caused considerable loss of life, but the details are too hazy to be used. The data you have there are to be taken as fact."

Garfield said, "And there are additional data, inexact but important. Pete?"

Pete recounted his second dive in the minisub and his observations of the ledge, the apparent fracture lines, his judgment that the entire mass was unstable.

Garfield said, "And as far as we know, the underwater nuclear testing is still going on." He looked meaningfully at Bert Robinson.

Again the white teeth showed in the thicket of beard. "You mean, could I ask a few questions here and there?"

"It would be helpful. Harry Saunders—"

Robinson nodded. "I get the message." He looked at Pete. "Just as a matter of curiosity, how big do these things get, these—tsunami?" He stumbled over the last word.

"The largest measured," Pete said, "was about two hundred and ten feet high, and their force can be roughly judged by the fact that a sixty-ton ship in one area was lifted on a wave sweeping through the harbor and left several miles up a shallow valley thirty feet above sea level. It's still there."

Robinson pursed his lips in a silent whistle. "The man mentioned," he said, "that you considered these data important. You weren't just whistling 'Dixie,' were you?" He stood up. "Okay, gents. Give me a few days, a week at the most, and I'll have a program ready."

Pete said, "How long will it take on the computer when you feed it in?"

For a third time the black beard parted to display the astonishingly white teeth. "I'd guess about twelve minutes."

Pete shook his head in disbelief.

"We don't fool around either," Robinson said. "I give baby the data and ask the questions, and baby gives out the answers almost before I'm finished." He touched the printout sheets. "Putting these out is the slowest part, and that isn't what you'd call leisurely. Twelve minutes—make it fifteen at the outside. You'd like to be here? I'll give you ample warning of kickoff time."

Pete was almost ebullient, driving back to Encino Beach. "The last thing I expected was . . . cooperation at this level. You—"

"Harry Saunders came to see *you,*" Garfield said, emphasizing the last word.

"But he only really perked up when I told him you were involved." Pete glanced curiously at Garfield's face. "And I still don't know why you are."

"I'm . . . enjoying it," Garfield said, and realized that he spoke only the truth. Call it therapy, he thought, something to take my mind from that . . . humiliation at the hands of Atlas, Case and Carmichael.

8

Walker Carmichael appeared unexpectedly at the Winslow house, driving a shiny new Mercedes. "I had the hell of a time finding you," he told Garfield. "You didn't leave much of a trail." He seemed resentful, but almost at once his hearty salesman's good nature reappeared. "How are you, boy? Enjoying the free life? No worries. Quite an improvement, no?"

"You're working up to something, Walker," Garfield said. "I know the signs. What is it?"

Carmichael sat down. He looked out over the bay. "Nice spot. I've thought sometimes about getting into sailing, boating myself." He looked at Garfield. "Holding a grudge? Because Paul and I wouldn't go your way for once? And made you lousy rich in the bargain?"

"What is it, Walker? Spell it out."

Carmichael sighed. "Okay. Just like you always were, all business. Did you ever learn to relax, Dan? Never mind. Strike that." He was silent for a few moments, contemplative. "We had a deal, you remember," he said at last. "The DOD wanted our analysis *and* cooperation in development of one part of—hell, what everybody calls it is Star Wars. Right?"

"Go on."

"You aren't very friendly, Dan."

"Stick to the point."

Carmichael sighed again. "Okay. The DOD have called the deal off. And Atlas wanted to know why. You know what the DOD's answer was?"

"No."

"Because they wouldn't be dealing with you anymore. You're who they wanted overseeing the show. They're used to you. They—" Carmichael stopped. "Okay, goddamn it, they don't think anybody else can do the job as well. So they're calling it off. That's the bottom line."

"I'm flattered."

"No, you aren't, Dan. You know how good you are. You've always known. And you couldn't care less how long it ever took other people to realize it. You—"

"The DOD will find somebody else."

"Sure they will. But that's just the point. Atlas wants to get *into* that project, get a foot in the door. It's worth—who knows? Maybe hundreds of millions if it works out. Maybe billions."

"Probably."

"Damn it, Dan, they, Atlas, came to me. They want you. They asked me—"

"Was that all you had in mind, Walker?"

There was a silence. For long moments Carmichael studied Garfield's face and then looked away, out at the water. For the third time he sighed. "That was all. Yes."

Garfield stood up. "Then you'll excuse me. I have an . . . engagement."

"Doing what? What's so damn important?"

"I'm going surfing. Sorry you made the trip for nothing."

❦

Garfield sat on the beach at San Onofre with Lucy and Todd Wilson, their three surfboards planted upright in the sand nearby. Todd and Lucy drank from cold cans of diet cola.

"You did real good," Lucy told Garfield. "That last run was really neat."

"Pure luck. But you're also good teachers." Garfield could smile despite fatigue, his growing stiffness and the faint discomfort of sunburn. He felt good, relaxed, filled with a sense of accomplishment. Still fresh and clear in memory was the *feel* of that last exhilarating plunge over the crest of the breaker, the surfboard suddenly tilting down and the gathering power of the wave surging beneath him, knowing that he had caught it just right, neither too far ahead nor lagging behind—and then the breathtaking ride down the front slope, confidently balanced at last, totally in control.

Running through his mind during that final experience had been the childish chant of glee "Look, Ma, no hands!" It was a long time since he had felt like this.

"You're smiling to yourself," Lucy said. "What's funny?"

"I'm just thinking of something. Somebody." Walker Carmichael, to be precise. Walker, Garfield was thinking, would almost drop dead of surprise if he were here now. As would Paul Case. And probably hundreds of others who had known only the expert business side of Dan Garfield. "Sorry Pete isn't here."

Lucy laughed aloud. "He'd flip if he saw you. We'll bring him maybe tomorrow and show you off." Her eyes sparkled, and there was pride in her young voice.

Todd set down his can of cola, scooped up a handful of sand and watched it contemplatively as it trickled between his fingers. He looked at Garfield. "I went to the library after I was with you and Dr. Williamson," he said.

"Come on!" Lucy said. "He's still Pete."

Todd emptied his hand of sand and dusted it automatically. He shook his head. "Not to me. Not anymore. I know his . . . reputation with the people in his field. He's one of the best." He looked again at Garfield. "And he scared me," he said. "Hearing him talk about the size wave it would take to move those rocks way up there. And then reading about tsunami."

"What rocks?" Lucy said, looking from face to face. "Where? And what's that funny word?"

"Up in the hills," Todd said. "You heard me telling Dr. Williamson. Big rocks I couldn't lift, and he thinks they may have been carried up there by a wave. One wave!" He shook his head in wonder.

"You're kidding!" Lucy said. She looked at Garfield. "Rocks that big?"

Garfield was smiling no longer. "I'm afraid so."

"I don't believe it! It's something you made up. Or—" Her face changed quickly to an expression of annoyance and sudden understanding. "Or is that what you and Pete have been all uptight about, talking together and shutting yourselves up in Daddy's office? Is that it?"

Garfield nodded faintly. "Broadly speaking, yes."

"And that . . . man in the Mercedes who came to see you? The same thing?"

"No. That was a different matter. Entirely different." Until this moment he had not seen the enormousness of the difference between his association with Pete and the association Walker Carmichael had wanted him to engage in with Atlas. The first was unselfish, noncommercial, important, *real.* The second was merely business as usual, profit-motivated, even, in a way, sordid. And it came to him with something of a shock that he could think of it so dispassionately in those black-and-white terms.

"Everything's so hush-hush!" Lucy said. "You guys get together and . . . whisper! Like you're telling jokes I shouldn't hear the way guys used to do at school."

Garfield was smiling. "Male chauvinist pigs. I seem to have heard the phrase somewhere."

"You better believe it!"

Todd said, "Hey! Slow down! You're racing your motor."

Lucy breathed deeply, straining the scant halter top of her bikini to its limit. "Okay." She could even smile ruefully, looking from face to face. "I'm sorry. But it does . . . make me mad. Why does it have to be such a . . . secret?"

"Because we're not sure," Garfield said. "Yet. Maybe in a few days we'll know better just how we stand." He smiled in what he hoped was a reassuring way. "And even then a lot of things have to come together before there's any immediate . . . problem here."

Lucy's eyes watched him steadily. "But there *could* be? Is that what you're saying?"

Even mild evasion was impossible in the face of this scrutiny. "We're pretty well convinced that it is possible, yes."

Lucy looked around at the sand, the clear sky, the surf sweeping in, all of it familiar, dependable, safe. "It's . . . hard to believe," she said. "And I don't think I want to believe it anyway."

"Smart girl," Garfield said. And when she looked at him sharply, suspecting patronization, he added, "A healthy skepticism is sensible, honey. Things shouldn't always be taken at face value."

"You sound just like Daddy." There was disappointment behind the words.

❦

Tom Winslow came down from town that Friday afternoon late. Despite the air conditioning in his car, he looked heated and tired as he walked into the house. "Freeway traffic," he said, and managed a wan smile. "Sixty-five miles an hour, and suddenly there's a traffic clot that takes ten minutes to clear up. Then more speed up and stop." He shook his head, and the smile turned full and happy. "Never mind. I'm here and I can relax." He looked out at the bay. "And tomorrow we can spend the whole day out on the water, no phones, no crises." He looked at Clara. "Okay?"

"Lovely," Clara said. There was a glow of happiness in her face Garfield had not seen in a long time. He felt a pang of envy.

Showered, refreshed and carrying a drink, Tom came out on the porch a half hour later wearing shorts, sailing shoes and a faded tee shirt. He sat down and studied Garfield. "Picked up a little color instead of that prison pallor," he said, and nodded approval as he tasted his drink. "But I understand you're already involved with Pete Williamson in some kind of—what? Research?"

"More or less. Pete has a theory that makes too much sense to ignore." Garfield sketched in the major points of the potential tsunami threat. "Briefly," he finished, "that's where we are."

The doctor tasted his drink again, and his eyes watched Garfield over the rim of the glass. "Science fiction," he said as he lowered the glass. "But, then, that's been your thing all along, hasn't it? Far-out ideas transformed into reality?" He was silent for a time, looking out at the water, the moored boats. "Hard to believe, but if you're convinced—"

"Almost convinced," Garfield said. "When we have the deeper analysis, I may lose all hesitation."

The doctor nodded, but his thoughts seemed to be elsewhere. Again he stared at the water. "And Clara tells me," he said without looking at Garfield, "that Maude Anderson is down here, too." The question was implied.

"She is. I've seen her."

The doctor still stared fixedly at the water. "Clara and I are not matchmakers. But it did seem that at last you had found somebody who lived up to your high standards. None of our business, of course, but we have known you well for a long time." He did turn his head then and faced Garfield.

"You've turned shrink, have you?" Garfield was smiling. "Or is it advice to the lovelorn?"

"Damn it, boy, you've been alone too long. I would have gone mad long ago if I hadn't had Clara. And Lucy. Everybody needs somebody." He, too, was smiling now. "And you may quote me."

"I'll give it due heed, Doctor."

"Maude's a stunning woman."

"Granted."

"And bright."

"All of that."

"And I think in love with you. Clara thinks so, too, and I'll trust her judgment in that kind of matter ahead of my own."

"So I'm the problem?" Garfield was smiling still. "You may be right. I think probably you are. So I'll just flounder around until I get the problem sorted out."

"Are you even trying?"

"Right now, frankly," Garfield said, "I'm too wrapped up in Pete's theory for much of anything else. There's too much at stake."

"You were too wrapped up in Garfield Associates, too."

Again the difference between what he was doing now with Pete and what he had spent his adult life doing, building Garfield Associates, suddenly seemed stark and clear. "There is no comparison," he said. "This—what Pete has uncovered is—*real.* From this distance, the other, inventing and manufacturing electronic gadgets, now seems somehow . . . artificial." It was as simple and as clear as that.

The doctor finished his drink. "I'd say you've got religion bad." He stood up. "And maybe that's good. Who knows? Let's join the ladies. I have trouble getting enough of them just during a weekend."

❦

The City Council meeting was short and decisive. The vote in favor of the new marina was unanimous. It just went to show, Jimmy Silva thought, what a man who did his homework could accomplish in the way of persuasion. As a matter of fact, Brown, the lawyer on the Council, and the orthopod as well were beginning to sound as if the marina had been their idea to begin with.

"It will enhance property values," the lawyer said. "They're already high, but this will make them even higher. If I can find a place that even comes close to being a good buy, I'll snap it up and hold it until I can turn it over at a nice, fat profit once the marina is in being."

Jimmy made no comment, but he remembered well that this was the same man who had explained at tedious length once during a Council meeting that for a Council member to use what the lawyer referred to as insider information was a gross breach of the trust the citizenry had shown by voting the Council members into office. It was also, he had said, sometimes actionable. Jimmy did not bother himself over other men's morality. He figured that being responsible for his own behavior was job enough.

And Jack Barnes was living up to his reputation as a real estate whiz, a reputation Jimmy had researched very carefully long before Barnes had walked into his office. All in all, Jimmy was thoroughly satisfied with the way matters were progressing. The bond issue would be on the ballot in the next election, and Jimmy had no doubts of his ability to twist enough arms, if necessary, and even put up a little cash to be judiciously distributed, to ensure the bond issue's passage. So he foresaw nothing but clear sailing, and a pleasant profit for himself in the bargain.

❧

Joe Hines, harbormaster, took his gray and white workboat up the harbor at a leisurely pace from its float in front of his office just north of the Yacht Club, leaving no wake to speak of, sending out no waves to disturb the yachts on their moorings, because of their number jammed together with scarcely room to swing from wind or current without fouling one another.

Almost unconsciously he noted that while the high-sided power cruisers were pointing west into the morning breeze, the deep-keeled sailing yachts, obeying the outgoing tidal current, were without exception pointing north, up-channel.

Locally born and bred, Joe Hines had been around boats and the water all his life and had long ago learned to accept without complaint such matters as tides and currents, weather and storms and even the sometimes apparently capricious happenings that were all part of life on or near the sea.

During his five wartime years in the navy, in destroyers—"tin cans"—which in any kind of weather seemed to spend more time on their beam ends than on their bottoms, he had served under a chief boatswain's mate with more years at sea than he cared to remember, filled with endless tales of happenings which maybe were, and maybe were not, to be believed. From this chief, he had absorbed wisdom along with the lore, and it was part of this wisdom that was bothering him now.

"There's no way in God's world of knowing what may happen either in wartime or in peace," the chief had been fond of saying to the water-wise kid he had in a sense taken under his wing. "But when you're dealing with the sea, you'd goddamn well better make sure you prepare for everything and anything you can think of that just *might* decide to happen whether it seems likely or not. You may be in calm, well-charted water, but there still could be floating wreckage, or unexpected newly formed shoals, or weather that comes out of nowhere without warning, and as near as you can, you'd better be ready to fall to the moment anything happens."

And what had brought the chief's words to mind again, Joe thought now, pipe between his teeth, eyes constantly on the alert for anything out of the ordinary, handling the workboat with the unconscious ease of long experience, was something as simple as a little sign he'd seen a thousand times in the greasy spoon where each morning he had a sociable cup of coffee with whoever happened to be around.

The sign read: OCCUPATION OF THESE PREMISES BY MORE THAN 35 PERSONS IS UNLAWFUL. BY ORDER OF THE FIRE MARSHAL.

Joe Hines had sat and just stared at that sign for a matter of minutes, mentally kicking his own ass that he had not seen the parallel long before this.

The implications of that sign were too obvious to miss: In the event of fire or any other immediate danger—here in California earthquake came to mind—getting more than thirty-five people out of the greasy spoon in a hurry would be difficult, if not downright impossible. That was what bothered Joe.

Because how many boats were there in this harbor under his care? He didn't remember offhand an exact figure, not counting visiting yachts on the club's spare moorings, but there were sure as hell more than could possibly get out to sea through the one narrow channel in less than a matter of days, let alone minutes or even hours. It was as plain and as startling as that.

What kind of immediate danger could arise that would require getting all the boats safely to sea? Joe had only the foggiest idea, but hadn't that been exactly the chief's point? That you couldn't foresee everything, but you'd damn well better be prepared for it, no matter. Think of Pearl Harbor, with the Pacific Fleet caught at anchor when the waves of Japanese bombers suddenly came diving in out of the sun that quiet Sunday morning?

He was coming back down-channel now, running with the current, and without even thinking, he throttled down a trifle more, maintaining only bare steerage way past the hundreds of moored or tied-up craft.

All the way down the bay of the channel itself, narrow, well dredged, wide enough, but with the larger yachts only just, for incoming and outgoing craft to pass safely.

He took the workboat out between the jetties and the newly added hundreds of tons of great rocks that built up the breakwater. Once he was clear of the jetty's ends, closing upon the bell buoy and immediately into deeper water, the motion of the workboat changed, falling into the rhythm of the incoming swells.

One of the fishing fleet was coming in, and the captain, at the controls on the flying bridge above the wheelhouse, waved at Joe, who waved back. Joe had grown up and been through school with half the current fishing boat captains. He wondered now if anyone but himself had seen the problem of an overcrowded harbor. He doubted it. It was *his* responsibility.

And there was one more thing, too, and it was really this, lurking in his thoughts, that had prompted the sudden realization of that little sign's implications.

Todd Wilson, whom Joe had watched grow up summers down here at Encino Beach, had dropped into his office only yesterday. Todd was a big, good-looking kid now, a better-than-competent hand on a sailing yacht or navigating somebody's big power cruiser in one of those predicted-log races the club sponsored outside. Joe could remember when Todd was first sailing dinghies in the kids' in-harbor races.

"Hi, Joe," Tod said. "How's it going?"

"No complaints. What about you?"

Todd helped himself to a chair. He seemed uneasy, the way young ones were when they were trying to get to a point. "You've been around, Joe. I mean, at sea. I used to listen to you talk about it." He grinned suddenly. "When you weren't chewing me out, that is, and reading me the rules of the road."

"A harbor hot rodder, that's what you were."

Todd's grin remained unabashed and then faded. "You ever heard tell of big waves, Joe? I mean, really big, big enough to make the biggest breakers San Onofre can produce look like nothing?"

"I've heard tell." Joe took out his pipe and rubbed its bowl slowly against the side of his nose, remembering. "Chief I served under had spent time out on the China Station, and he had stories about the kind of waves you're talking about down in the South China Sea. He had a funny word for them, foreign word, I seem to recall." He had the pipe back between his teeth again, and he smiled around it. "That chief, you never knew whether to believe him or not."

"Was the word *tsunami,* Joe?"

Joe took his pipe out again, looked at it and then pointed it, stem first, at Todd. "Where'd *you* hear it?"

"It's a real word, Joe. Oceanographers use it. Ask Dr. Williamson."

"Pete?" Joe nodded thoughtfully and put the pipe back in his mouth. "What about them? These—what you called them."

Todd told him about the big rocks up the hillside and about what he had read. The trouble was, Joe thought, it all sounded entirely too damn much like what the chief had yarned about down in the South China Sea. "You wouldn't be making this up, would you?" Joe said, already knowing that the answer was negative.

Todd stood up. "Kind of scary, isn't it?"

Now, taking the workboat back into the harbor, seeing again the hundreds of pleasure craft riding serenely on their moorings, looking, too, at the low-lying land of the peninsula, all that separated the bay from open ocean, still not knowing whether to take seriously what Todd had told him along with what the chief had spun his yarns about, and, above all, remembering that little sign in the greasy spoon, Joe Hines, harbormaster, had a sudden sinking feeling in his stomach and an unpleasant taste in his mouth and in his mind.

Another of the chief's favorite sayings came to him. "Times when you can't do a damn thing, even when it's sure as hell needed," the chief had said, "they're worst of all. Like watching a torpedoed troopship go down in flames, and men in the water screaming for help, but you can't help because your job is to find the goddamn sub, and blow it to hell before it sinks another ship. That's the kind of thing that curdles your stomach and waters your bowels. And you don't forget it. Not ever."

Interlude

The Aleutian Islands chain sweeps in a great uptilted southwesterly arc fifteen hundred miles down into the North Pacific from the mainland of Alaska. "All more or less part of that same broad cordillera," Pete had told Garfield, "that goes down from Alaska to Cape Horn, young, still in a sense in the process of formation, unstable. Tremors are almost the norm."

Early that Saturday morning, July 12, three undersea earthquakes rocked the tip of the island chain. The largest of the three measured 7.7 on the Richter scale. Its epicenter was approximately ninety miles northeast of the island of Adak, about twelve hundred miles from Anchorage.

Walls were cracked and windows shattered by a tsunami wave at the naval air station on Adak; but the five thousand residents of the island, mostly navy personnel, had already been evacuated to high ground, and there were no casualties.

Seismgraphs around the world recorded the shocks, and from reporting stations encircling the Pacific Basin data were sent to the International Tsunami Warning Center headquarters at Ewa Beach, Honolulu, Hawaii, whereupon a Pacific-wide tsunami warning was issued.

Officials in the Aleutians, Alaska, Washington, Oregon, California and Hawaii immediately recommended evacuation of low-lying coastal areas.

❧

"It's nonsense," Pete Williamson said. "An alert, maybe, but a warning, no. That's putting out the red flag, and I'll bet my shirt it isn't necessary. Earthquakes in the Aleutians are not quite a dime a dozen; but they're common enough, and this one isn't so big that it will raise that much hell."

Pete and Garfield had walked across the peninsula and were sitting on that same stone bench they had first chosen. Garfield said, "That's your studied opinion?"

"Yes, damn it!"

"And yet what we're thinking about—"

"Bigger! Because of the circumstances! Maybe eight-point-five, even eight-point-seven. The scale is exponential, you know, and eight-point-seven would be *ten times* the strength of this one! Then we'll really have something to worry about. This—" He stopped, studying Garfield's face. "You're thinking what?"

"Not very happy thoughts."

"Such as?"

"You think this will turn out to be a false alarm?"

"Definitely."

"Then what do you think will be the reaction when the next alarm is raised? Will anyone respond?"

"Damn it, they've got to!"

Garfield was silent for long moments, staring at the water. "Maybe," he said. "But I doubt it. And I think we'd better try to find out." He sighed as he got up from the bench. "A little stiff from surfing yesterday." He was smiling.

❦

It was early evening of that Saturday, and cars filled the parking lot of the Dunes shorefront restaurant a little north of Encino Beach. From within came sounds of voices, music, laughter. The headwaiter said, "If you want a window table, gents, they're all taken. Have been for a couple hours. Sorry."

Pete said, "Why the crowd? Far more than usual."

"Haven't you heard there's a tidal wave coming? People want to see it."

"But the waves aren't supposed to come this far south," Pete said. "Only way up on the northern coast."

"Well," the headwaiter said, "people aren't sure the folks who predict these things really know what they're talking about, and if there *is* anything to see, they want to watch it. You know how it is."

Walking back out to the car, "Yeah," Pete said, "we know how it is." He glanced at Garfield's face. "That's five restaurants, same thing at each. I give up. You were right. As usual."

"Let's go down on the beach," Garfield said. "See what's doing there."

Pete walked to the edge of the parking lot and walked back. "You can see from here," he said. "There're three, four fires, picnics, drinking beer, cooking hamburgers, waiting for the show." There was disgust in his voice.

"Like going down to see the grunion run," Garfield said. All at once he was smiling as he looked at Pete. "Do you know about them? You're not a Californian, are you? California grunion are silversides, family Atherinidae, small shore fishes that come in on high tide to lay their eggs as far up the sand as they can. When I was a kid, we came down to watch them. It was, of course, full moon. Very exciting for a small boy." His smile spread, as he remembered the sight of the small, wriggling fishes, thousands of them, gleaming damply in the brilliant moonlight, a sudden explosion of nature.

Pete studied him in silence and shook his head in wonder. "You know," he said, "I don't think I'd ever have thought of you as a small boy, excited. Funny, isn't it?" He waved one hand in vague apology.

"Never mind. Like I said, these people"—he gestured again to include the restaurant and the beach beyond—"behave just like the people Jerry Matsuo tells me who turn out in droves whenever Kilauea acts up in Hawaii, regardless of the possible danger. Like those damn fools who went down to the beach at Hilo to watch the predicted tsunami come in—and were wiped out to a man." He looked as if he wanted to spit. "People."

"My opinion of herd behavior," Garfield said, "is not very high. I know that's not a popular view, but I see no reason to change it." He was silent as they walked back to the car. "The major problem," he said as they got in, "is that once these people have been thoroughly disappointed because there are no spectacular waves, and certainly no danger, why should they place any credence in the warnings that will be issued if and when the real seismic disturbance has taken place and tsunami waves of enormous force have actually been generated?"

"You want me to answer that?"

"Not really," Garfield said, "but I'm afraid we do have to recognize the answer: People will pay little or no attention, no matter how urgent the warnings are. Agreed?"

Pete took his time. "Oh, hell," he said at last, "yes. You're right again. As usual." He started the engine and then sat back in his seat, deep in thought. "One thing. We don't really know how folks are behaving up north and in Hawaii, where there *are* going to be some waves, do we?"

"We'll find out tomorrow," Garfield said.

By the Associated Press

PACIFIC TIDAL WAVE A WASHOUT

Sunday, July 13

Thousands of Pacific Coast residents fled to higher ground after sirens and loudspeakers warned of a tidal wave triggered by yesterday's earthquakes off the Aleutian Islands, but the biggest wave was a human one.

A tsunami warning was posted from Alaska to California as well as to Hawaii and Japan after a major quake, measuring 7.7 on the Richter scale, occurred undersea near the Aleutian island of Adak. About 21,000 fled low-lying coastal areas in Hawaii, Alaska, Washington, Oregon, British Columbia and northern California, and many boats headed out to sea to ride out the waves.

But there was a festive atmosphere in the emergency shelter in Copalis Crossing, Washington, and several hundred evacuees who gathered at the Campbell High School parking lot in the Oahu, Hawaii, community of Ewa Beach threw a tailgate party with six-packs of beer and decks of cards. Southern California seaside restaurants were crowded with customers anxious to watch the waves come in.

Waves were less than 8 feet high in Hawaii, 2 to 3 feet in Washington, and only 5.8 feet on Adak Island closest to the epicenter. Japan's Central Meteorological Agency said a tsunami of 9 inches was observed there.

No casualties were reported in any area.

The Federal Tsunami Warning Service called off its warning six and a half hours after the quake struck.

Garfield, Daphne and Pete sat over beer in Pete's kitchen, the morning papers spread on the table before them.

"So now we know," Pete said. His eyes were on Garfield. "You had it figured out right from the start. Can you pick horse races the same way?" There was a blend of admiration, awe and a small amount of resentment in his voice.

"As I understand it, chaps," Daphne said, "you are in agreement that when the balloon goes up and warnings are issued, probably no one will pay any attention, is that correct? They cried 'Wolf!' yesterday, and there was no wolf." She looked from one face to the other and found her answer. "Then," she said, "the question becomes, does it not, just what do you intend to do about it? Merely shake your heads sadly?"

Part II

9

It was early the Monday morning following the tsunami warning. Tom and Clara walked slowly out to the doctor's car. Despite the early chill, Clara wore only a robe and slippers; the doctor wore shirt, tie and suit trousers and carried his suit jacket over his arm. "I wish—" he began, and stopped, smiled and shook his head. "I always wish after a weekend that I didn't have to go back to town."

"So do I." Clara held his arm tightly against herself. "The weeks are long, and the weekends short, too short, always." She managed a smile, too. "You'd better hurry to miss the heavy traffic."

"Yes." Tom kissed her. It was a long kiss.

"Call me from the office."

"After rounds."

"All right."

The doctor got into the car, started the engine and rolled down his window. "Is Dan too much in the way? He could just as well stay in a hotel. God knows he can afford whatever he wants."

"I like having him here. And Lucy is—" Clara shook her head. The smile this time was genuine. "Lucy would be heartbroken if he left. She's taken him surfing, and she's so proud of him she could burst. Her own pet celebrity."

The doctor said, "What about Maude Anderson?"

"Yes." Clara's smile disappeared. "I'll have to try to do something about that."

"I told him we were not matchmakers."

"Then," Clara said, "I'll have to be subtle. If I can." She bent and kissed him again quickly. "Hurry, darling, or you'll be fighting freeway traffic all the way to town." She stepped back and waved him away. When the car backed and turned in the alley and drove away, out of her sight, she at last turned and walked back into the house, suddenly feeling very lonely. Tears were very close.

🌀

Pete had a caller that morning at his office at the institute. Joe Hines, harbormaster, had a little trouble coming to the point. "Todd Wilson," he said. "You know him?"

Pete nodded. "What about him?"

"He came to see me the other day." Joe puffed thoughtfully on his vile-smelling pipe. His eye caught the big Pacific Basin map on the wall, and he got up to walk over to it and stand studying its immensity. With his pipe stem he delineated the vast area bounded by Midway, Guam, Port Moresby, Pago Pago and Hawaii. "I spent the big war down there aboard a destroyer." He turned to look at Pete. "Gets rough sometimes, what they call typhoons."

Pete nodded. He was beginning to catch the drift of the conversation, but both politesse and prudence dictated that he refrain from trying to hurry it. Joe Hines was a man who made his mind up slowly on broad matters and resented being pushed.

"Over in the China Sea and the Sea of Japan," Joe said, "I hear tell they get all kinds of winds and seas. Never been there myself."

His look was questioning, and the pipe was firmly settled between his teeth again as he waited.

"Pays to know your way around there," Pete said, nodding. "And sometimes not even that will do much good. That whole area is unsettled, volcanoes, earthquakes—the Japanese in particular are well acquainted with earthquakes and what they produce."

Joe thought about it. He took the pipe out of his mouth. "There's a funny-sounding word—"

"Tsunami."

Joe sighed. "That's it. That Todd Wilson said you'd know about them." He was obviously not finished with his train of thought, and Pete waited. "Chief I served under," Joe said, "had yarns that were hard to believe. People by the thousands drowned, boats smashed in harbor, even buildings wrecked ashore—" His eyes had not left Pete's face.

"All true," Pete said.

"That warning last Saturday—" Joe said, and stopped. He looked at Pete in silence, question plain.

"A foul ball. It never ought to have been issued. We knew it right from the start."

Joe walked slowly back to his chair and sat down. "I figured," he said. "Didn't seem to add up to what I'd heard—" He looked a trifle embarrassed. "And read," he finished. "Library, after Todd talked to me. I couldn't remember the word—"

"Tsunami," Pete repeated.

Joe nodded. "But the librarian knew right away what I was asking about. She went right to it. Whole row of books. Papers of yours."

Pete sat silent, waiting.

"We could get *them* here?" Joe said. "Bigger waves than anybody's ever seen?"

"We think so. We're pretty sure so. A lot of things would have to happen, but—yes, we could get them here." Pete couldn't leave it there. "But if we do, we'll have warning."

"How much?"

Pete's eyes went to the small *x* marked on the big chart near the equator in the vast South Pacific. He estimated distance. "Maybe three hours. Maybe a little more."

Joe blinked. "And every boat in the harbor trying to get out that channel?" He shook his head. "Just one piss-to-windward landlubber at the wheel of a sixty-foot cruiser running hard and fast aground on the way out"—he shook his head again—"and the cork's jammed tight in the bottle." He looked around as if for a place to spit. "Jimmy Silva talks about the money we put into the breakwater, but with the kind of waves I think you're talking about . . ." He left the sentence unfinished, hanging, a question demanding answer.

"The breakwater probably wouldn't do a bit of good," Pete said. "Tsunami come in series, and the first wave would probably tear the breakwater apart."

Joe stood up and turned for a last look at the map. He sighed again. "You sure know how to make a man's day," he said, "and that's a fact." Pipe in mouth again, he walked out.

❧

The telephone call caught Garfield in the kitchen, in swim trunks, as he was about to go out with Lucy. "For you," Clara said, holding out the phone, "*Dr.* Garfield." She emphasized the title, smiling.

A pleasant, brisk female voice said, "Dr. Saunders calling."

And in a brief moment Harry Saunders was on the line. "Robinson said you wanted to know what, if anything, we know about our Gallic friends' plans," Saunders said. "Can you talk?"

Garfield was conscious that both Clara and Lucy watched him. "I can listen."

"Roger." There was a short pause. "We *know* very damn little," Saunders said. "We *infer* considerably more. Indications are that they're planning another test on or about the thirtieth. That's this month."

Garfield was silent, eyes closed, concentrating.

"You still there?" Harry Saunders said after a moment.

"Right here. I was . . . calculating." Garfield smiled wryly. "That's full moon."

"Is it? What—" Harry Saunders stopped. His voice changed. "Oh. I see. One of your factors, spring tide."

"Exactly."

"Ginger-peachy. Well, that's the first bit of joyful inference. There's more. You want it all?"

"I'm listening."

Saunders hesitated. "It may be H type. We can't be sure, but that seems to be the way the wind blows."

Garfield closed his eyes again momentarily. H type, hydrogen, *fusion,* he was thinking, rather than fission. The difference was of kind, not merely of degree. "That *is* good news," he said. His voice was flat, expressionless, the irony muffled.

"I thought you might see it that way." Saunders's voice, too, was carefully casual. "And I have a little story you might also like to hear. I got it from one of the Los Alamos people who was there at our first H test. It seems that Teller came out that morning and said he'd been going over his calculations all over again, and it looked as if maybe they'd underestimated the yield. Their underestimation, he said, could be on the order of ten."

Garfield shook his head gently. "Such a minor error."

"Yes, wasn't it?" Harry Saunders's voice held a smile. "The possibility of a yield of twenty megatons when they were expecting a yield of no more than two." His voice turned brisk again. "Luckily, with their situation, it didn't matter, so they went ahead, and twenty megatons was almost exactly the yield they got. End of story."

Conscious of Clara's and Lucy's presence, "Possible similar . . . uncertainty this time," Garfield said carefully, not even making it a question.

"Exactly. We've . . . hinted at the possibility of miscalculation, but they're not buying it." Saunders's shoulder shrug was almost visible across the thousands of miles. "Thought you'd like to know."

"I appreciate it."

"Keep in touch," Saunders said, his voice brisk and businesslike again. "I'd like to know the results of Robinson's program."

"Will do."

"Ciao." The line went dead.

Garfield hung up slowly and stood for a few moments, pondering the information. Then he looked up, smiling. "I'm afraid," he told Lucy, "that we're going to have to postpone our surfing lesson. I'm sorry."

Lucy hesitated, her smile uncertain. Clara watched in silence. "That's okay," Lucy said at last. "I mean, I've got other things to do, too, so I know what it is when you . . . can't—you know—sometimes do just what you want. Bye now." She waved one hand in a vague gesture of farewell as she turned quickly away and was gone.

Garfield looked at Clara. "That tore it," he said. "I didn't mean to—"

"Dan. It's not your fault. She . . . doesn't understand yet. But she will." Clara gestured vaguely. "It's part of growing up, learning that sometimes men have different priorities. It's just the way things are."

"That doesn't make it any easier."

"No." Clara was smiling almost sadly. "It doesn't. It just makes them . . . bearable. If Maude hasn't learned it yet, she will. You saw her." It was a statement, no question. "You didn't tell me. Tom did."

Garfield stood as uncertain as Lucy had and at that moment felt kinship with the girl. "We—Maude and I—" He spread his hands and smiled helplessly. "There's nothing to say."

Clara's smile now was full-blown, amusement tinged with gentleness. "So don't say it. Go do whatever it is you have to do. Lucy will be all right, and there will be other times for you to indulge her."

"I don't indulge her. I enjoy her company, and I enjoy surfing."

It did not seem possible, but Clara's smile grew even brighter, more amused, more gentle. "You're beginning to relax, Dan," she said. "Just when I was beginning to . . . despair. You'd better put some clothes on before you go . . . wherever it is you're going."

❧

J. G. Brown, attorney-at-law, one of the three minority members of the Encino Beach City Council, considered the matter that was on his desk. The waterfront property offered for sale consisted

of two adjoining lots, for a total width of sixty feet, a one-story house
built to the legal maximum, which was within eighteen inches of the
perimeter property lines, a small pier and a slip capable of accom-
modating a fair-sized power cruiser, altogether a most desirable
package. And the price was right, suspiciously right, Brown had first
thought and had searched out the reasons.

Item one, the owner had experienced financial difficulties, which
he hoped were only temporary but which necessitated a quick sale
for immediate cash, and, item two, the location of the property
within the bay was not the most desirable location, being close to the
unsightly mud flats which Brown knew would shortly be transformed into the new, expensive and undoubtedly highly desirable
marina complex with the full blessings of His Honor Jimmy Silva,
mayor of Encino Beach. The value of the property in question would
undoubtedly increase immeasurably once the news was out. It was
all Brown could do to refrain from rubbing his hands together in glee
and shouting aloud.

As a rule of thumb, Brown considered the use of inside information unethical because it usually worked out that what was the
insider's gain was also the public's actual loss, as, for example, when
insiders, knowing that corporate trouble would soon be revealed,
sold their stock, and outsiders innocently bought the stock and suffered financial losses when the facts of the corporate trouble came
to light.

But this matter he considered wholly different because no one
would suffer, except, possibly, the present owner, who was already
in the position of having to sell at almost any price and would have
no real justification for complaint.

On the telephone to the realtor handling the property, Brown
said, "Make him an offer ten percent beneath his asking price. If he
is adamant, and only if you are convinced that he *is* adamant, raise
the offer to ninety-five percent of the asking price and tell him that
it will be a cash transaction, neat and tidy with no loose ends. I will
have a check for twenty-five thousand dollars earnest money in the
mail this afternoon."

And that, Brown thought as he hung up the phone, deserved a

leisurely lunch at the California Club, where no doubt he would find someone to join him, with maybe a few rubbers of bridge afterward.

❧

His Honor Jimmy Silva sat patiently in his office, the door closed, and made himself listen while Joe Hines talked. And when Joe stopped, "That all you got to say?" Jimmy demanded.

"It's your turn," Joe said equably, and stuck his pipe in his mouth.

"Okay." Jimmy hammered softly on the desk with his clenched fist. "You listen to young Todd Wilson. You go look up books at the library. You go see Pete Williamson. Right?" Rhetorical question; he waited for no reply. "Well, I listened Saturday when they put out that scare warning. And I watched what happened. Nothing! Not a single fucking wave! Did you see anything? Anything at all? Did you?"

"Nope."

"Neither did I. And I was right there on the jetty, watching! This is my town, and I care about it as much as anybody! More! So I was there to see what happened!"

"Not real bright," Joe said. "A wave had come, the starfish and the spiny lobsters'd be feeding on you now."

"You trying to scare me, Joe? Because—" Jimmy stopped, breathing hard. "Okay, tell me why. Tell me why you still believe all this crap after what didn't happen when they said it would! Tell me that!"

Joe was unperturbed. "Times at sea," he said, "we were piped to battle stations because sonar thought they'd picked up a Jap sub, sometimes, mostly in the middle of the night. Maybe they'd picked up a whale, or a school of fish, something, but no sub. After a time we'd stand down, try to get some more sleep. There was bitchin' and grousin', but it didn't make no difference."

"What's your goddamn point?"

"Because the next thing sonar picked up, or maybe the one after that, would be the real thing—a Jap sub with torpedoes that didn't miss the way some of ours did, torpedoes that could blow a hole the size of a house in the side of a twenty-thousand-ton troopship or blow us clean out of the water. That's why when the next siren sounded, no matter how soon or when, we hit the deck running, no matter."

Jimmy leaned back in his chair and studied Joe's face carefully. "You're serious, aren't you? Don't shit around, answer yes or no."

"Yes."

"Jesus!" The mayor hammered softly again on the desktop. "We don't *know* a thing, not a single fucking thing! You know that? You say Pete Williamson *says* it can come! What in holy hell does that mean? We take it serious, get our balls all in an uproar, start hollering 'danger,' and maybe somebody listens and maybe they don't—and then nothing happens, like last Saturday, not a single goddamn thing! Then—" Jimmy stopped, breathing hard. "All you do is sit there and suck on that goddamn pipe. You're serious, you say. You trying to scare me? Because I don't scare! You ought to know that! You—"

"I'm trying to make you see sense. This here isn't going to go away just by you saying it is. You—"

"Goddamn it!" Jimmy said. "You've known me all my life. You going to believe me or those bastards with their computer shit and all their fancy ideas?"

For emphasis Joe took the pipe out of his mouth very slowly. "Them," he said, got up and walked out.

❀

Pete sat at his desk and listened to Garfield's account of Harry Saunders's phone call. "He said 'ginger-peachy' when you told him the thirtieth is full moon?" Pete grinned. "That's just the way I feel, too. Three factors that have to go together to make the worst possible situation, right?" He held up his hand, three fingers extended. "Spring tides. That's one. Big underwater test shot. That's two. Big storm pushing higher water ashore. That's the third." One by one he had folded down the three fingers. "So what have we got? Not only a test shot, but likely a big one, biggest yet, multimegaton range." He sprang one finger to a counting position. "We've got a date, right smack on the full moon, highest tides of the month."

Another finger. "All we're lacking is bad weather. What's the forecast?"

"That's over two weeks," Garfield said. "Forecast has to be uncertain as of now." He smiled suddenly. "You're thinking Murphy's Law?"

"Yep. Whatever bad can happen will."

Garfield's smile spread. "I was thinking the same."

The phone on Pete's desk rang then, and he picked it up and spoke his name. "Oh, yeah," he said. "Hi." He listened for a moment. "Okay," he said then, "thanks. Will do." He hung up and looked at Garfield. "Let's saddle up. That was Robinson. He's ready for us, and I must say I'm sure as hell ready to hear whatever his wizard computer baby has to tell us."

10

The French oceanographer said, "We have a warning from the Americans that our proposed test shot *could* have . . . *dire* is the word they use consequences."

"Nonsense," the director said. "They have been trying to stop our testing for years. A matter of jealousy. They would like to maintain a . . . monopoly, which is already impossible, but still, they continue the pretense. America must learn that when they snap their fingers, the world no longer obeys."

"This is not a matter of political thinking."

"No? Then?"

"A matter of geological results. Not certain, but possible, even probable."

"A pretext."

Inwardly the oceanographer sighed, but allowed nothing to

show. "There was, you will remember, a similar warning years ago. We . . . discounted it and lost our atoll base as a result."

"That was then. We are far better informed now. That is your field, your responsibility to study and understand."

"And I don't like the . . . import of this message."

There was a short silence. "What, precisely, is its content?"

"That our testing has at least . . . hastened certain submarine geological changes until the situation is now precarious. The fear is that our proposed test shot may trigger an underwater seismic disturbance of enormous proportions. The analogy is that of a cannon shot setting off a massive Alpine avalanche, which, of course, can and does happen. The magnitude of this proposed test—"

"Did the Americans mention magnitude?"

"Yes."

"They are guessing. Our security—"

"Does it matter whether they are guessing or not? We know, or at least we *think* we know, what the magnitude of the shot will be, although I have been told that even the Americans were quite astonished by their original results."

"We are not Americans."

"As for whether they are guessing," the oceanographer said, "frankly, I doubt that they are. They have always seemed to know exactly what our plans are. But as I say, does it matter? If the facts are as they represent them—"

"*If!* And how do we know that they are not . . . bluffing, as they do so often?"

"We don't."

"Then?"

"The only way to find out," the oceanographer said, "is by carrying on with the test. And then we may find out too late that they were not . . . bluffing." He waited in silence, knowing well what the answer would be. He was right.

The director shook his head decisively. "Boldness. We must be bold. We have set our course, and we must follow it. To the letter. Is that clear?"

The oceanographer shrugged.

"And I want no word of this . . . message to reach the rest of the company."

He had done what he could. Further protest would not only be futile but be, as international leaders were fond of saying these days, counterproductive. *"Naturellement,"* the oceanographer said.

❦

Bert Robinson, the computer man, was waiting for Garfield and Pete in Pasadena. "You said you wanted to watch the show," he said, and smiled through his beard. "Not that there's much to see except printout sheets emerging."

He turned to his keyboard, and his fingers busied themselves for a matter of seconds, no more, and almost immediately the swift, quiet clacking of the printer began, and the first of a continuous flow of printout pages began to emerge and settle into neat folds in the receptacle. "Baby already has the answers for us. He's way ahead of the printer," Robinson said.

Pete watched the process in awe. "How fast—" he began.

"Does baby work?" Robinson said, and again the smile appeared through the black beard. "A few million calculations a second. A number of countries, Russia, for one, would give their eyeteeth for one of these." The smile spread. "Of course, the gigo law still applies—garbage in, garbage out. That's my job, to see that what goes in isn't garbage, so what comes out can be believed. And I'm pretty good at my job." He glanced at Garfield. "But I gather you'll want to check me out in detail." He nodded. "I'm used to that."

Pete, watching the printout sheets pouring out and piling up almost an avalanche of paper, shook his head in wonder.

"Beats a slide rule," Robinson said. "Beats counting on your fingers and toes, too."

The printer stopped. Robinson glanced at a digital clock face. "Twelve minutes, seventeen seconds," he said. "I'd already fed the data in as I worked them into the program." He tore the top printout sheet from the continuous roll of paper, picked up the neat pile of printed pages and held it out. "Here you are. As promised." Again he looked at Garfield. "You'll call Saunders when you've gone through it?"

"I will. First thing." He studied Robinson's face. "You pretty well know the results?"

"I've done some peeking, and some guesswork, yes."

"And?"

"Good luck with whatever you're planning to do," Robinson said. "I don't know what else to say."

Garfield was smiling. "Maybe a prayer?"

In the car Pete at the wheel said, "It sounds as if the results are pretty much as we expected."

"I expect so."

"But you'll want to check them out."

"Of course."

"And then? Do we plug Boggs into it, my boss?"

"I think not yet. Saunders will want to know immediately if the threat of predictable tsunami is real, although I would imagine they're already laying on precautionary measures in likely danger areas now that he has a probable date for the test shot."

Pete kept his eyes on the road. "But we need weather information before we—"

"Before *we* start shouting, 'Fire!' in a crowded theater, yes." Garfield glanced at Pete's face. "That's about what we'll be doing, you realize?"

"I'm beginning to appreciate it. And I can't say I like it much, laying my reputation right on the line. Suppose we're wrong?"

Garfield nodded. "You'd like reassurance? Of course, you would. But I can't give it. There is always the possibility of error in judgment. We've reduced it as far as we can, but we can't eliminate it."

"You make my day."

"I know," Garfield said, "and I'm sorry about that." He smiled faintly. "You could pray for fine weather the end of the month. Then we'd probably be protected here, wouldn't we?"

"That," Pete said, "yes. Probably. I'll cling to the thought."

❧

It had begun, as tropical disturbances do, as clusters of cumulo-nimbus clouds in the high, humid air over the sun-warmed waters of the Pacific. Summertime is the breeding season.

A drop in barometric pressure supplied original impetus, and the clouds slowly began to gather and stir themselves almost lazily into counterclockwise motion around a vaguely defined central vortex.

This was as far as the process had progressed.

❧

Daphne, barefoot, wearing cutoff jeans and a halter top, was sitting cross-legged in *Lydia*'s cockpit, frowning in concentration as she worked a Turk's head into the end of the motor sailer's bell lanyard.

Olaf Hansen sat on the seat opposite, a *Coast Pilot* open in his hands.

"It was the Water Rat, I believe," Daphne said, "who said that there was absolutely nothing to compare with simply messing about with boats."

"I believe you are right," Olaf said without looking up. "It was, and is, perceptive observation."

Daphne said without expression, "Does Peter enjoy sailing?"

"He does. He's a good hand." Olaf raised his eyes from his book and regarded Daphne's bent head. It told him nothing he had not already guessed. "Pete is a man of many parts," he added, and went back to his reading, or pretended to.

"Has he ever married?"

"I believe not."

"Not gay, is he?"

"I believe I can say with assurance that he is not. On the contrary, I would say that he is quite . . . receptive to feminine wiles."

"I'm lacking in wiles," Daphne said. And then: "Damn! It doesn't go there; it goes *there!* Over *and* under!"

Olaf looked up again and studied her appreciatively. A lovely young woman. "But not lacking the wherewithal."

"Comment noted, and appreciated." Daphne's head remained bent, and she kept her voice carefully casual. "He seems to wear well. Peter, I mean."

"He is a good shipmate. And one learns to know another in a small boat on a cruise."

"The cruise I have in mind," Daphne said, "could be an extensive one." She raised her head then and faced Olaf steadily, the green eyes quite open, somehow revealing. "You are a wise man, Olaf. Am I being foolish?"

"I think," Olaf said, "that you are the only proper judge of that."

Daphne considered it briefly. "One is forever hearing that aggressive females tend to frighten away their quarry. But how else does one make one's feelings known? Particularly when the competition is threat of impending disaster?"

"I believe," Olaf said slowly, "that there are times when one suspends the amenities. It was so during wartime."

"You give me heart." Daphne held up her handiwork. "There. I think three passes are ample, possibly even excessive. A bit of trimming, and, *voilà!* a proper bell lanyard, *n'est-ce pas?*"

"Just so," Olaf said, "thank you," and hid his smile as he bent to his reading again.

❦

On the phone the National Weather Service meteorologist said, "All I can tell you is that we have a couple, no, several tropical disturbances on the satellite photos right now, out in the Pacific, north of the equator. This time of year it would be unusual if we didn't."

"And?" Pete said.

The meteorologist's voice was unconcerned. "Any one of them could go either way, gather momentum and work itself into something big, or just futz around until it runs out of steam and as a system collapses." The tone changed. "Why the interest now? If any one of them does achieve hurricane status, which is unlikely, that's one thing. Any hurricane is dangerous. And unpredictable. But if the system just collapses, it becomes nothing more than a low on outdated meteorological charts, of no interest to anybody except as a statistic."

"Do you track these tropical disturbances with aircraft?"

"No. Only by satellite photos. They're not that important yet. It costs money to keep aircraft and crews in the air. If there's a sudden change in one of them for the worse"—Pete could almost see the shrug that accompanied the conditional statement—"then we assess the situation and decide."

Pete had a new, unpleasant thought. "You say there are several disturbances right now. What happens if they . . . merge, become one big system?"

"Whoosh!" For the first time the meteorologist's voice showed emotion. "Then you're talking about real trouble, friend. The kind that makes headlines if it even comes close to land almost anywhere."

"You have my name and number," Pete said. "If there's any significant change—"

"We routinely notify your oceanographic institute. And Scripps. And a few others, along with official organizations and—oh, hell, the list is long, and notification is automatic."

"I meant a personal phone call," Pete said. "It . . . could be important. Very important as we approach the end of the month."

"Mind telling me why?"

Pete was silent, lips pressed tightly together.

"Okay," the meteorologist said after a few silent moments. Again his tone had changed; it now sounded conspiratorial. "I catch the drift. Mum's the word. I'll see to it myself that you're called."

"Thanks."

"Glad to help."

Pete hung up and sat quiet, staring at the chart of the Pacific on his wall. "I don't know who you are, or were, Murphy," he said aloud in a low voice, "but your law is probably the biggest thing since

Newton, and it seems to be just about as inexorable as his law of gravity." Unhappy, dismal thought.

☙

Clara Winslow answered the call and went to find Garfield. She found him in Tom Winslow's study, the computer printout sheets on the desk in front of him. "A smooth, professional female voice," she said, "asking for Mr. Daniel Garfield." She smiled. "They're always almost deferential when they ask for you."

"Your imagination." Garfield was smiling, too, but he waited until the door closed before he picked up the phone and spoke his name.

"Mr. Hawkins calling," the voice said, "Mr. Geoffrey Hawkins. A moment, please."

Garfield sat expressionless, remembering Hawkins flying out in one of the Atlas corporate jets for the closing—jovial manner, confident handshake, nautical term, gold Rolex watch and all.

"Garfield," the hearty, assured voice said. "How are you? Enjoying your seaside rest?" There was an audible chuckle. "Surfboarding, I understand. Bit energetic for me. Tennis is my game. Doubles."

No doubt with lessons from a name professional, Garfield thought, and made a polite noise of understanding.

"The reason I called—" Hawkins began, and broke off, his voice suddenly muffled by his hand over the mouthpiece. The words were barely comprehensible. "Be with you in five minutes," the voice said. And then into the open phone again: "Sorry. Interruptions."

"You're a busy man," Garfield said. His eyes were on the printout sheets. He thought he knew what was coming.

"Well, yes. You know how it is, I'm sure. What I called about was a telephone call I had with Wally Carmichael."

"Walker. It's Walker Carmichael."

"Yes. Of course." There was a smooth shift of vocal gears. "He said he had spoken with you."

"He had."

"And he seemed to have the impression that you were—"

"Not interested," Garfield said. "He was correct."

There was a short pause. "Perhaps he did not make the situation clear," Hawkins said. "He may have misunderstood—"

"What he told me," Garfield said slowly, distinctly, without inflection, "was that Atlas had run into a snag with the DOD over the agreement that had been made, but never formalized, with Garfield Associates, over a matter that you quite rightly think could turn out to be far-reaching, important, extremely costly and a possible source of considerable profit. Does that sum it up accurately?"

There was another short pause. "Those are the broad . . . parameters, yes," Hawkins said. "Of course we, Atlas, can, through our own personnel, resolve the situation, I am confident, but—"

"Then," Garfield said, "my suggestion is that you do precisely that."

The silence was a trifle longer this time. "Okay," Hawkins said at last, in a new, different tone, subtlety set aside, the voice of a man getting down to the meat of the matter, "I'll grant that you are a shrewd, tough, crafty bargainer. You proved that when you played hard to get with the sale of Garfield Associates, knowing full well that we wanted it badly in order to fill a rather important . . . gap in our defense-vendor capability. I repeat, I grant you that."

Garfield sat, eyes closed, remembering what Clara had told him about the appearance, rather than the reality, being the important thing. So this is my reputation, he told himself, and it is wholly undeserved. Strangely, this time there was not even a vague sense of shame. Instead, what he felt was sudden, easy amusement. "I'm flattered," he said. He was smiling.

"And so," Hawkins went on as if Garfield had not spoken, "I won't even try to haggle. I won't make any bones about it, this particular DOD contact. A foot in the door in this ongoing project is important to us. I won't say vital, but it is damned important." There was another pause. "Come back and set our relations in this matter back on track, and you . . . can write your own ticket, name your own price. The sky is the limit."

Garfield sat quiet, staring at the pile of printout sheets, the thoughts running through his mind taking strange, new directions into unfamiliar territory. All at once it was as if the last twenty years, starting, nurturing, expanding and building Garfield Associates into the position of importance it obviously now occupied, it was almost as if these years had not been; as if all that time and all that devotion and effort had been illusory, unreal, a frantic pursuit of . . . nothing. He felt stunned.

"Take your time," Hawkins's voice said, quieter now, still assured, but softer and almost patronizing. "Call me back when you've had time to think it over. Maybe tomorrow?"

"That won't be necessary," Garfield said. Suddenly he was smiling again, and some of the earlier amusement remained, but it was mixed now with awe and wonder at what had all at once become so clear and bright and shining. He took his time, savoring the feeling.

"It may come as a surprise to you," he said at last, thinking: As only a short time ago it would have come as a surprise to me, "that not everything and not everybody has a price. That is not, repeat, *not* a bargaining ploy; it is a simple fact. I even harbored a grudge against Walker Carmichael and Paul Case and, yes, against you because of Atlas's takeover, and this could have been an opportunity for retaliation, revenge, if you will. But for reasons I'm not sure I understand, I don't harbor that grudge anymore because I no longer care. I am simply not interested, period." He paused. "As I told Walker, I am sorry you had your trouble for nothing. Good day, Mr. Hawkins."

He hung up and leaned back in the chair for only a few moments. Then he sat up again and bent over the computer printout sheets, feeling, he suddenly realized, better, easier, looser and more at ease with himself than he could remember.

Daphne, barefoot and wearing the cutoff jeans and a halter top, appeared as soon as Pete got out of his car at his house the afternoon of that day.

Pete was tired and depressed after the day's events: Garfield's recounting of his conversation with Saunders, Bert Robinson's admittedly horseback judgment concerning the conclusion his computer analysis had reached and, more recently, Pete's disturbing talk with the meteorologist.

"You look," Daphne said, "as if the woes of the world are in your care. Is it truly that bad?"

"Only close." Pete held the door wide. "I'm going to have a beer. Join me?" It came to him that he was in no mood for solitude.

"Delighted."

They sat again at the small table in the kitchen, cans of beer in front of them.

"Do you know, Peter," Daphne said, "you are beginning to interest me?" She was unsmiling. "A scientist, of some note, I am told. A surfer. An accomplished sailor, Olaf tells me, and a good shipmate." She gestured vaguely around the small house. "Obviously something of a nonconformist. A number of facets."

Pete sucked on his beer. Daphne's halter exposed more of her splendid breasts than Pete found comfortable. He labored to keep his eyes from them and steady on those disconcertingly penetrating green eyes. Daphne seemed quite unaware.

"Did you ever marry, Peter?"

"Negative." He grinned.

"Attachments?"

"None of lasting importance. Am I applying for something? This sounds like a job interview."

"Not exactly. But I do like to learn the pertinent facts."

Pete drank deep from the beer can. Those eyes watched him relentlessly. "Life began," he said, "when I came here as a junior oceanographer. All that came before was . . . make-believe. Childhood in the East, some athletic and scholarly aptitudes in school, college and graduate school, some girls, a few friends—" He shook his head. "The sea, the surf, sailing, scuba diving and serious study as compared to the once-over-lightly of schooltime—these were reality. They still are."

"Enter Dan Garfield," Daphne said. "You revere him, don't you?"

Pete thought about it and shook his head. "I don't think that's the word. I admire him, and I'm a little awed by him."

Daphne leaned her chin on her hands. From across the small table the green eyes studied Pete carefully. "Tell me why."

"You bore right in, don't you?" Pete said, as once he had said to Garfield. "Okay." He took his time setting his thoughts in order. "He grasps things, concepts, facts and theories more quickly than anyone I have ever known, more quickly than I would have believed possible." He was silent a moment, following the direction his own words pointed.

He made a vague gesture of dismissal. "I have a sketchy idea of his business and commercial success," he said, "which was considerable, more than considerable. But I wasn't prepared for the range of his acquaintance"—he was thinking of Harry Saunders—"or for the obvious high esteem in which he's held." The memory of that monster lightning-swift supercomputer in Pasadena was still vivid. "Otherwise we wouldn't have had access to . . . what we have had, a highest-priority piece of government hardware."

He spread his hands. "Those are some of the reasons. There are others." He was thinking now of the ease with which Garfield had outmaneuvered Howard Boggs in the matter of arranging for Pete to devote his entire attention to the tsunami research. "He's quite a fellow."

"And that is quite an assessment." Daphne appeared to be trying to make up her mind about something. Her eyes did not leave his. She, too, raised her can of beer and drank deep. With her forefinger she wiped away the small white mustache that remained. "I am twenty-nine years old, Peter. Like you, I have never married or even formed important lasting attachments. And like you, I seem to have found my little niche right here near the water. I believe that gives me some kind of proprietary interest. Are we truly threatened?"

Pete hesitated. Well, he thought, why not? "Afraid so. Dan's view—"

"I would prefer yours. I believe it would be more personal, less dispassionate. I am not sure I completely trust dispassionate observers."

Pete sighed. "It's coming," he said. "As I told you before, I've known it in my gut for a long time and just tried to ignore the implications. He, Dan Garfield, made me take a good, long look at the facts and at myself. Most of us tend to turn our backs and look the other way when something unpalatable comes along. I guess we hope that if we ignore it, it'll go away. Maybe that's why too many people shy away from the Xrays or the tests they ought to have— until it's too late and the malignancy has already metastasized beyond control." He gestured with the hand that held the beer can. "Sooner or later we're almost certainly in for a very rude shock. Is that what you wanted to know?"

Daphne nodded, her mind at last made up. "It is." Her tone was emphatic. "Sign me on for the entire cruise. If there is anything I can do, tell me. If there is not, I'll be around, quite close, in the event something does turn up." Her eyes had not left his, and for long moments she was silent. Then: "Understood?"

"I think I get the message," Pete said slowly, in sudden, almost bewildering wonderment. "Uh, let's have another beer."

Daphne's instant smile was brilliant, and the green eyes seemed very bright indeed. "Absolutely," she said. "At least that."

๛

Garfield got up from the desk and stretched, arms wide, rising on tiptoe, working his shoulders gently to relieve some of the tension that had developed during his time of concentration over the computer printout sheets.

He glanced out the window and was surprised to find that it was still broad daylight. Dusk would have been more appropriate, he decided, a fading day to match his somber thoughts. He sat down again and glanced at the closed door as he reached for the telephone.

Across the country a male voice answered his eleven-digit dialing on the first ring. "Dr. Saunders? Yes, sir. Let me patch you through."

And in only a moment the familiar voice said, "Saunders."

Garfield said, "Garfield here. Can you listen?"

"Shoot."

"I've been through Robinson's analysis. A good job. Better than good, first-rate." Garfield paused. "The conclusions are pretty much as we expected, although perhaps a bit more drastic. All merely probabilities, of course, but—"

Saunders said dryly, "The mathematics of E equals MC squared are also based on probabilities—and have a way of living up to expectations."

Garfield smiled faintly. Quantum mechanics itself was based on probabilities. Saunders did not need to expound. "Quite. And we have about the same situation here. Sooner or later, and probably sooner, there is going to be a massive—underline *massive*—submarine seismic disturbance in that area Pete Williamson has been studying. In short, an avalanche of enormous scope and enormous consequences. Tsunami are bound to be generated. I'm not familiar enough with the mathematics of tsunami to give any kind of opinion on their magnitude, but it will be . . . considerable."

"Emanating in all directions from the epicenter," Saunders said, "yes. As we . . . feared. We have already taken some . . . precautions at what we consider our more . . . vulnerable spots. We'd better increase those measures. The target date, by the way, seems still to be the thirtieth, which, as you pointed out, is full moon and high spring tides."

"Pete tells me," Garfield said, smiling faintly again, "that the word is syzygy"—he spelled it—"when the earth, sun and moon are in a direct line and gravitational pulls are at their maximum. Splendid timing, no?"

"*Vive la France!*" Saunder's tone turned serious again. "Assuming a test yield in the multimegaton area, what is your and Williamson's educated guess? Do you think the projected avalanche, as you call it, *will* be triggered this time?"

"Pete isn't here. I haven't told him my conclusions from the analysis."

"But?"

Again the faint smile without amusement. Right up to you, Garfield told himself and decided that he had expected no different. "My guess is yes."

"Good man," Saunders said. "Thanks, Dan. We'll crank that into the equation." He paused briefly. "None of my business, really, but I've also asked our air force people to keep a sharp weather watch with your area in mind. Your third factor, following test and spring tides, as I understood it from Williamson, is storm pressure at sea pushing higher surf than would otherwise be the case. He mentioned Murphy's Law"—his voice turned light again—"which, by the way, I don't recall ever reading about in scholarly journals but which I have seen in action myself on entirely too many occasions. 'Whatever bad can happen will' ought to be taught as a policy in every science course along with the second law of thermodynamics. They seem to apply with equal inevitability."

"Hear, hear," Garfield said. "You'll keep us posted if your air force people turn up anything pointing in our direction?"

"Will do. And if you have further thoughts, I'd like to hear them. Ciao!"

Garfield hung up and again got out of the chair. A little exercise, he thought, at least a stretching of the legs. He was astonished how at ease mentally he felt as he walked out of the study and started through the house.

Clara was on the porch, reading. She put down her book as Garfield walked out and smiled up at him. "Hard at work?" she said. "At whatever it is that you and Pete have going?"

"More or less." Garfield leaned against the porch railing, feeling strongly the sense of ease that always seemed to increase in Clara's presence. "I was thinking a walk."

"I just got back from one, Dan. If that was an invitation." She was smiling at herself now, mocking her own weakness. "It always takes me the rest of the day to get hold of myself after Tom goes back to town from the weekend. Silly, isn't it?"

"No. Not many are as close as you two. I . . . envy you."

"You should try it, Dan."

"I'd be a rotten husband."

"No, I don't think you would. After you learned to . . . open yourself up a little, that is. There has to be . . . relaxation and ease." Smiling, Clara shook her head, admonishing herself. "I'm lecturing. Go have your walk."

Garfield looked around. "Where's Lucy?"

"Surfing at San Onofre. With Todd." The smile reappeared, filled with amusement now. "Jealous, Dan? Do you think he's . . . beating your time, as we used to say?" Smiling still. "Go have your walk. Lucy will wait. She won't forget you."

It was good in the warm sun to feel the freshness of the sea breeze, clean and salt-smelling. Sails were out in the harbor. They made pleasant, changing patterns against the wide sky and the back-drop of the houses crowded together along the shore. A peaceful, easygoing—what was the current phrase?—laid-back locale, in its way epitomizing the life-style of Southern California—a world of tanned, healthy youngsters in trunks or bikinis, so active, so *physical,* intent on their sailing and surfing almost to the exclusion of all else.

He had grown up in this atmosphere but had never really been an integral *part* of it, possibly, probably because his out-of-step age had always set him apart—college, Cal Tech, at fifteen. There had not been much time for the easier, more physical side of childhood. No regrets, or maybe only occasional, fleeting wistfulness, as he wondered what it might have been like otherwise.

"Hello, Dan." Maude, in shorts that displayed her slim, tanned legs to advantage, a light blue short-sleeved blouse, sandals. "I was just coming out, and I saw you—oblivious, as you walked along, probably on some important mission." She was smiling.

Garfield shook his head. "No . . . mission. No responsibilities. No—"

"That I won't believe, Dan," Maude said. She was smiling still, but there was now an undertone of seriousness in her voice. "Not now, not ever. I think you are the most responsible person I have ever known."

"A damning accusation if I ever heard one."

"Not meant." She hesitated only a brief moment. "Out for a walk? Want company?"

He put all thoughts of computer printout sheets, of Harry Saunders and of Pete behind him. Strangely, it was easy to do. "I'd like that," Garfield said. "Let's cross to the ocean side." His voice was light, easy. "I've been . . . cooped up, and I want to look at . . . infinity."

The tide was coming in, succeeding breakers reaching farther and farther up the beach. They walked slowly, eyes on the water. "There are rhythms," Garfield said. "You can feel them."

"Yes." Maude's voice was quiet.

"A kind of music, I suppose, if you could make it out."

"Can't you hear it?" Maude looked up at his face in mild surprise.

"I can't say I ever have. Not really."

"It's there."

"Maybe you're right." He was smiling again. "Or maybe we're talking about different things."

"I think we frequently are, Dan. I'm afraid we always have."

She shook her head and was smiling again. "Oh, there have been times, not many, but some, when we were on the same wavelength." She was silent for a few moments. "But mostly you have been—how do I say it?—wrapped up in your world, what you were doing, what you were going to do, deciding whether it would work or not, although I have an idea it always did work. You are . . . used to success."

"I've left that world." Odd, tangential thought coming from he knew not where. And yet, as he considered it, maybe it was wholly true. It seemed to be a day for new concepts.

"I think you'll always carry your own world with you, Dan, wrapped around you like a serape. It's something I'm not sure I've ever become used to. Or . . . ever could." The brilliant smile appeared briefly and was gone. "It's the . . . air down here, and the . . . openness. They make it seem like the normal rules don't apply, so you can think, and say, things you wouldn't dream of saying or even thinking up in town. Sorry."

Garfield was remembering his telephone conversation with Hawkins. He, too, was smiling again. "Funny," he said, "I was . . . feeling almost the same thing myself."

"Were you? Now you're just being . . . sweet, easy on me. You know, sometimes you *are* very considerate, did you know that?"

"Frankly, no." Smiling still, he shook his head. "Mostly I've been told I am self-centered, which is probably true, that I wear blinders, maybe also true, and that—"

"That you don't suffer fools gladly, which is definitely true." The brilliant smile had not reappeared. Instead, Maude wore a small frown of puzzlement. "And yet, somehow, there's a change in you just since the other day. Why, Dan? Has something happened?"

"Maybe I've started looking at myself a little differently." Another odd concept coming out of nowhere. "Maybe I've picked up some of Pete Williamson's . . . irreverence."

"You have always been . . . irreverent. Institutions, establishments don't impress you. You have your own . . . icons." Now the smile did break through again. "Although I've never been able to find out what they are." She flung out one hand. "Look at the pelicans!"

There were six pelicans, flying in a rigid line ahead, no more than ten feet above the incoming swells. From time to time the leader ceased his wingbeats and glided easily for some distance before he resumed. In perfect sequence, the trailing birds ceased and then resumed their wingbeats at precisely the same points, an airborne ballet.

Maude clapped her hands in delight. "You can hear the music now, can't you? You have to! It's choreographed! They're crossing from stage right to stage left, every movement planned to the beat!"

Garfield shook his head slowly, smiling, almost laughing. "You must be right, I'll have to admit."

"And they're so serious about it! Beaks tucked in, shoulders held just so—that takes practice, Dan, endless practice!"

"Ah-one, ah-two, ah-three?"

"Exactly." Maude caught his arm impulsively. "Maybe there's hope for you after all."

They walked back around to the bay side and in front of the Barneses' house stopped. "I won't ask you in," Maude said. "It's not my house, and besides, Jack Barnes would probably try to get you to invest in some real estate scheme. He says you'll have to put all that money somewhere."

"There are people taking care of that. I hope."

"I've enjoyed the walk, Dan."

"So have I. We can maybe do it again?" The mood of ease was still very much with him.

"No. I'm afraid not. I'm going back up to town. Enough lotus-eating. Back to work."

Garfield was frowning. "Why, I thought—" He stopped. "When did you decide that?"

"About ten minutes ago."

"Am I the cause?"

"I don't think I want to answer that, Dan. Let's just . . . leave it as it is." Her smile was less than full. "Maybe I can sell a house or two before the end of the month."

The end of the month. Full moon. Syzygy. Nuclear test shot. Would Murphy's Law provide a storm? A big one? This low-lying beach and peninsula so damned vulnerable! "Maybe," Garfield said, "it's just as well you do go back." He made himself smile, some of the ease no longer with him. "I'll come up to town sometime soon. I can call you there."

Maude hesitated. She seemed about to say something and then changed her mind. She nodded and smiled faintly. "Of course. Until then, Dan." She was gone, up the path, up the steps, long, slim, tanned legs moving quickly, almost running.

12

At the test site in the area of the South Pacific under French control, preparations were almost complete. The underwater structure which had caused problems was finally completed to proper specifications, sunk in the lagoon and firmly anchored to the bottom. The nuclear device had been lowered and fixed in place, but not yet armed. And most of the ships filled with personnel and monitoring gear had already been withdrawn to presumably safe positions. Only a handful of scientists and technicians remained aboard the command ship anchored at the site.

In his large cabin the director conducted a final briefing. The oceanographer was there, along with the mathematician, the head physicist, the ship's captain and the chief technician.

"We have had unavoidable delays," the director said. "I will not try to fix blame for these, and in any event they are now behind us.

"All is now in readiness for the July thirtieth target date, no?" He looked around the cabin.

The chief technician nodded enthusiastically. The sooner, the better, he was thinking, because so many problems had without warning appeared to be dealt with at urgent speed that he had begun to fall into the habit of thinking the entire project was somehow jinxed. In his long experience, he had known other jobs that had started badly and continued to grow worse rather than better as if some malignant force were attacking them. He would be glad when this test shot was over and done with and he could go home.

The head physicist said, "Frankly, I don't see what else could possibly go wrong, so I agree—we're ready to go." He was thinking of the most recent ridiculous fact that inexplicably the underwater structure, when originally completed, had failed by a matter of centimeters to fit the dimensions of the nuclear device, and the cutting, reframing and welding operations necessary to remedy the problem had taken an interminable time. The physicist had a low opinion of engineering draftsmen who altered dimensions on drawings as easily and probably as often as they changed their shirts. They frequently seemed incapable of designing anything without error.

The director looked at the mathematician. "Georges? You are strangely silent."

The mathematician took a deep breath and let it out in a long sigh. "I have been told," he said, "that when the Americans tested their first fusion device, the yield exceeded by a factor of almost ten the predicted results." His smile was sympathetic. "It could have been embarrassing. Happily, under the circumstances, it made little difference."

"It's a large ocean," the physicist said. "It is not infinite, of course, but it is immense. It can absorb a great deal of energy and dissipate it quite easily."

The director was still studying the mathematician. "Are you hinting, Georges, that your calculations may be at error? If so, it is rather late to come forward with your . . . concerns."

The mathematician took another long breath and let it out slowly. "On the basis of the data I have been given," he said, "I believe my calculations are correct. However"—he hesitated, choosing his words with care—"we are dealing with forces we do not yet completely understand, and there are, consequently, imponderables that defy specificity. You must comprehend that I am faced with wholly theoretical factors. I do not have ocean waves to look at or tables to consult."

In the silence the oceanographer cleared his throat. It was a loud sound. The director looked at him. "Yes?" the director said.

"July thirtieth is full moon," the oceanographer said, and watched the director smile wickedly.

"Mysterious forces are abroad then?" the director said. "Perhaps witches on broomsticks?"

The oceanographer flushed but shook his head stubbornly. "Full moon," he said, "means the highest ocean tides of the month."

The director was frowning now. "How does that possibly concern us in this project?"

The oceanographer spread his hands in a gesture of disclaimer. "I don't know." He was thinking of the warning the Americans had hinted at, the possibility of drastic geologic reactions to their test shot, and in his mind he was extrapolating those possible underwater structural changes into the generation of tsunami which, combined with high tides at various places around the Pacific Basin *might* produce unpleasant results. But the director had made that subject off limits for discussion, so the oceanographer's tongue was silenced. "There *could* be . . . consequences," he finished lamely, "even though I don't know what they might be."

The director was smiling again, satisfied. "Then," he said, "I think we can safely ignore them." He looked around the cabin. "Any questions, gentlemen?" He waited, but there was only silence. "Then," he said, "I think we may adjourn. It is almost lunchtime."

❦

Todd Wilson and Lucy sat on the sand at San Onofre, their boards upright in the sand nearby. "I think," Todd said, "that you and your mother ought to move back to town. I mean, like now."

Lucy waved one hand broadly at the sand, the sea, the sparkling curl of an incoming wave and the surfers riding it. "And miss all this?

You're out of your skull." She studied him carefully. "You're serious, aren't you? And all because of what Pete says?" She shook her head. "No way. I don't even believe it, those big waves and all. Not really, I mean."

"I do."

"Okay," Lucy said, "you go right ahead. Guys always stick together."

"And girls don't? Now who's being sexist?"

Lucy was silent, considering this new concept. Guys, of course, were *known* to be sexist; that was accepted fact. But come to think of it, girls *did* kind of stick together, too, and they *did* have their whispered and sometimes giggled secrets, and she supposed that seeing this kind of behavior guys just might think that girls were sexist, too, couldn't they?

She had never thought of it in just this way before, and the concept made her vaguely uncomfortable. It was just one more example of the kind of discovery that could pop up and startle you. So how could grown-ups be so sure of everything? Had they exhausted their capacity for surprise?

"Anyway," she said, brushing the thoughts aside, "why should we move back to town? We just got here."

"So you'll be safe."

"That's silly."

"Maybe to you, but not to me."

"You sound like a bad TV show."

"I can't help that. It's how I feel. Maybe that's silly, too."

It was, Lucy thought, using a phrase she had read somewhere, too close to the bone, almost embarrassing, the kind of thing you were only supposed to say, or hear, at night, in a garden, with music in the background and maybe a full moon overhead. She jumped to her feet. "Come on," she said. "This surf is too good to miss."

❧

Garfield came back from his walk, saw Pete's car in the alley behind his little house and knocked on the door. It was a time before Pete appeared, in shorts, bare to the waist, looking a trifle tousled.

"Oh," Pete said in a voice that seemed overloud, "it's you. Ah—come in." He held the door open.

Daphne appeared in her cutoffs and halter, smiling, wholly at ease. "Aren't you going to offer the man a beer, Peter?" Her tone was mildly admonishing, and her hand as she touched his bare arm was gentle. "And if I may, I would like one, too." She sat down at the kitchen table. "We were talking about you a short time ago," she told Garfield.

"I wondered why my ears were burning," Garfield said. Obviously he had walked in on a . . . situation from which he could not easily extricate himself. But instead of embarrassment, what he felt was a sudden envy—Clara and Tom, now these two. He could still see Maude hurrying up the stairs as if running from something. Maybe she had been. Running from him? Uncomfortable thought. He accepted Pete's proffered can of beer. "Thanks," he said as, smiling, he looked from one face to the other. "Cheers."

Daphne was smiling, too, and all at once Pete seemed more at ease as he sat down, looked at Garfield and waited, question plain.

"Yes," Garfield said. "I finished going over the printout, and the answer is as we expected." Words that were purposely guarded.

"She knows about it," Pete said, nodding toward Daphne, "warts and all." He hesitated. "It's certain?"

"As certain as it can be. The probabilities are . . . overwhelming." He told of his call to Saunders. "I took the liberty, in your absence, of saying that I, we, thought that this test, assuming multimegaton rather than kiloton yield, will kick off the whole . . . disaster." He paused. "You told me that during the last dive both the biologist, whatever his name is, and the other observer saw flaking from the cliff structure. That seems to clinch it."

Pete nodded. "They did. Henry Larson, the biologist, didn't report it because he didn't know what to make of it. That was why he called me. I told him it was a long story, but that they'd do well to postpone their next dive a little. That's something I wanted to talk to you about." He waved one hand. "To get back. If you're satisfied with Robinson's analysis, then I'll go right along with you that this test shot, assuming it's a big one, will bring down that cliff that, if it's flaking, is already obviously more unstable than it was when I saw it last. And when that happens"—he spread his hands, palms up—"it's 'Kitty, bar the door.' There's going to be hell to pay."

Daphne looked from one to the other. "I dislike appearing ignorant, chaps," she said, "but although I have heard the words *kiloton* and *megaton,* I do not know their precise meaning. Elucidate, please."

Garfield said, *"Kilo* means 'thousands,' *mega* means 'millions'—thousands of tons versus millions of tons."

"Tons of what?"

Garfield's sudden smile was crooked and unamused. "TNT," he said, "Trinitrotoluene, high explosive. Nuclear explosions are measured in the terms of their equivalent in TNT."

There was silence. Daphne said at last, "Haven't we perhaps . . . exceeded any . . . justification for our existence?"

Again it was Garfield who answered, wearing still that unamused smile. "A case can certainly be made that we may have. But those are the facts as they stand. We are expecting this new underwater test to be in the multimegaton range."

Daphne sipped her beer in silence, her eyes again going from one to the other. She lowered the can and wiped away the small white mustache that remained on her upper lip. "And what, pray, do you intend to do about it?"

Pete looked at Garfield. Garfield said, "A good question. As far as we are concerned here, unless the weather factor becomes important—" He told them what Saunders had said about alerting the air force people.

"And the Weather Service type will call me with any change," Pete said. He was now wholly at ease. "But regardless of weather, we still have the larger question: How do we broadcast a Pacific-wide . . . warning?" He still watched Garfield and waited.

"I had hoped," Garfield said, "that there would be time for you to carry the word, in person. You have contacts, no? At the prime danger spots around the Pacific Basin?"

"Pen pals, most of them, yes. Some I know." Pete shook his head. "But—what, less than a week? Not enough time, obviously."

"Then," Garfield said, "you get on the phone, and, I'm afraid"—his tone changed—"lay your neck on the block with a flat-out prediction to each one of big trouble dead ahead, timed to coincide with high tides."

"Thanks a heap." Pete sat silent, wearing a wry smile, shaking his head slowly. He glanced at Daphne.

"You can do no other, Peter," Daphne said.

"As you British might say, 'queen and country and all that'?" Pete made a quick, angry gesture. "Strike that. My . . . scientific timidity was showing."

"I don't blame you," Daphne said, her voice suddenly soft, gentle. "It is a not very appealing decision. I entirely understand that. Putting your reputation at risk—"

"The hell with my reputation," Pete said suddenly. "It's what has to be done, and that's that." He shook his head in wonder. "But the phone bills! Do you know what international calls cost?"

"Minor detail." Garfield was smiling, finding it hard not to laugh aloud in sheer ebullience and joy that at last they were coming to grips with the problem.

"What about Boggs?" Pete said. "We'll have to plug him in now because I'll be in a sense involving the institute."

"Of course. I'll talk to him, if you like."

Pete looked relieved. "I like."

"We'll do more than talk to him," Garfield said. "We'll lay the printout in his lap and let him draw his own conclusions. I assume he is receptive to . . . overwhelming evidence?"

Daphne said, "Who is—Boggs? He sounds like one of Bernard Shaw's less-than-heroic characters like the dustman in *Pygmalion*— or, as you Yanks renamed it, *My Fair Lady.*"

"My boss at the institute." Pete waved one hand, smiling. "And Dan has him buffaloed." The smile disappeared. "To answer your question, yes, he'll accept solid evidence. He's . . . careful, but he's not intellectually dishonest." He jumped up from the table and was gone for only a few moments, returning with a large yellow pad and a pencil. "I think we need a list. Who or what else?"

"For me," said Daphne, pulling the pad toward herself. "You

two talk. I'll take notes." She wrote quickly. "Boggs," she said. "You head the list, Mr. B. Continue, chaps."

❀

The clouds stirring counterclockwise around the vaguely defined central vortex of the tropical disturbance had by their motion gradually regularized the boundaries of that vortex until they were definite and real, and maintained their definition as with growing strength they began to expand.

Condensation of moisture from the humid air rising and cooling within the core released enormous quantities of heat, energy equal to and surpassing that of the detonation of multiple hydrogen bombs, gradually turning the entire mass into a gigantic thermodynamic engine.

The resulting cloud crown spread outward for tens and then hundreds of miles, blowing downwind, a cumulonimbus cloud formation of such enormous proportions that it could be seen at sea for hundreds of miles.

Within the growing monster, intense line squalls spiraling inward reached velocities upwards of 100 mph. Its irresistible strength consolidated, the entire system began to move inexorably northeastward at an unhurried pace of about ten knots.

❀

"Mr. Daniel Garfield? This is Colonel Hargroves, sir, U.S. Air Force. I have been instructed to notify you that our weather people have under close scrutiny a tropical storm carrying winds that are approaching hurricane force. The present location of the storm center is approximately a thousand miles off the coast of El Salvador, and its course is northeasterly, moving at a speed of approximately eleven knots. As with all tropical storms of this magnitude, sir, its behavior is unpredictable. I am afraid that is all I can report at the moment."

"Thank you, Colonel."

"Not at all, sir."

On the phone the Weather Service meteorologist told Pete, "You asked to know if and when changes occurred. Well, they have, and what we've got now is a full-fledged hurricane. His name is Bob, and I must say he is a fine, healthy specimen."

"Lovely," Pete said. "Murphy's Law is alive and active."

"We're tracking Bob, of course," the meteorologist said.

"And you're predicting it will go where?"

"No prediction. We follow hurricanes; we don't try to lead them. Like six-hundred-pound gorillas, they go where they want."

"Understood, but could you make a guess at its northerly limit?"

"No. I can give you statistics and averages, none of which means a damn thing. We have a hurricane on the loose with winds in excess of a hundred miles per hour. At the moment it is moving northeastward, as they tend to do. We're warning shipping and any pleasure craft that have the sense to cover our frequencies. We are not issuing a shore alert yet."

Despite his thoughts, Pete could not help grinning at the irony of the situation. "You will," he said. "You will. I'd make book on it. Thanks for the word."

He hung up and looked at Daphne. "You could hear?"

She nodded. Her face was thoughtful. "It means what?"

"Hard to tell."

"Peter!"

"I mean it," Pete said. "There is no way of knowing."

"But you *are* sure. I heard you."

Pete was silent for long moments. He said at last, "Worst-case scenario." He nodded. "Yes. That's what I'm . . . expecting. Gale-force winds can extend as much as three hundred miles from the eye of a hurricane, particularly on its right side as you face in the direction of its travel because on that side the resulting winds are the vector sum of the cyclone winds and the speed of the hurricane as a whole."

" 'Vector sum'? Never mind. I believe I understand."

"Total wind velocity. What that means is that just the fringe of the hurricane, let alone the main body, can pile up and drive waves ashore far beyond the limits of the normal surf, as I said once before."

"And then," Daphne said, "*if* a tidal wave—tsunami—adds *its* force—" She caught her lower lip between her teeth in an expression of dismay and then released the lip and smiled. "You paint a splendidly dismal picture, I must say."

❧

Joe Hines listened on the telephone without expression.

"Just an advisory, Joe," the coast guard voice said. "They haven't even issued a shore alert yet. But we've got a rogue hurricane named Bob, *possibly* heading in our direction. As of now, the storm center is almost a thousand miles southwest and moving northeast rather slowly. It is being tracked, and any change will be passed along."

"Every so often," Joe said, "you get a feeling, you know what I mean? I came off watch at sea one midnight, and I didn't even take off my shoes because I knew, sure as I was standing there, that I'd want them on my feet too damn soon."

The coast guard voice was silent.

"Not one sub," Joe said, "but near as we could tell four of them, like those wolf packs they talked about in the North Atlantic. We lost four ships from the convoy and took a hit ourselves but managed to stay in action. Quite a night."

The voice said, "This isn't by any means sure, Joe. It's just an . . . advisory."

"But the smell of trouble is in the wind. Okay, thanks."

Joe hung up and sat for a moment, looking at the far wall. A large calendar hung there, featuring the full-length front-view picture of a nude smiling seductively. Joe did not even see her. This time, by God, he was thinking, Jimmy Silva, that thickheaded Portugee, was going to listen if Joe had to knock him down with whatever was handy and sit on his chest to talk to him.

The telephone rang again, and Joe snatched it up and spoke his name.

"Jimmy here," His Honor's voice said. "Haul ass over to my office on the double. We got a date with J. Howard Boggs at the oceanographic institute, me and you and Pete Williamson and that rich bastard was in *Time* magazine a few weeks back, Dan Garfield. They think the stuff's going to hit the fan any minute, and they want us to know about it. You—"

"Stop clicking your teeth," Joe Hines said. "I'm on my way."

13

J. Howard Boggs sat behind his large desk. Garfield, Pete, Jimmy Silva and Joe Hines faced him in a rough semicircle. The pile of computer printout sheets, neatly stacked, sat on Boggs's desk. He endeavored to keep his eyes from them.

"I must apologize," Boggs said, "for the lack of notice. But apparently what we have is an emergency situation. At least it is so represented to me." He looked at Garfield. "You will take over?"

"Pete first," Garfield said.

"Okay." Pete nodded. "I'll make it brief." He stood up and walked to the wall map of the Pacific he had brought from his office. His hand moved quickly as he talked. "Here, and running down in this direction roughly here"—his hand crossed the equator into the South Pacific—"and meandering around more or less like this and then swinging in this direction"—he looked at them all—"a fracture zone of the earth's crust, the largest geologic formation on earth, most of it submarine, in places deeper than Mount Everest is high, in places large enough to take the Grand Canyon and lose it in its depths—this formation meanders around the earth for a distance of about forty thousand miles. The earth, you'll remember, is only about twenty-five thousand miles around at the equator, so you see this fracture zone formation has to do a lot of meandering. Okay?"

He moved his finger to the small x he had marked just off the equator. "In this area we have actually seen, photographed, examined about forty miles of this huge undersea formation. Forty miles, out of about forty thousand! And I've been on the bottom twice in nineteen months right here, at a depth of about thirty thousand feet in a minisubmarine.

"But what we're interested in now is right here, at a depth of about forty-five hundred meters—just under fifteen thousand feet. There's a broad rock ledge there that runs for a hundred miles in this general direction. That's all plotted by depth-finding devices, and you can find it on charts. Nineteen months ago, when I first saw that ledge, actually looked at it, it looked something less than stable, cracks visible, rock debris that had broken from the sheer walls, that kind of thing typical of instability. And we had been having, and have continued to record, periodic but minor underwater earthquakes in the area."

His hand moved quickly southward. "Down here," he said, "the French have been conducting underwater nuclear tests for years. I ran some comparisons and found a definite correlation between the underwater nuclear test shots and the periodic minor earthquakes in the vicinity of that ledge. Not proof of anything, of course, but unmistakable correlation.

"A month ago I dove again in the same area, saw the same ledge and could definitely see structural changes since I first saw it nineteen months ago. Far more cracks, rock debris, even what looked like a separation of the ledge from the cliff. Last week two scientists on another dive noticed that the rock was flaking, pieces falling through the water, they said, like dead leaves in autumn, definite, further indication that the ledge was becoming increasingly unstable. Probably, although I can't prove it, all hundred miles or so of the ledge is in the same condition.

"That's where we stand today." He looked at Garfield.

Garfield stood up. "Another nuclear test shot is scheduled for the thirtieth," he said. "It will almost certainly be the largest shot so far since it is planned to be fusion—that is, hydrogen bomb stuff—rather than fission. The Department of Defense in Washington is sufficiently concerned that they are already taking precautions around the entire Pacific Basin to protect their installations from tsunami—huge waves—that will be caused if that ledge does collapse from the force of the explosion. They have also placed at our disposal to help us in our analysis of the situation one of their top-priority computers, the kind that exist nowhere else but in the U.S., to process the data Pete has compiled concerning tsunami waves over the centuries caused by underwater earth movements in that general area of the Pacific. The results of that computer analysis are right there on the desk, and I have given the DOD our opinion in the matter, which is that this next, probably multimegaton explosion— that is, an explosion with the force of not thousands, but millions of tons of TNT—will trigger the collapse of that rock ledge, and the resulting underwater avalanche will set in motion tsunami, huge so-called tidal waves, that will spread in every direction from the point Pete has marked on the chart."

His voice changed, hardened. "The DOD has accepted our conclusions and are taking further steps to protect as best they can their installations. They are also bearing in mind that the date of the test shot, the thirtieth, is full moon, which means that in all oceans of the world there will be the highest tides of the month."

He looked around the room. "All clear so far?"

Jimmy Silva said, "Jesus H. Jumping Christ!"

Joe Hines said, "And now they're talking hurricane-force winds heading this direction!" He shook his head. "Troubles come in litters, like kittens. Seen it before."

Howard Boggs cleared his throat. "Please continue, Mr. Garfield."

Garfield nodded. "Pete."

Pete stood up again. "I've set up to run some moving-picture film I want you to see." He walked to the table where the projector stood. "Lights, Dan, please." And as the room turned dark and the film began, he said, as he had said before to Dan, "This was pure luck, an amateur photographer filming what he thought was going to be incoming tide in a picturesque harbor."

They watched in silence as the film rolled and the water level began to drop, exposing debris, mud flats, the bottom itself.

Joe Hines said softly, "Jesus! My chief talked about this kind of thing. I didn't know whether to believe him or not."

Pete said, "Here it begins. Watch!"

The water rose, filling the harbor, and then in the channel the monstrous, smooth swell appeared approaching swiftly, filling the channel and then the harbor, rising as it swept forward, plucking the trawler from its anchor line like a toy, sweeping onward toward the shore and the men working on the dock.

In the office there was only the faint whirring sound of the projector, otherwise dead, strained silence.

"There they go," Pete said as one by one the seven men disappeared and the swell continued its inexorable sweep covering the dock buildings, moving up into the town. The film ended suddenly, as it had before, and again there was only the flapping sound of the film's loose end as it spun emptily.

Pete said, "I think it's time for lights again." His voice was not quite steady, and he cleared his throat. "No matter how often I watch this, I—" He shook his head apologetically. "That," he told them all, "is a tsunami. Any questions?"

In the hushed silence Boggs cleared his throat quietly. "Your thesis, I take it," he said, "is that if there is underwater geologic change, specifically, collapse of that ledge, in effect, an underwater avalanche of large proportions, tsunami such as this are bound to be generated?"

Pete confined himself to saying merely, "Yes."

"And," Boggs said, "your further thesis is that with a combination of spring tides *and* hurricane-induced surf well above normal limits, the low-lying coastal area here is also in danger from those tsunami?"

Pete nodded. "Yes again."

Boggs looked at Garfield. "You concur?"

"Without hesitation."

Boggs took his time. "I am afraid," he said, "that I do, too. I'll want to examine these, of course." He indicated the computer print-out sheets. "But I am afraid that the . . . indications of trouble are too compelling to ignore."

"Trouble, hell!" Joe Hines said. "This here is . . . disaster!" He looked at Jimmy Silva. "Goddamn it, you convinced yet?"

Jimmy stood up. "Let's haul ass," he said. "We got things to do."

❧

There were seventeen boys ranging in age from sixteen to twenty in Joe Hines's harbormaster office. All bore the Southern California trademarks of deeply tanned faces, arms and bodies, and most also showed sun-bleached hair. They stood silent in Joe's presence.

"Ain't one of you I haven't eaten their ass out," Joe said, "for hot-rodding in harbor or other shenanigans, some I'll admit I hadn't even thought of before you did them."

There were universal smiles and a general sense of relaxation.

"How you managed to survive," Joe said, "beats me all to hell; but you have so far, and you've all turned out to be fair to middling good seamen, too. That's why I got you here this morning."

"To eat our asses out again?" a large nineteen-year-old said.

"Pipe down," Joe said. "You'll have your chance to talk up when I'm through, not before." He looked around at them all. There was no comment. "Now," Joe said, "you all know about that big wave warning we had couple weeks ago." He watched grins appear. "Yeah. Pure bilge, wasn't it? Well, one of these days it's not going to be. Never mind the details, but just because the squall you see coming turns out to be no more than a small breeze don't mean the next one won't knock you down if you get caught unready. You all know that. Or ought to."

He walked over to his desk and perched on a corner of it. "We got thousands of boats in this harbor. And there's only one way out—through the channel and between the jetties. Time comes, and it will, when we want to get as many boats out to sea as we can, we don't want some piss-to-windward landlubber from town running his sixty-five-footer hard and fast aground and blocking the channel for all the rest. You all see that?"

A sun-tanned and bleached twenty-year-old, big, solid and muscular in droopy swim trunks, said, "Why would we want to get the boats out to sea? Safer in here if it comes to a blow."

"Mostly you're right," Joe said. "Even in a good blow like the ones we get every now and again, you're better off inside, maybe double up on your dock lines or ground tackle." He paused. "But if that warning couple weeks back had been real, one of them big waves coming from an earthquake somewhere, you'd have been far better out at sea, well beyond the ten-fathom line, where all you'd catch would be a swell maybe three, four feet high that wouldn't start building into something big until it got into shallow water. You all ride surfboards, God only knows why, but you know that you get out beyond the surf line, all you got to contend with is swells, nice and easy, just sitting there like in a cradle."

"I guess you've made the point," the twenty-year-old said. "Where do we come in?"

"You've all crewed," Joe said. "Maybe mostly on sail, but every one of you has crewed aboard one of the big power cruisers we got here in harbor. I gone to some trouble to make sure about that." He reached back across the desk and into the top drawer and came out with a paper. "Got a list here. There's seventeen big power cruisers I'm worried about, the smallest is a fifty-footer, and a couple are sixty-five-footers. They're all owned by weekenders from Hollywood, Brentwood, Beverly Hills and like that, folks who don't know much about handling their boats. That's where you come in."

"Doing what?"

"I got the key to every one of them boats," Joe said. "I got the owner's permission. In writing. Just in case, I told them, to try to save your property if worse comes to worst."

The big twenty-year-old said, "Hey, you're quite an operator, Joe. I know some of those people like Paul Harmon who wouldn't trust anybody—"

"But who wouldn't like to lose their half-million-dollar boat either," Joe said. "So Paul Harmon gave me the key and told me it was only for use in an emergency. I said it sure as hell was. He didn't ask, and I didn't tell him that if that emergency comes along, I was going to turn his half-million-dollar boat over to one of you and tell you to take her out to sea and stay there until radio contact says it's safe to come back in wherever. He'd have pissed in his pants if I'd told him that. But I'm telling you."

The office was suddenly very still.

Joe said, "Anybody here thinks he can't handle it? You all grew up in boats. Command scare you?"

The sixteen-year-old said, "Jesus, Joe!"

His name was Tommy Parks, and although he could hold his own with, and sometimes exceed the performances of, every other youngster in the room at swimming, surfing or sailing, there remained the barrier of age to keep him on the outside, looking up with envy at the eighteen- and nineteen-year-olds who had always been his seniors.

He was aware now that everyone in the room was watching him.

Joe said, "Your daddy sailed an eighty-five-foot motor sailer to Japan and back, ten–twelve thousand miles round trip. You were aboard, and you stood your tricks at the wheel all by yourself out in the middle of the ocean with nothing in sight and you responsible for the safety of the boat *and* seven, eight people asleep below. You can't take a sixty-five-foot twin-screw cruiser like *Lubelle* down-channel and out to sea by yourself? You scared? You've crewed on her how many times?"

Tommy swallowed hard and produced what he hoped was a confident smile. "You put it like that, no, I'm not scared. It's just—" He stopped. "Oh, hell, sure I can do it. Be fun."

"That's what I thought," Joe said. He looked around at them all. What he saw satisfied him, and he nodded approvingly. "Maybe your owner will be aboard. I can't say. But even if he is, you take the wheel. He'll be glad to let you. He'll be thinking about all the times he couldn't cut it when it didn't matter much, when maybe he rammed a dock instead of laying alongside, or tried to pick up a mooring and missed two, maybe three, four times with everybody in the anchorage watching and laughing. It'll be an emergency, and he'll be pissing in his pants and damn glad you're there to take over.

"If he isn't there, it's all yours anyway. Just don't block that channel, get out to sea and stand off and on until radio says it's safe to come back in." He paused. "Could be you won't be able to come back in here. Can't say. If that's it, the radio'll tell you where to go, maybe Long Beach, Pedro, no telling." He looked around the room again and waited.

The twenty-year-old said, "If we can't come back in here, how's to give a compass course to the best destination? Plotting a course when you're alone at the wheel could be a little unhandy especially if there's any sea running."

"Good thought," Joe said. "We'll do her. Anything else?"

Tommy Parks, the sixteen-year-old, said, "Some of these owners don't keep their boats fueled up all the time. They always want to stop at the gas or diesel float on the way out."

"Another good thought," Joe said. "I'll see to it."

Telling Jimmy Silva about it later, "Good youngers," Joe said. "Sailors. Seamen. I watched them grow up."

"You're taking the hell of a chance."

"I'm aiming to keep that channel clear. That's the best thing, hell, just about the only thing I can do, and I'm going to do her."

Jimmy said, "Maybe you're right, at that."

Joe said, "Man taught me a long time ago to try to figure out everything that *could* go wrong and get ready for it. That's just what I'm doing, best I can."

❧

Jimmy Silva was not wasting his time either. He had called an extraordinary meeting of the City Council, and he made no pretense this time that the Council president had anything to do with it.

"Reason I called you," he said, "we got a problem, what I guess you call a dilemma."

He had their attention. "First thing," he told them, "the marina project is out, dead. It—"

"A moment." It was J. G. Brown, the lawyer, minority member of the Council, with immediate, urgent thoughts surging through his mind of the house purchase now in escrow and beyond recall. Stunned, he wanted time to regain his balance. "Precisely what are we to infer from that?"

"Simple," Jimmy said. "There ain't going to be no marina. Not now. Maybe not ever."

In court, Brown had long ago discovered, pointless but innocuous questions were always good in order to gain further time for thought. "This is a unilateral decision?" he said. "I trust you have reasons?"

Jimmy did not have to close his eyes to see in memory the picture of that huge, smooth tsunami swell sweeping in toward the camera, the shore and the town, lifting the heavy trawler as if it were a toy boat in a bathtub, overwhelming those seven poor bastards on the dock and continuing unchecked, menacing and relentless as the film ran out.

"Yep," he said, "I got reasons. In spades." He sketched briefly that session in Howard Boggs's office. "Up to then I was dragging my feet." He shook his head. "The people in Washington are convinced. Joe Hines is convinced. So am I."

He paused to let it all sink in, especially since he knew that mention of Joe Hines would be a clinching point with at least the majority members, all of whom were longtime Encino Beach residents who knew Joe and his frequently intractable ways.

"Now," Jimmy said, "what we got to do is figure how we handle it. First off, I want emergency powers to handle the police and the fire people like I see fit. Then there's the question of do we talk about it now or—"

"I would prefer," J. G. Brown said, "to dwell a little longer on the marina. We are committed, and I do not see that we can now in good faith back out. The reputation of Encino Beach is at stake, and—"

"Maybe you didn't hear me good," Jimmy said. "I'll admit the idea takes some getting used to, and I don't like it any better than you do. But what we're talking about ain't the reputation of Encino Beach. What we're talking about is something that maybe won't even leave enough Encino Beach to have a reputation. What we're talking about is maybe a ruined harbor, and no houses left on the peninsula, maybe the whole beach washed away, like in some of those big storms at places up and down the coast a few years back. What we're talking about, I'll admit, scares the shit out of me, and I grew up as a waterman and I've never been scared of the water before. Screw the marina. That's dead, like I said. Now let's get down to how we handle it because whether we like it or not, we're responsible for making the decisions. That's what they elected us for."

"Noble sentiments," Brown said. "But—"

"No goddamn buts!" Jimmy's voice had not risen, but its tone was suddenly implacable. "Up in L.A. in a courtroom maybe you can fancy-foot around and get away with it, but here, goddamn it, you face up to being on this City Council and deciding what it has to decide, or by God, you get the hell out if I have to throw you out myself! You got that?"

The large room was still. One or two among the majority remembered when Jimmy had called out the movie star's bodyguard and whipped him good and decided that old Jimmy hadn't lost his fire, no matter if he *had* put on a few pounds and a number of years. The minority of three on the Council, relative newcomers all, sat in stunned silence.

"Okay," Jimmy said at last. "Let's get down to her. Joe Hines is already thinking about his boats and the whole damned harbor. We got people to think about."

14

The name of the director of the County Office of Disaster Preparedness was Wilbert Ellis.

"I didn't even know there was such a thing as Disaster Preparedness," Pete Williamson said. They were driving to a meeting with Ellis, and Pete glanced at Garfield on the seat beside him. "You did. You would."

"I ran into them sometime for some reason. It doesn't matter."

"Just like you ran into Harry Saunders and God only knows what other important characters, too."

Garfield was smiling. He seemed to find it easier to smile these days. Strange. "A lot of different people were interested in some of the electronic gadgetry we produced." The smile spread. "Which is precisely why we produced it." Somehow all that seemed long ago and almost hazy in outline. "But I don't know Ellis."

Wilbert Ellis was small and stocky, with a firm chin to match his handshake. He led them into his office and closed the door after them. "If you're interested in that tsunami warning that was issued a short time ago," he said, "I mean, if that's what you've come about, I'll admit right off it was a . . . disaster. National Weather Service, which is an . . . instrumentality of the Department of Commerce, was—shall we say?—hasty in issuing that warning. But once it was issued, we had no option but to . . . set our defense mechanisms in motion." He glanced at the closed door, took a deep, angry breath and lowered his voice. "It was a total fuck-up," he said suddenly, and there was no mistaking the bitterness in his voice.

"We didn't come about the past," Garfield said, "although it is unfortunately germane because it may influence future reactions." He nodded toward Pete. "I'll let . . . Dr. Williamson explain what's on our mind."

As he had in Howard Boggs's office, Pete sketched in background, present situation, specifically the threat of hurricane fringe winds, and, following a nod from Garfield, testing plans in the French South Pacific.

Ellis listened carefully and in silence and, when Pete was done, let out his breath in a long sigh. "This is not another . . . San Andreas rift scare?" he said. "It doesn't sound like it, but—" He smiled suddenly. "Maybe after that last . . . foul ball, I'm gun-shy."

Garfield said, "You're already aware of the hurricane threat. For the rest, you could check with the DOD. A man named Saunders, Harry Saunders, scientific adviser."

Ellis swallowed visibly.

"Or you could go over the computer printout sheets from the DOD's big mainframe computer in Pasadena," Garfield added. "Howard Boggs of the Encino Beach Oceanographic Institute should have been through them by now."

Ellis's smile this time was rueful. "I withdraw my . . . skepticism." He hesitated. "Until we have actual . . . warning, of course, we can do nothing officially. Except stand by. But—"

"It is possible, I understand," Garfield said, "that if what we anticipate does in fact take place, Encino Beach may well be the prime danger area." He glanced at Pete, who nodded.

"It has to do with coastal configuration and bottom contours,"

Pete said. "San Onofre is an analogy—on a much smaller scale, of course—with its headlands forming a cove and the submarine ridge that bisects the beach providing the mechanism that bends the swells inward, concentrating their energy and producing larger surf than elsewhere. On a far larger scale, we have the same kind of situation here with the point as one headland, the bend of the coast below us as the other, and a spine of near-shoal water extending out from the bell buoy. Incoming tsunami swells would be enhanced by this configuration exactly as the swells are enhanced, built up, at San Onofre."

"I've done a little surfing," Ellis said, "so I know Onofre and its surf." He nodded.

"That's not to say that other areas would not also be at risk," Garfield said. "Much would depend on the fringe winds from the hurricane they're calling Bob, or, heaven forbid, the hurricane itself coming ashore, and on the severity of the tsunami generated." Again he glanced at Pete for confirmation. "So what we had in mind," Garfield went on, "was some kind of coordination among the low-lying communities that might be affected, coordination that would best be set up in advance if possible."

Ellis was scribbling notes on a pad. He looked up and nodded. "Good thinking," he said. "I'll get on it immediately and get back to you soonest." He was studying Garfield's face. "You have other matters in mind?"

"The real question," Garfield said, "is, given the fiasco a little time ago, will your disaster system respond again as it's supposed to?"

Ellis leaned back in his chair. "We hope so. We think so. We have, of course, considered the possibility of a succession of disasters—earthquakes, flood, out-of-control fire, even the, ah, unthinkable, nuclear explosion from whatever cause. And we realize that there could be a breakdown in communications. But the . . . systems, as you call them, are programmed to function automatically once warnings are issued."

"Radio? TV?"

"All of that. And more. At need, loudspeakers, sirens, cruising patrol cars with bullhorns, deployed law-enforcement personnel, even if necessary the military. I don't want to boast, but it is likely that California leads the nation in disaster preparedness. We know we are . . . vulnerable. But frankly, this scenario you outline—" He shook his head. "Will there be warning?"

"At a minimum," Pete said, "three hours. Even at five hundred miles per hour, it would take the tsunami that long to reach here. Other places would not be so . . . lucky."

"Is three hours enough to set things in motion?" Garfield said.

"From any Touch-Tone telephone," Ellis said, "I can set our defense mechanisms in operation. That is all it takes." He hesitated and then opened a drawer and took out a card which he handed to Garfield. "Normally we rely on our own warning channels." He paused. "But a call from you to that number, anytime, day or night, and I will see to it that action is taken." He smiled. "I'll be in touch shortly in any event."

Riding down in the elevator from Ellis's office, Garfield was silent, contemplative.

When they reached the ground floor, "What do you think?" Pete said.

"A stout little man," Garfield said. "I think we're very damn lucky."

❧

The secretary thought about what Harry Saunders had told them. All present waited for the secretary's thoughts.

"Am I to understand," the secretary said, "that we are accepting at face value Daniel Garfield's and Dr. Williamson's assessment of the situation? Our own people have no input?"

"Not quite," Saunders said. "A copy of the computer printout was transmitted to us simultaneously while the printout copy for Garfield was being run in Pasadena. I considered Garfield's independent assessment too valuable to ignore, so I asked him for it, and you have it in front of you. Beneath it you also have my assessment and that of three others competent to judge. All five assessments agree that this coming test, if it is as anticipated, will almost certainly trigger a geologic change of almost incalculable force, from which tsunami will be generated that, combined with spring tides, as Garfield points out, will threaten low-lying land areas around the entire Pacific Basin."

"All of this, of course," an assistant secretary said, "is based on no more than probabilities, as I understand it."

"Yep. Sure is." Saunders's voice held an impatient, whiplike quality, the voice of a man who gave stupidity or ignorance short shrift. "The uncertainty principle applies just as it does in E equals MC squared and every other atomic equation that's ever been devised. Does that answer your question?" He relented a trifle and added, "In matters such as this, there is no such thing as certainty. Not ever. Certainty is a chimera those who don't understand the facts pursue like the Holy Grail."

The secretary said, "And what are you suggesting we do about this . . . threat?"

"Issue Pacific-wide orders," Saunders said, "that all ships in harbor put to sea immediately upon receipt of tsunami warning; that all shore installations within a minimum of three hundred feet of mean high-tide level be evacuated immediately, personnel and what equipment can be moved taken to higher ground, and that all aircraft on the ground at similar dangerous low elevation be flown to safer airfields." He smiled quickly, apologetically. "No doubt there will be other precautions that will occur to those who are more experienced than I am. My field is physics, not military installations."

The assistant secretary said, "Three hundred feet above mean high-tide level? Isn't that . . . excessive?"

"The highest measured tsunami wave," Saunders said, "was two hundred and ten feet. I am leaving a margin of error." He paused and looked around the room. "Anyone who is in doubt concerning the potential destructive power of tsunami waves might do well to talk to someone who was at Hilo, Hawaii, in 1960, or Anchorage, Alaska, in 1964."

The secretary said, "Apparently you place great faith in the judgment of this man Garfield, Dr. Saunders."

"I do. I have worked with him."

"Then might we not do well to have him here for . . . consultation?"

Saunders smiled. "Frankly, I'd like nothing better. But I think Dan Garfield has his hands full with a very special situation that seems to be developing off the coast of Southern California, where they have always thought themselves immune to tsunami damage. We already have his broad assessment, and I doubt if he could give us anything more if he were here."

❧

Again Garfield felt the need of exercise, an opportunity to stretch his legs and think a little alone. And as before, he crossed the narrow peninsula to the ocean side, where he finally settled on the stone bench he had chosen before to gaze comfortably out to sea at the vastness of near infinity. The only sounds were the quiet thunder of the surf and the occasional scream of a gull. It was there that Lucy found him.

She was barefoot and wearing her scant bikini with total unselfconsciousness typical, Garfield thought, of the local attitudes and laid-back life-style. "Hi," she said. "I sort of thought I'd find you here. I've seen you on this bench before, with Pete and with that woman Mom knows but I don't." The words were without guile or accusation. She sat down on the bench. "This is your . . . kind of secret place?"

"I guess you could say that. Everybody needs one, don't you think?"

Lucy smiled quickly, pleased with his understanding. "Where you can go," she said, "and, like, think, all by yourself. I have one. I found it a few years ago. A cave, out on the point. It looks shallow, but it isn't; it goes back I don't know how far, I've never even tried to find out. But when I sit just inside, nobody can see me from above and only the seals in the water and maybe a gull or two can watch me." She shook her head gently, the smile suddenly gone, her face serious now. "I've never told anybody before."

"I'm honored. And I will respect the confidence." Dealing with this child, or with any young person, Garfield thought, was like negotiating in unknown territory; he was without experience to draw on, without guidelines to follow. I've lived too long isolated in an adult world, he told himself.

"Do you want me to split? I mean, leave you alone so you can . . . think?" The young voice was anxious. "Mom and Dad have always said you think a lot."

"That's just a bluff, a front so I can sit still behind it and do nothing." He smiled. "Don't go. I enjoy your company." Simple, rather astonishing truth. Garfield found himself wondering at its cause.

"Todd," Lucy said, "keeps talking about those . . . waves, whatever their name is."

"Tsunami."

"Yeah. Well, he's all spaced out on them. All of a sudden geology's his thing and he can't think about anything else." There was a question implied, an oblique request for advice or at least comment.

Garfield said cautiously, "What do your other friends think?"

Lucy scuffed one bare foot on the scattered sand in front of the bench. "I guess I don't have many friends. They, people, always want to know everything."

Garfield hid his smile. "I know the feeling."

"You do?" There was genuine surprise behind the words, and she studied his face carefully, the original implied question forgotten. "Or are you just putting me on?"

"No put-on. It's for real."

Lucy took a deep breath. "Do you, you know, sometimes have the feeling you'd like to . . . talk to somebody, really talk, I mean, let it all hang out? But you can't quite do it?" Unsmiling, serious now, her eyes searched his face.

"Welcome to the lodge," Garfield said. "I know that particular frustration well."

Lucy stared seaward for a long time in silence, and there was, as before, only the low, booming sounds of the surf and the occasional harsh scream of a herring gull. "No wonder Mom and Dad have always thought you were so neat," Lucy said suddenly. She

looked at him then, wearing a shy, half-smile almost of embarrassment. "So do I. You're easy to talk to. Most grown-ups aren't."

"You flatter me."

It was the full, brilliant smile now, lighting her face, her eyes.
Lucy jumped up from the bench, all cares suddenly wiped away. "I'll
bet you can bear up under it," she said, and was suddenly gone,
almost running, out of sheer ebullience.

❧

Mayor Jimmy Silva had one more thing to do on this day, and
because it seemed to put the stamp of finality on predictions of
disaster, and in the bargain shattered what had been very pleasant
dreams, he found it a distasteful task to perform.

But he had always prided himself on his sense of loyalty as well
as on his willingness to face facts. And so as soon as he got back to
his office, with reluctance, but also with firm resolve, he made the
telephone call to Jack Barnes, real estate operator par excellence.
Jack answered his private phone immediately.

"Jimmy here," His Honor said, "and the whole goddamn project has blown up."

There was a brief silence. "Fill me in," Jack Barnes said then
in a surprisingly mild tone. He was and had always been a gambler,
and although winning was far preferable to losing, he had long ago
discovered that the wrong roll of the dice or turn of a card was not
the end of the world. He listened carefully and in silence.

"How do you like them apples?" His Honor said in conclusion.

"You wrote my insurance," Jack said. "Do I have flood damage
on the house?"

Jimmy pursed his lips in admiration at this demonstration of
practicality. "I don't think so," he said.

"Can I get it before news of all this breaks?"

"I'll see what I can do."

"On the other hand," Jack Barnes said, "I've had several offers
for the place. Maybe I'd better take one of them. Yes," he added
shortly, "forget the insurance. Now about the boat." Another short

silence. "Three hours' notice, huh? And out to sea will be safe? Okay, we'll manage that. Thanks for the warning."

Jimmy said almost explosively, "All that planning shot to hell! And all that money we were both going to make!"

"It's been said before," Jack said, "but I'll say it again: 'You win some, and you lose some, and that's the way it goes.' *Sayonara.*"

Jimmy hung up, feeling, if anything, worse than he had before making the call. "Cold-blooded bastard!" he said beneath his breath, but nonetheless felt again that surge of admiration. He even allowed himself a smile of understanding, kinship.

At the other end of the line Jack Barnes hung up the telephone and sat quietly for some time while he considered this new intelligence and how to deal with it.

The morality, or its lack, of selling a house that was presumably doomed did not even occur to him. Caveat emptor was an established principle long before Jack Barnes came upon the scene and would undoubtedly continue long after he was gone. His single guiding consideration was, and had always been, what the market would bear; and his affluence demonstrated that the guiding consideration was sound.

Worth of an object or a property was precisely the amount someone was willing to pay for it, neither more nor less, and all other attempts to define such an intangible were silly.

Jack and Betsy owned two original Picassos, which they kept in their Brentwood home. As art, Jack had never liked them, and he didn't think Betsy had either, but that was beside the point. A Picasso, no matter how silly it might look, was money in the bank, and that was the bottom line. In this sense the two paintings were a source of great practical pleasure, even pride.

Jack consulted his desk telephone file. Bert Flanagan first, he thought, and if Bert either was not available or had lost interest, there were two other interested parties, and Jack had no doubt of his ability to close a deal with one of them. Before he dialed, he checked the tape recorder in his desk drawer.

Bert Flanagan was in his office, and still interested in the Encino Beach house, but immediately wary that Jack should unexpectedly be willing to sell. "How come the turnaround?" Bert Flanagan said. "Has it suddenly developed termites?"

It was nothing like that, Jack explained. It was simply, well, that keeping up two places—and that didn't even count their part owner-ship of the condo at Big Bear—was just too damn much of a drag. "You know," Jack said. "Betsy and I have talked about it"—not true—"and, well, you know how it is."

"No," Bert Flanagan said, "I don't know how it is. I've envied you that place for years, and now, all of a sudden—" He stopped. "So, okay, what's the real reason? Give!"

Jack produced a sigh that was clearly audible on the phone. "Okay," he said, "but keep it to yourself, huh? Word gets out, and—well, I just don't want any talk. It . . . wouldn't be good."

"I'm still listening," Bert said, and then, quickly: "Wait a min-ute! You mean Jack Barnes has finally stubbed his toe? Is that it?"

"No, damn it," Jack said. "It's not that. It's just—well, a matter of cash flow, temporary, of course, but I don't want it to get out of hand, you know how these things can be, suddenly blown out of all proportion. But if you're not interested—"

"I didn't say that."

"You sure as hell sounded like it."

"Damn it," Bert Flanagan said, "I've got to protect myself, don't I?"

"Sure." Jack's voice sounded hurt. "Get somebody down to go over the place, check it out till hell won't have it. That's fine with me, but . . ." He left it hanging.

"But what?" Bert Flanagan said.

"There's a time factor," Jack said. "I want cash soon. That's the bottom line."

Bert Flanagan's voice altered, and the smile behind the words was clear. "Message received loud and clear. But if it's a fire sale—"

"Damn it," Jack said, "it isn't a fire sale. It's—well, a sale would be handy, that's all."

The smile behind the words was even plainer now. "So, okay, buddy boy," Bert Flanagan said, "we'll get on it right away. But you're willing to talk price, no? In return for the hurry?"

Jack hesitated as long as he thought necessary for the effect he wanted to achieve. "Okay," he said at last, "I'll talk price, but I'm not going to give the place away, you understand that?"

"Of course," Bert Flanagan said, and found it hard not to laugh aloud at his good fortune.

Jack Barnes, expressionless, hung up the telephone, opened the side drawer of his desk, checked that the tape recorder had recorded it all and leaned back in his chair, satisfied.

His next call was to the Encino Beach house, and after a few rings Betsy answered. "Hon," Jack said, "there'll be some people coming around to look the house over. Show them through, huh? Tell them whatever they want to know."

"Who are they," Betsy demanded, "and why are they coming?"

"We're selling the place, hon."

There was a lengthy silence. Betsy said at last, "Have you lost your mind? We like it here! We—"

"Have I ever steered us wrong? Answer me that."

There was a pause before Betsy's sigh of resignation was clearly audible and carried over into her voice. "I suppose you have reasons. You always do. It's just that I never know what they are."

"That's my girl."

"What about the boat? Are we selling that, too?"

"It's just fine where it is, right on its Yacht Club mooring. And we can use it, just as we always have."

There was more silence.

"Got it, hon?" Jack Barnes said.

"I guess so. You just bowled me over, is all." Betsy's voice changed suddenly. "You're sure about this?"

"Trust me."

Another audible sigh. "Okay. Only next time I'll marry a guy who doesn't wheel and deal."

"You do that and you'll live in a little apartment and do all the cooking and the laundry." Jack's voice was only partly jocular. "Look," he said, "you'll want to move all our stuff out—"

"The furniture, too?"

Jack thought about it. "No," he said. "We'll make that part of the sale. But all your clothes, and mine, and the little personal things—"

"It's been a long time since I've felt like crying," Betsy said. "But this, damn it—"

"Okay. Tell you what you do. Get Maude Anderson down again to keep you company. How about that?"

"I don't think she'll want to come. She feels she struck out with Dan Garfield. In that swimsuit, too. I think he's crazy."

"If you tell her you need her?" Jack said.

Yet a third silence, longer than the others. "Yes," Betsy said. "She'll come then. And maybe it's best after all. That Garfield character can't keep on being an idiot forever. Okay."

"That's my girl," Jack said again. "I'll either call or come down myself tonight. Bye now."

Countdown

Saturday, July 26

Dr. Tom Winslow came down to Encino Beach early that Saturday morning for the start of his annual vacation. He was in a jacket and tie and looked out of place against the backdrop of open sky, flat water and boats riding serenely on their moorings.

"Sorry I couldn't make it last night," he told Clara, "but I've got a patient in intensive care, and I couldn't leave him." He paused. "I'm a little uncomfortable about leaving him now, as a matter of fact. I went to the hospital to see him this morning before I left, which is why I'm in store clothes, and—" He shook his head.

"What's his problem?" Long ago Clara had become accustomed to hearing about cases Tom could not shake from his mind, and sometimes she could share, if not ease, his worries.

Tom was already shucking off the city clothes as if they were anathema. "He's grossly overweight and out of condition from total

lack of exercise. All smoking is bad, worse than bad, but the amount
he smokes is ridiculous. And he drinks far too much."

He pulled a tee shirt over his head and emerged through its neck
with a faint smile. "I have an idea some of the interns have a betting
pool on whether heart attack, liver cirrhosis or lung cancer will get
him first. I would have when I was their age."

Clara said, "What can you do for him?"

Tom pulled on a pair of sailing shorts. "Unless we put him in
a straitjacket, gag him and strap him to the bed, there isn't much.
He's used to having his own way, and what he can't get by demanding, he's sure he can buy with all the money he has. He'll keep on
smoking, drinking and eating too much no matter what I say."

Clara folded the trousers and hung them neatly on a hanger,
added the jacket. "I hate patients like that," she said. "They . . . take
advantage of you."

"They pay for the privilege."

"But not for the worry they cause you."

Tom had his sailing sneakers on and tied now, and he straightened, smiling, the transformation complete. "He's up there, and I'm
down here, and the sun is shining and I'll wager that the sea breeze
will be stirring shortly, so I'm going to forget all about him, and all
the others. I'm on vacation."

"The trouble is," Clara said, "you never can completely forget.
You're too . . . conscientious, too caring."

The doctor grinned. "How about some breakfast? All I had was
a cup of coffee."

❧

It was scarcely first light when Daphne said, "Wake up!" She
shook Pete's arm until he stirred and made unintelligible but obviously conscious sounds. "You were dreaming again," Daphne said.
"We're going to have to do something about that."

Awake in the dimness, the memory of the nightmare, the gigantic tsunami wave, still hovering at the edges of his mind, Pete could
smile nonetheless. "Yes, ma'am," he said. "What do you have in
mind?"

"Why, Lady Daphne's sovereign remedy for troubled dreams, of course. Handed down from mother to daughter since before the Conquest."

Daphne threw back the light coverlet and sat up. In one motion she peeled her nightie over her head and tossed it to the floor. Her full breasts stood out in sharp profile against the faint light of the window as she turned toward him. "It goes something like this," she said, and, bending, found Pete's mouth with her own.

It was a long, deep kiss. "Are you beginning to catch the drift?" Daphne whispered. Her voice was not quite steady.

"I think so," Pete said. "But let's make sure." The hell with tsunami, he thought. Let them come. I couldn't care less.

☙

Garfield knocked on Pete's door while Pete and Daphne were at breakfast. Pete sighed and went to the door. "Come in," he said as he held the door wide, "perch, guzzle a cup of coffee and tell us what's on your mind." His tone was ebullient, and a smile seemed to have been deeply engraved in his face, accentuating the happiness in his eyes.

Garfield glanced at Daphne. She wore, as usual, the cutoff jeans and halter top, and she was smiling a secret woman smile, unmistakable.

"I hope I don't interrupt," Garfield said, and thought: The hell I don't.

"Nope." Pete was at the stove, pouring a cup of coffee, his back to the room, but the exuberance in his voice was plain. "I am . . . ready to start the day with a fresh mind." He turned and held out the cup, that engraved smile still plain on his face. "Speak up! What scheme have you hatched now?"

Garfield sat down. "I've made up a list—"

"The damnedest, most organized man I've ever known," Pete said. The smile had not faded a whit. "Early in the morning on a day like this he already has a list—"

Daphne said, "Peter!" Her smile, too, was unchanged, but her voice held fond, mild reprimand. "Settle down, Peter."

Pete sat down at the table, and his smile turned vaguely sheepish. "Yes, ma'am," he said, and to Garfield: "Shoot. What kind of list?"

"Places I think you should call with anticipatory warning. I'm hoping you can fit names to most of the places, so the calls won't be entirely impersonal."

Pete's eyes swept the list. "From Chile to Japan to Hawaii and Central America among others—you've done some homework. These are all places that have in the past had tsunami damage."

"They came from your data in the original computer printout."

"And you just happened to remember them?" There was awe in Pete's voice. He glanced at Daphne. "See what I mean?"

"I'm beginning to."

Pete looked again at the list. "Names, people, yes, for most of the places."

"Good. As I hoped." Garfield held out a card. "International telephone credit card. Talk as long with each as you think necessary." He paused. "If you're still willing to go all out with a prediction, that is."

Pete's engraved smile faded and then reappeared in milder form, turned inward, mocking his own thoughts. "We've gone this far," he said, "there's nothing else to do but go the whole distance. In for a penny, in for a pound. I'll get right on it." He made a sharp gesture of dismissal. "Party tonight at Olaf's. You're invited. You'll come?"

Garfield pushed back his chair and stood up. Again he found it easy to smile. "With pleasure."

❧

Maude Anderson and Betsy Barnes sat over second cups of coffee after breakfast. Through the picture window they could look out over the bay, the moored yachts, the open channel and, across the bay, as on their own side, the houses, cheek by expensive jowl, filling all available shorefront space.

"Bless you for coming down," Betsy said. "I slept better last night with you here. I'm not even embarrassed to admit it. Jack—" She shook her head. "When there are no kids—" She looked directly at Maude. "And that, for the record, was a matter of mutual consent, as much my decision as Jack's, maybe both selfish, I don't know. But when there are no kids, and you more or less go your separate ways, I'm not sure you ever really get to know each other because there's no single common meeting ground—if you see what I mean?"

"I think so."

"I don't know a . . . damn thing about Jack's business. I don't think he is, but for all I know he might be into drug peddling. *Real estate* is an elastic term."

Maude smiled. "There are wheelers and dealers, and there are good solid folks." She lifted her slender shoulders and let them fall. "All kinds. But for what it's worth, Jack's reputation is solid."

"Thanks, hon." Betsy had a sip of coffee. She set the cup down carefully, her eyes avoiding Maude's. "No rumors that he's . . . hard up?" She looked up then and waited for the answer.

"None that I've heard. His reputation is sound, as I said. Some, everybody knows, are always skating right on the edge of disaster or maybe even prosecution. Jack is nowhere near that category."

"You make me feel better and better." Betsy looked around. "But I still don't know why we're selling this place."

Maude had wondered, too, but she said nothing.

"Now what about your man?" Betsy said.

Somehow she had not expected the question, and it caught her off-balance. "Dan?" The name emerged automatically.

"Who else?"

Maude had thought of little else since her walk with Dan and her sudden decision to go back up to town. And face it, she told herself sternly, she had reached no firm conclusions. "I think that's finished," she said, and wondered if that was what she truly meant. She was not, repeat *not,* a dewy-eyed young chick; she was an allegedly mature woman, wholly capable of making up her mind. The only trouble was that in this matter she found herself being consistently both evasive and indecisive even in her own thoughts.

She had been fond of Dan Garfield. She still was. But what, no, *how much* did that mean? In some ways, perhaps many ways he had always been . . . unreachable, but maybe she had expected or hoped for the impossible. He had his world, just as she had hers, and was it logical at her age and his, or even likely, that those worlds could ever merge completely, all barriers destroyed, all frontiers wiped out? What did she really want?

"Somebody else?" Betsy said. "Open up, hon."

Maude showed a faint smile that was meaningless. "I don't think there's anyone."

"Then it's not finished." Betsy's voice was definite. "Men can change their minds. Believe me, that's true. They may think they know what they want, but most of them really don't. They have to be shown."

"I'm not . . . aggressive," Maude said. "If I tried, I'd just make a fool of myself."

Betsy smiled and shook her head. "You underestimate what you've got going for you. In that swimsuit—"

"Betsy. Please."

"No, hon. It's my turn to lend a hand. If you want him—and you do, it shows—then you have to go after him."

"Betsy. I—"

"I know Clara Winslow pretty well," Betsy said. "Maybe between us we can do some good. Clara's known him since year one, and—"

"Betsy. I wish you wouldn't do anything. Please!"

Betsy picked up her coffee, looked at it and set it down decisively. "You don't even look like what's her name who pined away and finally went floating downstream dead because the other what's his name, the big boob, wouldn't even look at her."

Despite herself, Maude smiled. "Elaine, I believe, and Launcelot."

"So, okay. I won't have it. You hear?"

❦

The Weather Service chief meteorologist studied the computer-enhanced time-lapse satellite photos on his drafting board. "Bob," he said, "is afflicted, I would say, with what the shrinks would probably call schizoid paranoia. He doesn't seem to know what he wants to do, and there is sure as hell no way *we* can predict his movements.

Look here, and here, and here: advance, retreat, advance again, all the time gathering strength. Will you look at the size of that eye!"

An assistant said, "He could swing in below Baja, Mazatlán, maybe even as far inland as Durango—"

"He could," the chief said, "and you can be sure our Mexican friends are watching carefully. On the other hand, he *could* swing even farther north, threaten San Diego, that Southern California coast—it *has* happened! And with the population what it is now—" He shook his head. "Can you imagine what a mess that would be?"

"It hasn't happened often. A hurricane getting that far north, I mean."

"You cling to that thought," the chief said, and reached for the telephone to call Pete Williamson. When Pete was on the line, "You asked for blow-by-blow coverage," the chief said. "Well, I'm looking at photos of Bob's latest antics—and they don't tell me a thing. Not a thing, except that he's big and dangerous and hasn't made up his mind what he wants to do. His position as of noon, our time, was a little more than three hundred miles west of the coast of Mexico at about Manzanillo, and about the same distance south of the tip of Baja California, not far from an island called Socorro, which is currently catching hell, no doubt, although we have heard nothing about it or from it—if, indeed, they have any reporting facilities there."

Pete got up from his desk and carried the phone over to the large wall map of the Pacific. He spanned distance with his thumb and spread fingers. "That puts its center about eleven hundred to twelve hundred miles south of here," he said.

"About that."

"And maybe," Pete said, "just maybe, he'll behave himself and stay down there." Memories of Daphne's warm, exciting body and urgent whispers and small cries were undimmed, and it was not possible on this day for him to look on the world with anything but ebullient optimism. "You don't suppose they've repealed Murphy's Law, do you?" he said.

"What?" The chief meteorologist chuckled suddenly. "Not the last I'd heard," he said, "and I sure wouldn't count on it whatever you have in mind. Bob could just as easily start north at a trot, and that could get him in your vicinity in maybe two, three days. If that's what he finally decides."

"I'll think positive," Pete said. "Thanks. Keep me posted, please." He hung up and carried the phone back to his desk, where Garfield's list of places to call was spread out.

❧

At Woods Hole on Cape Cod, Walter Yorke, director of the lab, hung up the phone and leaned back in his chair after a long talk with Pete. He was a quiet, contained, usually placid man, but he was upset now. He roused himself at last and buzzed for his secretary. "Get Henry Larson, please," he said. "It's . . . urgent. He got back yesterday."

Henry Larson was the biologist who had been with Pete in Pete's second minisub dive. He had also been down during the last descent. He sat now in Yorke's office and stretched his legs. "What's up?" he said.

"Your last dive," Walter Yorke said. "You saw rock flakes drifting down like autumn leaves?" The analogy had stuck in his mind.

"Well, yes." Henry Larson made a grimace. "That's what they looked like. Never seen it before."

"And was there something strange about that ledge? The broad one at about the forty-five-hundred-meter depth?"

"That, too," Larson said. "It looked almost as if it wasn't really attached any longer. Couldn't have been, of course, but that was how it looked."

"So you called Pete Williamson out in California about it and about the falling rocks?"

Larson nodded. "Geologist, you know, or geophysicist, and he'd been down and would know what I was talking about. I thought he might have some idea what it was all about." He paused. "Was that out of line?"

Yorke dismissed the question with a gesture. "Did he?"

Larson smiled. "All he said was that it was . . . interesting. And he thanked me for calling."

Walter Yorke sighed. "Okay," he said. "Stick around. I want to make a phone call."

The phone call took a little time, through channels, but Harry Saunders came on the line at last. "Yorke," Saunders said. "Woods Hole. Of course, I remember you." There was a smile in his voice now. "I have an idea I know what's on your mind, but tell me anyway."

"Williamson out in California."

"Right. *You* can judge Williamson better than I can. He's more or less in your field."

"Garfield?"

"There are only a couple or three in this world I'd believe," Saunders said, "if they told me the Apocalypse was tomorrow morning. Dan Garfield's one of them. If he's ever made a mistake of fact or judgment, I don't know about it."

"It's still theory."

"And the uncertainty principle does apply, yes. As it always does. But I've gone over the computer printout, and so have others, and we all agree. There it is. You disbelieve it at your peril."

"It's quite a handful to accept."

"I'll agree to that. *E* equals *MC* squared raised a lot of eyebrows, too, I seem to remember reading." He paused briefly. "I don't want to seem abrupt, but was that all you had in mind?"

"It was. And—thanks."

"Glad to oblige."

Wally Yorke hung up slowly. "In a nutshell," he said to Larson, who sat frowning, perplexed, "there we are. The consensus is that we are diving in unsafe waters, and I don't like it." He paused. "Not even a little bit."

❧

Pete sat in his office, staring at the phone, and at last picked it up and called the Winslow house. Lucy answered. "Hi, Princess. Is Garfield there?"

"Leave him alone. I'm taking him surfing."

Pete could smile. "I won't eat him. I just want to talk to him."

"Okay." Reluctantly. "Here he is."

Garfield said, "Trouble with your calls?"

"Not really. I'm just thinking of the . . . goddamn it, the enormity of this! If they do go on with that test shot—"

"That route," Garfield said quietly, understanding immediately what Pete was getting at, "has been tried. And the answer is that they'll go on testing no matter what. National pride. Witness the sinking of the Greenpeace ship in the New Zealand harbor. *Vive la patrie!*"

Pete took a deep breath and let it out slowly. "Okay," he said at last. "I guess I'll have to accept that. It's a goddamn shame—"

"In spades," Garfield said.

Lucy's voice came clearly in the background. "Come on! The surf's up!"

"I am summoned," Garfield said.

Pete smiled ruefully into the phone and nodded. "Stay in one piece. See you tonight."

❦

Encino Beach life-style what it is, Betsy Barnes's unannounced visit to Clara Winslow aroused neither comment nor curiosity. "Just passing by," Betsy said. "I haven't seen you in ages. Is the celebrity still staying with you?"

"Dan?" Clara could not help smiling. "Right now he's off surfing with Lucy."

"That," Betsy said, "is a side to him I wouldn't have expected." She dismissed the subject with a fleeting smile. "We're selling the house, you know. Or did you?"

Clara had not heard and was surprised. "Such a lovely place."

"Jack's idea." The two words neatly conveyed the conviction that men were unpredictable and sometimes prone to infantile impulses. "Maude Anderson's come back down to help me organize the packing. So much to decide about. You're still on the Charity Board? We'll have quite a few things for you."

Clara made pleased, polite sounds. "Maude will be a great help, I'm sure."

"I don't know what I would have done without her." This much, at least, was true and held the ring of conviction. "Such a darling person."

"I always thought so." Clara hesitated. "I just wish—" She stopped and smiled apologetically. "None of my business," she said.

"The Garfield man?" Betsy nodded. "Jack and I were sure that was going to be a thing, a lasting thing. I don't know what happened, and of course, I haven't asked. Pity."

"Yes," Clara said. "Dan is—" She shook her head helplessly. "Atypical?"

She had not expected to find an ally, let alone a confidante. "All of that, and more. Would you like a cup of coffee? I was about to have one."

"I'd love it, hon. I really would."

❧

Harold Smith, chief scientist of the expedition, sitting now in the salon of the minisub's mother ship almost on the Pacific equator, read the radio message through twice, searching for, and failing to find, hidden explanation for its order. He set it down at last and shook his head in resignation.

"We're to suspend diving until further notice," he said. "No reasons given. And we're to buoy our spot and move out of the area." He looked around the table. "How do you like that?"

The skipper of the mother ship said, "No foul weather reported." He shook his head. "There's a tropical storm that's worked itself up to hurricane strength, but it's well to the north and doesn't affect us at all. In fact, it's moving away from us, north and east." He shrugged.

Someone said, "When does this order take effect?"

"Immediately." Harold Smith gestured with the paper.

" 'Until further notice' could mean—"

"Indefinitely," Smith said. "Then again it could mean for only a day or two."

"Can't you ask?"

"I did." Smith's smile was humorless. "All they did was repeat the message."

The skipper stood up. "That's it then? I'll start things moving." He left the cabin.

Geraldine Adams, marine biologist, said, "Something to do with the area, of course, but what? It isn't as if we were sitting above a guyot that's about to turn active again, and we'd have indications anyway." She paused. "Henry Larson's in Woods Hole now. He could probably tell us what's doing." She shrugged. "Pity."

"Obviously," Smith said, "it's felt that diving is too risky. Wally Yorke wouldn't have taken this step otherwise. So we comply. No choice."

ૹ

The University of Alaska geophysicist, whose name was Phil Brown, said, "We're not talking this time about the kind of quake we had out near Adak two weeks ago. At least, that's the message. We'll have warning, of course, but how long, just for example, would it take a big tanker loading at Valdez to cease operations and get safely out to sea? Or a cruise ship at Juneau to recall its passengers and get under way? And would Cook Inlet be affected directly, and if so, how about Anchorage?"

The coast guard commander said, "You're painting the hell of a gloomy picture."

"I didn't make it up. I'm just passing it along."

"Do you know this fellow Williamson down in California?"

"Only by reputation. Which is high. They don't fill the Encino Beach institute with dummies."

"Hard to believe," the commander said after a short, contemplative silence. "On the other hand, underwater blasting is tricky stuff, and when you're dealing with nuclear blasts—" He shook his head. "Well, we appreciate the word anyway."

"I hope," Phil Brown said, "that it's off the mark." He was unsmiling. "But somehow I don't think it is. It makes too much sense."

❧

In Hilo, Hawaii, Jerry Matsuo listened quietly on the phone. After a time, "Fun and games, huh?" he said. "There isn't anything we can do, of course, except watch for the warning. But thanks, Pete, anyway. When are you coming over? I'll show you some waves to ride that make Onofre look pretty pallid."

"That," Pete said, "may be just what I'll need when all this is over."

❧

In Valparaíso, Chile: "Many thanks, Dr. Williamson. We have a long coastline, as you know, and we are—how you say?—vulnerable. But rest assured that we will make all preparations that are possible to take effect if and when this thing may happen—although I hope it will not."

"I hope not, too," Pete said. "This is one time I wouldn't mind being wrong." Well, he thought, not really. My reputation wouldn't be worth a plugged nickel if nothing were to happen. Some of the ebullience of the day had diminished.

"Again, Dr. Williamson, our thanks."

❧

Dr. Kanuko in Honshu, educated at the University of California at Berkeley, spoke almost unaccented, idiomatic English. "I have heard or, rather, read of you, of course, Dr. Williamson." He drew his breath in with an audible hiss. "I am sorry that we have not had the opportunity to meet, but this telephone call is a distinct pleasure."

"I'm sorry it may not continue to be," Pete said, and launched into explanation. It was obvious that Dr. Kanuko listened attentively, making only small noises of wonder and concern from time to time.

And when Pete had finished, "I'm afraid I understand all too well," Kanuko said. "We Japanese grow up aware of the threat of earthquake and tsunami, as I am sure you know, and we do have our own preparations to prevent total disaster. I am in your debt for this early warning."

"You'll have longer than the rest of us to get as ready as you can," Pete said.

"The factor of distance, yes, we are fortunate in that. I am looking at the map. We will have perhaps six hours of warning, as against your—what?—about three? That is not much time for you."

"And Hawaii will have less," Pete said.

"That," Kanuko said, "is the way the ball bounces—as a professor of mine used to say." Again the faintly audible hiss of indrawn breath. "I am deeply grateful, Dr. Williamson. Rest assured that we shall . . . alert ourselves immediately. I will be in touch with Hokkaido and other islands as well." His tone changed. "The time of the full moon—do you suppose the French are allowing their sense of the dramatic to influence them?"

"I'm damned if I know," Pete said, grinning now. "But it's a thought. *Sayonara.*"

"Adios, Dr. Williamson." There was a smile in Tanuko's voice.

❧

On the beach at San Onofre, boards standing upright nearby, Lucy shook the water from her hair and smiled at Garfield as she lowered herself gracefully to the sand. "Hey! You're doing great! I'm proud of you!"

"Thank you, teacher." Garfield, too, was smiling, savoring still the exuberance of that last ride: the frantic paddling as the swell approached; the feeling that this was the moment when the force of the wave was taking over, and the sudden, energetic spring to a squatting position and the slow rise, standing obliquely, arms outstretched for balance, leaning forward as the board changed angle and the exhilarating, swooping rush began, gathering speed; the shifting of his weight slightly and the feeling of triumph as the board responded by altering course and cutting obliquely across the wave front. . . .

"You're a natural," Lucy said. Her smile was brilliant, seeming to light the entire beach. "And you're . . . liking it, aren't you?"

"Understatement. The only other thing I've ever done that gave me the same thrill was soaring." Garfield saw and understood her puzzled expression. "Sailplane," he said, "what you call a glider. No engine, just . . . you and the air currents to ride. Utter silence."

"Wow!"

"But this," Garfield said, "has something else—a sense of competing with the water that's all around you, with the wave that's far more powerful than you are. It's something else! And I thank you for introducing me to it."

"Well, hey, you're welcome!" Her expression changed immediately, lost its happy exuberance. "You and Pete on the phone just before we left the house. You were so serious!"

"Sorry about that."

"No. I want to know. National pride, you said, and *Vive la patrie!* That's French, isn't it? What are they doing?"

Garfield's eyes went to the twin domes of the atomic reactor that dominated the scene. "Going their own way," he said. "Countries frequently do."

Lucy shook her head almost angrily. "Does this have something to do with . . . those waves you and Pete talk about, that Todd's all uptight over?"

"Yes. I'm afraid so."

"I don't want to believe it!"

"I don't blame you. I'd rather not myself." Garfield hoisted himself to his feet. He was smiling apologetically. "We'd better be getting back, honey. I'm an old man, and I've had it for today."

"Okay." Her face was averted as she rose to her feet effortlessly as if by levitation, brushed sand from her slim, rounded buttocks, stood for a few moments indecisively. She looked at him then, unsmiling now. "I don't like being . . . left out of everything. It's like you . . . pat me on the head and tell me it's only a movie, everything's going to be okay. Is it going to be okay? Is it?"

Garfield took a deep breath. He picked up his board and tucked it under his arm. The girl's eyes had not left his face. "I wish I knew, honey. I wish I knew."

"That's twice you've called me that—honey, I mean."

"Do you mind?"

"No." She shook her head emphatically. "I kind of like it, except—"

"Except what?"

"That you *are* patting me on the head, aren't you? Don't answer that. Let's talk about something else."

❦

Outside on a carving board that evening, Olaf had a huge steak which he had rubbed lovingly with lemon and garlic. The wood and charcoal fire was working up to proper temperature, and Olaf, in shorts, a tee shirt and sandals, capered around it, poking strategically at the coals from time to time with a long fork. He resembled a bald and energetic sorcerer tending his caldron.

Daphne said, "I don't know if the Druids, who practiced human sacrifice, also cooked and ate their victims—"

"They did not," Olaf said.

"—but," Daphne went on as if there had been no interruption, "if they did, I can imagine them prancing in a similar fashion around their fires and probably chanting incantations."

"I don't know any incantations," Olaf said. "None, at least, that would be appropriate. There." A final poke with the fork. "I think the fire is ready. Time for one more drink before we eat. This steak will take awhile to cook properly, even to proper rareness."

Lydia had prepared a vast mixed salad to go with the homemade garlic bread and the rough red wine.

"Inside, one dines," Olaf said of the wine. "Al fresco, one eats, and a fine vintage would be out of place. Besides"—he paused and looked around the trestle table—"we are in a sense, I believe, getting down to basics." He raised his glass. "Confusion to the enemy."

Pete said, "The underwater bombardiers?"

"All forces of darkness in whatever form they occur," Olaf said, and drank deep.

The meal finished, dishes cleared away and wineglasses refilled, Olaf said, "I believe a small lecture on meteorology is in order." He gestured with his glass. "Pete?"

Pete took his time. "Some of this is old stuff to some of you," he said, "but I'll go over it briefly anyway." He had a sip of his wine. "Full-grown hurricanes," he said, "are very nasty beasts, and their behavior is just about as unpredictable and potentially every bit as dangerous as that of a grizzly bear you might run into on a mountain trail in Alaska. They occur mostly during the summer and fall in the warm westerly waters of all oceans. They are sometimes called ty-phoons. If you're at sea, you stay as far away from them as you can, although clipper ship captains sometimes deliberately rode the fringes of hurricanes, which is how they set some of their sailing ship records that still stand. If you're on shore, you tie everything down and hope. In our Northern Hemisphere, they, hurricanes, tend to swing north and east, and their right side, as you face in the direction of their travel, is the more dangerous side, with higher winds and waves."

Pete paused and had another sip of his wine. "That's the book lecture. Any questions?"

Daphne said, "Lucid chap, isn't he?" Her voice was fond, and the green eyes seemed to smile.

"Worst-possible scenario," Garfield said. "That's what we're concerned about here. Let's explore that a little."

"Okay." Pet wiped his lips thoughtfully. "Hurricanes can pile water against land lying in their paths even hundreds of miles ahead of their centers, causing waves that crash ashore much harder and much farther inland than even heavy storm surf. Just by themselves, hurricane-caused waves can do enormous shore damage."

He regarded his wineglass thoughtfully. "Hurricane Bob is alive and well, a fine, healthy specimen, already far too close to us for comfort. Which direction he will choose to go is anybody's guess, but we will do well to be as prepared as we can be because we already have two other factors in place and threatening.

"First, we are approaching the full moon—the thirtieth is the exact day—which is when the sun, the moon and the earth are in a straight line—syzygy it's called—and the resulting concatenation of gravitational forces produces exceptionally high, or spring, tides, so any hurricane wave effect will be intensified by the already high surf."

He gestured with the wineglass. "And, second, we are convinced, Dan and I at least, along with the Defense Department and others around the Pacific basin, that the underwater nuclear test expected for the thirtieth down in the French-controlled Pacific waters will almost certainly set off submarine geologic changes of catastrophic force, causing without doubt tsunami, or what are sometimes called tidal waves, that can threaten places as far apart as Japan, Hawaii and the coast of Chile." He paused. "And this coast as well."

He smiled, without amusement. "Conventional wisdom in oceanographic circles is that this Southern California coast, because of its wide, shallow continental shelf, is more or less immune to tsunami damage. Our thesis is that large tsunami waves, combining with high spring-tide surf *and* hurricane-caused waves may very well roll over that continental shelf protection and cause nothing less than . . . devastation."

He raised his wineglass. "End of lecture." He drained the glass and set it on the table. "I may have had a little too much to drink, but I'll lay it right out on the table: If we're right, and Hurricane Bob does move only a few hundred miles farther in this direction, there is going to be hell to pay and no pitch hot." He paused, wearing now a crooked grin. "If we're wrong, and nothing much happens, then Pete Williamson's name in oceanographic circles is . . . mud. He will be remembered as the guy who rushed around shouting, 'Fire!' and there were no flames. I'll see if Jimmy Silva will give me a job as dogcatcher." He turned the crooked grin on Daphne. "You'll wish you'd never heard of me."

Daphne smiled. "Not so," she said with quiet conviction. "I'll be the assistant dogcatcher, and quite content." She touched Pete's arm with a gentle hand. "But you aren't wrong. Not you two."

Olaf cleared his throat and waited until he had the attention of the table. "In a fairly long life," he said, "as much of it as possible spent at sea, I have learned one lesson, and that is to hope for the best and prepare for the worst." He smiled at them all, looking like a benevolent Pan or Bacchus. "*Lydia* can accommodate in reasonable comfort five persons. Hear me out." He had a sip of wine. It was obvious that he was enjoying his role. "I have always regretted that I was not present at the Dunkirk evacuation, but I was some five thousand miles away, in the center of the North American continent, teaching, or trying to teach, history to unenthusiastic students while history was being made on the European coast. This time I do not intend to miss out."

Daphne said, "Hear, hear!"

"Daphne and Pete, Lydia and myself," Olaf said, counting on his fingers, "leaving room for—"

Pete said, "Include me out. Sorry. Win, lose or draw, I am going to be a very interested . . . observer. On shore."

Daphne turned the green eyes on him for a long, silent and concentrated appraisal. She said at last, "That is firm?" Her eyes still steady on Pete's face, she answered her own question. "It is." She nodded abruptly. "Then," she said, "in Peter's elegant phrase, include me out, too, chaps, and accept my apologies as well."

Pete said, "Now look—"

"Don't make a scene, Peter. If you stay, I stay, and that is an end to it."

Olaf smiled at Lydia, who smiled back. Olaf said, "This is not wholly . . . unexpected." He looked at Garfield. "Will you join us?"

He had known the question was coming, and he supposed his subconscious mind had already prepared the answer without his knowledge. "I think not," he said. "I don't accept the possibility of a false alarm, and I'm afraid there will be . . . much to do ashore, and although I don't know where I'll fit in—"

"At whatever command post there is," Pete said. "*If* we're right, decisions are going to be needed."

"Maybe something like that," Garfield said. "I'm afraid we can't really know how it will all work out."

"When it comes to the crunch," Olaf said, "history tells us there is pandemonium. The fall of Saigon is a fairly recent example. There seems to have been total confusion, hysteria, a breakdown of all authority, a *sauve qui peut* atmosphere nothing at all like the orderly evacuation we would prefer to imagine. How much anyone will be able to accomplish against that kind of background I do not know."

"You're going to have your hands full, too," Pete said. "You're going to have to get *Lydia* out to sea fast, before boats start jamming up that narrow channel the way freeway traffic jams up at rush hour and maybe nobody will be able to move." He paused. "And once outside—" He shook his head. "Hurricane-caused seas aren't to be taken lightly."

"I appreciate that," Olaf said. "On the other hand, if there *are* hurricane seas, *and* your thesis is correct, which I consider more than likely, then if we remain in harbor, we almost inevitably lose *Lydia*—I am referring to the boat, of course—and that is not, repeat *not,* a risk we choose to run. We will put to sea and take our chances with hurricane-caused seas rather than allow the boat to be caught inside like an animal in a trap, unable to escape. And we will put to sea at first warning. Not very heroic, perhaps, but—"

"Merely sensible," Garfield said. "Given your decision, immediate reaction is the only course."

"Hear, hear," Lydia said.

"And you—" Pete began.

"I told you that was all settled, Peter. Now don't fuss."

Sunday, July 27

C. Ward Struthers, who wore a Buffalo Bill hairdo, western hat and high-heeled boots with jeans and fringed buckskin shirts, and wrote unpublished seafaring novels badly imitating Jack London's work, had an open house at his small house on Sunday afternoon.

Struthers lived comfortably on Social Security checks, deposited to his account at the local bank on the third of each month, and on checks which arrived on the fifteenth of each month from a nephew in Boston who carried on the family tradition of keeping Struthers in funds as long as he remained at a considerable distance, out of sight, almost out of mind.

Helen DuBois came to the party. Helen taught watercolor painting and lived in the small studio above Tillie Burke's garage.

Tillie Burke also came. Tillie espoused *Causes* with money from the trust her grandfather had established in Cleveland. Tillie's views on anything tended to be tentative and almost apologetic, as if she had spent her life under a burden of shame for having been born rich.

Mayor Jimmy Silva came, too, as did Harbormaster Joe Hines. Both had known Struthers for years, and neither was at all bothered by eccentricities. "We got all kinds at Encino Beach," Jimmy the booster had been known to say, "from yachting dudes in blue coats with brass buttons to spaced-out beach bum kids who'll maybe grow up and maybe won't, but I could care less either way as long as they don't cause too much trouble on the way. We're like, you know, a what they call melting pot, whatever that is."

"I have discovered the true elixir of life," Struthers said to no one in particular. "It is vodka and cranberry juice, which sounds horrible, I know, but does have miraculous curative and therapeutic properties. Try it, you'll like it."

"All the same to you," Jimmy Silva said, "I'll stick with a shot and a beer chaser."

"Likewise," Joe Hines said.

Angelo and Flora Santini (Angelo's Market—Seafood, Prime Meats, Choice Delicacies, Sensible Prices) arrived late. "Always some character," Angelo said, "comes in Sunday the last moment, we've already closed the doors, he needs pickled onions and stuffed olives and maybe a lemon, or how else can he offer his guests a choice of martinis, gin, vodka, up or rocks, olive, onion, twist? His reputation's on the line, see what I mean? And while he has us open, maybe some Brie and some smoked oysters and how about those what-you-ma-call-it? carrot spears in dill juice? And then, for good measure, slice me some prosciutto and I'd like a good melon to go with it. For me good, honest, paisano red, Ward, baby, a big beaker. Flora's the same."

"I am not," Flora said. "I want vodka on the rocks with a twist. Customers!"

Jerry Diggs, fishing boat skipper, longtime friend of Jimmy's and Joe's, arrived even later, smelling of fish. "Radio says seas beginning to build down off Dago—" like Joe, Jerry had served his hitch in the navy, and San Diego's shore-leave name came easily to his tongue—"and beyond. Down off the Baja, one report has it, winds are building pretty good." He looked at Jimmy and Joe. "You heard about Hurricane Bob?"

"I get the Weather Service reports," Joe said.

"Thing like this happens," Jerry said, "and they start looking in all their old records. We *have* had hurricanes this far north. Raised some hell, so they say. Not like that crap warning a few weeks back—remember?—that one of them whatever they call it was coming ashore, and nothing happened."

"Tsunami," Joe said around the stem of his pipe, which he held tightly in clenched teeth. This was no time to start a panic report, he told himself. On the other hand, a fishing boat skipper like Jerry had everything he owned in the world tied up in his boat, and there wasn't enough insurance in Hartford to cover that loss if it occurred. Some things, along with pride and memories, were irreplaceable. "Pure bilge, that warning," he said, nodding agreement. "But the next warning might not be."

Jerry, drink in hand, stopped in the act of raising it, to study Joe's face carefully. "Battle stations," he said, "because the next alarm might be the real thing?"

"Exactly."

Jerry moved closer while across the room Ward Struthers was again touting his elixir of vodka and cranberry juice in a carrying, slightly nasal, upper-class New England voice.

"Joe," Jerry said in a hoarse, urgent whisper, "what do you know that I don't?" He seized Joe's arm and shook it. "Goddamn it, talk up! I'm lying in my slip, crew ashore and probably drunk by now! What in hell are you talking about?"

Jimmy Silva, standing close, shot glass in one hand and beer chaser in the other, listened carefully.

"You'd best keep your fuel tanks filled," Joe said. "That's all I got to say."

Jerry shook his head emphatically. "That's both too much, goddamn it, and not enough." His voice rose a trifle. "That word you used, soonamy, or whatever, I may not know how to spell it, but I sure as hell know what it means." He was unaware that across the room Ward Struthers had stopped his pitch for vodka-cum-cranberry juice and was listening. The room was suddenly still.

Joe Hines said, "How so?"

"Sixty-four," Jerry said. "I was on a crab boat up in Alaska. That was when that big quake hit Anchorage and sent out them big waves, whatever you call them."

"Tsunami," Joe said automatically.

Jerry shook his head emphatically. "Don't matter a damn what their name is. What they are is what's important, damned important." He took a deep breath. "We're in Kodiak Harbor, the whole damned crab fleet, when we get late word that one of them big waves is passing Cape Chiniak, twenty miles south. We hoist anchor and put to sea in one hell of a hurry and are out into Chiniak Bay when we meet that first goddamn big wave."

The room was still, frozen.

"It was maybe thirty foot high," Jerry said, "and breaking at its top—you never seen such a goddamn thing!" He shook his head, remembering. "We're all full speed ahead," he said, "trying to get out to open sea, and the next thing we know, we're making sixteen, eighteen knots of *sternway!* going right back into the harbor, the whole damn fleet!"

He paused for a long sip of his drink. "It's funny now, but it sure as hell wasn't funny then. Back into the harbor we'd just left, like I said, and clean over the mole into the inner basin, up and over the docks and right smack back up into the town. You never saw such a thing, and I don't never want to see it or be a part of it again!"

Joe Hines said quietly, "Much damage?"

Jerry shook his head. "Not to us, the fleet. They build crab boats some stout, and we were shook up bad; but that was about all. But when the wave receded, there we were, high and dry, with busted-down buildings all around us and nobody really able to believe what had happened."

Jerry looked around the silent room. "Jake Higgins, one of the skippers," he said, "he gets on the radio, coast guard, I think, and we all hear what he says. 'What's my goddamn position?' he says. 'Well, hell, near as I can make out, I'm right on top of the school-house!' He was, too."

Jerry was looking straight at Joe Hines. "So I know about your whatever you call them waves, and I never want to see another, so you better tell me, goddamn it, what you know that I don't. I got my boat to think about! One of them waves coming, I want lots of sea room around me, lots of it!"

Joe Hines hesitated still.

It was Jimmy Silva who said, "He's right! Tell him what we're up against—the hurricane, full moon and high tides, and that test explosion that's going to happen! He's got a right to know. Goddamn it, everybody does! So tell him!"

That was how the word was finally given general circulation.

Monday, July 28

Pete and Garfield sat again in the office of Wilbert Ellis, director of the County Office of Disaster Preparedness. With Ellis this time was a man named Heinz. "Mr. Heinz," Ellis said, "is attached to the director of the Office of Disaster Preparedness for the state of California. At my request he flew down this morning from Sacramento." Ellis hesitated. "I felt that this . . . threat was more than a local matter."

"Correct," Pete said. "I've talked with Alaska, Hawaii, Japan, Chile and a few other places, filling them in on the possibilities."

Both Ellis and Heinz looked impressed.

"In other words," Pete said, "I've stuck my neck way out."

"You are that convinced?" Heinz said. He shook his head impatiently. "Strike the question. Obviously you are. And you, Mr. Garfield?" He merely glanced at Garfield's face. "You, too," he said. "I see the answer." He sighed. "I had hoped—" Again the impatient headshake. "Never mind. We have to accept what is."

"And what is," Pete said, "is Hurricane Bob has started north. Weather Service man called me only a few minutes ago. Bob's in no hurry, moving about ten, twelve miles an hour, but he has apparently made up his mind at least for now. And that is bad news."

" 'Accept what is,' " Garfield said, "and do what?"

"What do you suggest?"

"Coordinate information among Mr. Ellis's colleagues for start-ers," Garfield said promptly. "The test is scheduled only two days from now, and it is extremely unlikely that it will be called off."

Heinz nodded. "That is in train. We would like your thinking on another aspect. Do we pass the warning word along quietly, or do we go public immediately with the possibility in order to try to counteract the effect of that unfortunate tsunami warning a few weeks ago?" He looked at them both.

Pete looked at Garfield. Garfield said, "You're damned if you do and damned if you don't. More premature public warning could be highly detrimental. Quiet word could backfire if it leaked or was not immediately translated into action at the proper time."

Ellis said, "I believe the question is already moot. My wife called me less than an hour ago to say that the cleaning woman had heard there was a real tidal wave threat this time, she meant tsunami, of course, and did I know anything about it?" His expression was solemn. "The cleaning woman had heard it from a neighbor who had heard it from—" He spread his hands. "In small or relatively small communities, word spreads fast."

Again Pete looked at Garfield and waited. "A leak was probably inevitable," Garfield said. He was silent for a moment, thoughtful. "What the general reaction will be is anybody's guess, but I should think the sensible course is to go public with all the facts. I see no viable alternative." He was watching Heinz's face. "You disagree?"

"Our policy," Heinz said, "has always been on the side of caution against premature disclosure. I asked your opinion, I grant, but I hoped it would reinforce our . . . thinking. I am sorry it does not."

Garfield said slowly, "I should have thought that government at all levels would have learned by now that attempts to hide the facts are inevitably futile—Watergate, Iran arms sales—" He shook his head and then smiled almost sadly. "But perhaps some lessons are never learned."

"But what we have here, Mr. Garfield," Heinz said, "are not facts but conjecture. *If* the test takes place, and *if* the geologic results are as you predict, and *if* Hurricane Bob does approach this Southern California coast closely enough—" He spread his hands, palms up to indicate uncertainty, and smiled.

Pete said, "You asked me was I sure." He nodded toward Garfield. "You asked him, too. You got your answers. Then why?" He stopped there, glanced at Garfield and shook his head helplessly. "Oh, hell," he said to Heinz. "Your mind was already made up." He looked at Garfield. "I think we're wasting our time here."

"I'm afraid I have to agree," Garfield said. He nodded to Ellis, to Heinz. "Gentlemen." He walked out with Pete.

They were silent until they reached Pete's car. "What now?" Pete said then.

Garfield had already been thinking about it. "What about the mayor?"

"Jimmy?" Pete began to smile. "Jimmy's hell on wheels once he gets started. Good thinking." He switched on the engine. "Jimmy Silva it is."

The mayor leaned back in his chair and scowled at the ceiling. "Goddamn bureaucrats" was his first reaction. He sat up straight. "Okay. What can we do? Joe Hines has kids lined up to take some of the bigger boats out to sea." He explained Joe Hines's plan. "But we'll have warning, you say, maybe three hours? That's enough, more than enough for them." With a swift gesture he dismissed that matter. "Auto traffic is what we got to think about. You ever go to a Rose Bowl game and see how long it takes to get those cars out of the arroyo when the game's over?"

Garfield said approvingly, "You've given this some thought."

"Hell's fire," Jimmy Silva said, "I haven't been thinking of nothing else! This is my town! I grew up here! I don't want anybody hurt! I have to, I'll tell our police guys to block off the roads and keep everybody out, make all the traffic one-way leaving the beach!" He stopped and looked carefully from Pete to Garfield. "You're sure as you can be this is what we're up against?" He nodded emphatically. "Okay. That's good enough for me. We're wrong, okay, so we're wrong, and it's my ass, that's okay, too. I'd the hell of a lot rather do what we can and maybe be wrong than not do a goddamn thing and get some folks hurt, maybe killed. You can rebuild a house, but except in the Bible I never heard of bringing anybody back to life, did you?"

Driving away from the mayor's office, Pete said admiringly, "Thing like this kind of separates the men from the boys, doesn't it?"

Garfield smiled. "It does indeed."

Pete was grinning now. "I wonder, does that remark make me a male chauvinist pig?"

❦

The Winslow house seemed unusually quiet when Garfield let himself in that evening. Both Winslow cars were in the small alley parking area; but no lights had been turned on, and as Garfield went from room to room it was evident that no one was at home—until Lucy burst in, excited and apologetic.

"Sorry I'm late!" Her voice was a mixture of worry and annoyance. "I mean, Todd and I got to talking or I'd have been here sooner. We—" She shook her head emphatically, and her short hair danced. "Never mind. I'll bet you thought you'd been deserted!"

Garfield was smiling. "I did wonder."

"Mom and Dad are out in the boat. They sailed this afternoon. They'll be back tomorrow, or maybe Wednesday—" She stopped, and her eyes searched Garfield's face. "Why, what's wrong?"

"Nothing, honey." And he added vaguely, "Wednesday's the thirtieth."

"Sure. Full moon, too. Sailing in full moon's fun! They're—" Lucy stopped again, and her smile was hesitant. "What I mean is they're not so old, Mom and Dad, and they don't get much time alone, you know? That's why I didn't sail with them. Mom said it was okay. You'd be here, so I wouldn't be all alone, and, well, I thought it would be better that way, is all." Her smile still lacked assurance. "If you see what I mean?"

"I see what you mean, honey," Garfield said. "And I think you are a very considerate daughter."

"It isn't a very big boat. There isn't much—well, you know what I mean, privacy!" Instantly she was off in another direction. "Now, what's for dinner? You as starved as I am? Todd and I—" Her smile faded, disappeared.

"Todd and you?"

Lucy was silent for a few moments, unhappiness plain. "Okay," she said at last. "We had a fight. Guys make me mad sometimes, Todd especially." The smile returned, sheepish now. "And you know what? You'll think I'm spaced out, or something, but when I get mad, I get hungry! Crazy, isn't it?"

Garfield, too, was smiling. "Maybe it's a good thing. Relieves tension. Would you like to go out to dinner?"

"No." Lucy was instantly contrite. "I mean, no, thanks, if it's all right with you. I'll fix dinner here. I'm a good cook. I like to cook. How about that?"

"Wild," Garfield said, and meant it.

Tuesday, July 29

In the protected anchorage at the island that morning, the water was almost flat, only small, choppy swells inches high to slap gently against *Westerly*'s hull as she rode quietly at her mooring.

Below, in the double bunk, stretching luxuriously, "I don't think I've ever seen the moon as bright as it was last night," Clara said. She was smiling, "You did notice?"

"I had my mind on other things," the doctor said, "but I did happen to notice that there was a moon." He was smiling, too. "Full moon is tomorrow, as a matter of fact."

"Then it should be even brighter tonight."

"Probably." The doctor looked at his watch. "Seven-thirty. No wonder I'm awake. Habit dies hard."

"Are you thinking of getting up?" Clara's smile now held a secret quality.

The doctor appeared to take his time to think about it. "No," he said at last, "getting up was not exactly what I had in mind."

"Of course," Clara said, "if you're hungry, I'll fix breakfast."

"Breakfast wasn't exactly what I had in mind either." His eyes were on her bare shoulder and one partially exposed, enticingly curved breast.

Clara looked down at herself. "Funny," she said softly, "I don't seem to have remembered to put on my pajamas last night."

"I can't think why."

"Neither can I," Clara said. "But since I didn't—" Her smile was brilliant, happy as she threw back the light coverlet and lay back on the bunk, one arm behind her head in the *Maja Desnuda* classic pose. "I'm not hungry either," she said. "For food, that is."

ʘ

The chief meteorologist called Pete at home that morning. Daphne watched Pete's face as he listened, gestured next door toward the Winslow house with a questioning look on her face and watched Pete's emphatic nod. She hurried out of the house and returned shortly with Garfield.

Pete was already off the phone. "Bob," he said, "is flexing his muscles and beginning to move north a little faster. All shipping off the Baja coast is being warned away. From Punta Santa Eugenia, which sticks well out to the west, to Ensenada less than a hundred miles south of the border, all shore localities are being alerted."

"I'll make fresh coffee, chaps," Daphne said. "Proceed with your council of war."

Garfield took a chair at the kitchen table. "I think it's time you talked again with your man Boggs," he said. "We'll want his backing when we talk to the papers."

Pete's eyebrows rose. "We're going all out with a warning?"

"Do you have an alternative? Ellis can't make a move, as I understand it, until Heinz gives the nod, and we saw Heinz's reaction yesterday."

Garfield's logic was impeccable, Pete thought. As always. He sighed and nodded.

"And I think Jimmy Silva ought to know," Garfield went on.

"He'll deal with the auto traffic as he sees best. He knows better than we do what needs to be done."

From the stove, Daphne said, "You're taking matters into your own hands?" She nodded her bright head. "Good. Onward and upward!"

"Rule, Britannia!" Pete said, smiling.

"But I must say," Daphne said, "that you are offering a Scylla-Charybdis choice to sailing people. With hurricane seas outside and tsunami threatened in harbor, they are caught, as I believe you Yanks say, between a rock and a hard place, are they not?"

"We Americans," Garfield said, straight-faced, "do tend to overdo things sometimes." He stood up. "I think I'd like a little walk. Maybe I'll think of other . . . precautionary steps we might take." He smiled at Pete. "I'll be over on the ocean side, staring at infinity, if you should want me." The smile spread as he shook his head. "Lucy wanted me to go surfing with her. I declined."

"At sixteen," Daphne said, "one tends to avoid unpleasant considerations such as threats of catastrophe. It is probably just as well. There will be ample time for that later, and decisions then will be unavoidable."

Outside, the sun had already burned away the morning mists, and the water of the bay lay flat and shining, no hint of breeze yet to disturb its surface.

All those boats in the harbor, Garfield thought as he walked, and all those people with, at most, three hours' warning if, as he was now convinced it would, the worst-possible scenario did develop.

And for perhaps the majority of the boats, millions of dollars worth of pleasure craft, there was probably no hope. He was not a sailing man, but he was sure that only the most seaworthy boats, both power and sail, would be able to cope with the kinds of seas Hurricane Bob would now be stirring up off the Baja coast as he moved northward in his inexorable pace, and would most likely within the next twenty-four hours pile up here on this coast as well.

As he thought about this, it occurred to him that he had never before in his life faced the kind of elemental threat that was now approaching. Even years ago, soaring in his sailplane during what had probably been the most adventurous period of his life, he had avoided severe weather, thunderheads, areas of dangerous down-drafts, all of the obvious risks inherent in the sky.

He had, in fact, he told himself with some surprise, lived a very safe and placid life, engrossed in matters that now were beginning to seem more and more inconsequential—inventing and manufacturing ingenious electronic gadgetry and making money. Humbling thought.

It was in this mood of introspection that he encountered Maude on the sidewalk on the outer side of the peninsula, with the endless ocean stretching to the horizon and beyond, not yet churned into frenzy by Bob's distant strength.

"Hello, Dan." Maude's smile was tentative, as if she were not at all sure of her feelings. "Are you wondering why I'm here when I said I was going back to town?" Her eyes studied him carefully as they fell into step automatically. "Or hadn't that thought or any other thought concerning me even occurred to you?"

"I'm sorry." The words were automatic, but the thought behind them was insistent. "I'm not sure exactly why, but I am truly sorry."

"You see?" Maude said, "you are basically a . . . considerate person. I said that once before."

"And I believe I rejected the concept." He was smiling, and the words were light; but his thoughts were more serious, even brutally analytical. I was in no way considerate of others, he told himself, because I was wrapped up to the exclusion of all else in my own schemes, plans and ambitions and in finding ways of carrying others along with me.

Paul Case and Walker Carmichael at that moment were very much in his mind. They had been oh, so patient and obedient for—how long?—before they finally reached their point of rebellion. He had never thought of it in that way before, but he saw it clearly now and did not much like what he saw.

"You are," Maude said, "you have always been a . . . single-minded person, Dan. That I will grant. You could not have been as successful had you been otherwise."

"Maybe *selfish* is the better word?"

"Dan!" Her tone reprimanded him. "A hair shirt does not become you. I have no idea what all has been happening that has

... changed you, softened you. And I will admit that in some ways I like the results. But spare me the contrition. You were what you were, and I . . . was fond of you both because of and despite it. You are different now, and I'm not completely sure what I think." She made an odd, swift gesture of dismissal. "End of speech. Damn it, Dan, you do tempt me into saying things that would probably be best left unsaid."

"I'm glad you said them."

"Now you're being kind. And I'm not sure I can stand that either." She had stopped walking suddenly and turned to face him. "If I were still in my twenties," she said, "I think I would stamp my foot in sheer frustration. You infuriate me sometimes, and I'm not sure why."

Suddenly he was smiling in a loose, easy, comfortable way, all at once relaxed. "I'm beginning to understand that I infuriated a lot of people," he said. "But I'm not going to spend the rest of my life going around apologizing to them."

"Good." Maude, too, seemed suddenly to relax. Her smile took on a new, friendlier quality. "Let's leave it like that. Agreed?" She held out her hand.

Garfield took it. It was firm and strong. He shook it solemnly. "Agreed."

"Now," Maude said, "would you care to have me walk with you, or would you rather be alone?"

"I'd like your company. Maybe we'll see some more pelicans and I can try to hear the music they perform to."

They walked in companionable silence. From time to time Garfield found himself glancing at the ocean swells marching in to end their long journey on the white sands. Was it imagination, he asked himself, or was he seeing an increase in the size of the swells caused, perhaps, by distant contact with Bob's peripheral winds? The effect of a hurricane, Pete had said, extended for vast distances. Were they already seeing the beginnings of that powerful effect?

"I came back down," Maude said without warning, as if explanation were required, "because Betsy Barnes asked me to . . . hold her hand. They are selling their house. Why, Betsy has not the faintest idea, and Jack won't tell her. It has upset her badly."

Garfield thought about it in his analytical way. "Jack Barnes is a . . . shrewd operator?"

"Apparently. He is very successful in real estate." Maude looked at Garfield's face. "There was a point to that question?"

"Maybe."

"I'm listening, Dan."

"It's pure conjecture. Cynical, too."

"I'm still listening. Please. If I can ease Betsy's mind in any way."

There *had* been leaks, Garfield thought; witness what Ellis had said about his wife and their cleaning woman. And a shrewd operator like Jack Barnes would have had his ear to the ground, probably constantly, wanting to pick up whatever might give him even the slightest edge.

He, Garfield, was beginning to think again in terms of competition, he realized, back in the habit of anticipating others' reactions to subtle forces he had already considered. Habit died hard, he told himself.

"It's possible," he said, "that Barnes is hedging his bet, selling while the selling is good."

"Now you're talking in riddles."

"It's a long story."

"I'd like to hear it, Dan, please."

He was silent, hesitant. Then, Why not? he asked himself. Others already knew. "It's like this," he began.

She listened quietly while he went through it all chapter and verse as they walked: nuclear underwater testing, geologic changes, careful analysis of all available data, predicted results, the concatenation of high tides *and* the approach of Hurricane Bob. In the bright sunlight, it all seemed vaguely unreal.

"The trouble is, it all adds up," Garfield finished.

"Tsunami." Maude was smiling now. "That warning two weeks or so ago? What about that?" Her voice was skeptical.

"Foul ball. Complete mistake. Pete Williamson recognized that from the start."

Again Maude stopped walking and turned to face him. "You are serious?"

"Entirely. That was why I thought it best for you to be back in Westwood rather than down here."

"So I wouldn't be in the way? One less person to worry about?"

"That wasn't it," Garfield said evenly, "but if that's the way you want to look at it—" He shook his head. "Never mind. We were talking about Jack Barnes and why he may be wanting to sell his house."

"Knowing—no, *believing* that it could be destroyed?" Maude shook her head slowly. "That *is* a cynical thought, Dan."

"You know him. I don't."

Maude was silent for long moments, indecisive, turning the matter over in her mind. She said at last, "You look at people without blinders, don't you? The way most people look at . . . things?"

No doubt true, he told himself, the result of all those years of performing successfully in the intensively competitive field of high technology. You learned the laws of the jungle, the methods, the tricks and the subterfuges, the not always gentlemanly means of gaining advantage. There was no other way if you wanted to survive. But looking back, he didn't have to like it. "It went with the territory," he said. "Jack Barnes would understand."

Maude was silent again, troubled. "Should I tell Betsy?"

"Up to you. She's your friend."

"I'm asking you, Dan. I'm not quite sure I believe any of this. Really believe it, I mean. But telling Betsy—"

"What good would it do? You see, I'm being cynical again. And if it wouldn't do any good, then why do it?"

Maude's eyes searched his face. "Is logic all there is, Dan, the only consideration?"

"I'm not a philosopher. Sorry. But logic can be the most important consideration. That's why I suggest again that you go back to Westwood."

"And leave Betsy?"

"Is she your responsibility?"

"She's my friend. Isn't that the same thing?"

Beyond Maude, Garfield saw Pete coming toward them at a brisk trot. "I don't know the answers," Garfield said. "Maybe I've

never really understood all the questions. I don't know that either."
He made a small gesture of finality. "But I'm afraid our tête-à-tête
is finished. Sorry." He hesitated, and the smile appeared, rueful, wry,
apologetic. "I mean that. I am sorry." He turned from her as Pete
pulled up, breathing deeply, but not hard. "Yes, Pete?" Garfield said.

"Conference," Pete said. "Boggs, Jimmy Silva, Joe Hines, Ellis,
you and me. My car's just back there." He jerked his head toward
the shore road.

"I repeat," Garfield said to Maude. "I am sorry." He turned
away.

❧

Chairs had been brought into Howard Boggs's office at the
oceanographic institute and set in a rough semicircle. Boggs sat
behind his big desk, facing the room. The door was closed, and there
was no one taking notes.

"I have called this meeting," Boggs said, "because, unfortunately, matters seem to be coming to a head." He tapped the pile of
computer printout sheets on his desk. "This exhaustive analysis is
. . . frightening in its implications." He looked at Garfield. "I don't
know, Mr. Garfield, if you were aware that the people in Washington
have also seen this printout? And that they concur in your opinions?"

"I certainly assumed they would have copies as soon as we did,"
Garfield said. "In a matter of this importance, what Harry Saunders
may think of my capabilities and judgment is beside the point. He
would automatically want other judgments as well. That would be
axiomatic. I am happy that we all concur."

Pete opened his mouth and closed it again in silence.

Boggs blinked. "Obviously," he said, "you are better acquainted
with officialdom than I am, Mr. Garfield. I had assumed that this was
for your eyes only." There was a new note of respect in his voice.

Jimmy Silva said in what was almost a growl, "Get on with it.
Washington can piss in its pants for all I care. I'm worried about
Encino Beach."

Boggs had quickly regained his equanimity. "I take your point,

Mr. Mayor, but what Washington has set in train will also affect Encino Beach." He paused briefly. "This was told to me in confidence, but I see no reason not to divulge it here." He paused again. "Convinced of the threat, no, of the *likelihood* that Dr. Williamson's, Pete's, theories are correct concerning the geologic changes that will probably result from tomorrow's nuclear test explosion, Washington has arranged aerial surveillance of the test scene, complete with photographs of the explosion itself." He smiled. "The aerial surveillance will be officially accidental, of course. That is how I understand these things are done diplomatically to avoid ill feeling."

"Screw the frogs, and what they may think." This was Jimmy Silva again. "They're at the bottom of all this."

"And," Boggs went on smoothly, ignoring the interruption, "video coverage of likely danger spots—in Hawaii, in Chile, in Central America and elsewhere—has been arranged and will be broadcast via satellite in order that the severity of the tsunami reaction may be judged with accuracy."

"That means," Garfield said, "that some time, perhaps an hour and a half, perhaps even two hours, before we are threatened here, we will know something of what we are probably up against." He nodded. "Harry Saunders's thinking, I'll be willing to bet."

"You may be right," Boggs said in that same new tone of respect. "We will, of course, monitor those transmissions carefully. In the meantime"—he raised one hand to forestall interruption or further comment—"the Weather Service *and* the air force meteorologists have kept careful watch over the movements of Hurricane Bob."

He consulted his notes. "As of thirty minutes ago, the center of the storm was approximately seven hundred miles southwest of Encino Beach and moving northeastward at a speed of approximately twelve knots—fifteen miles an hour, more or less. That speed may increase, decrease or remain constant; there is no way of predicting. The winds within the hurricane have reached velocities on the order of a hundred and twenty miles per hour. The seas in its path are . . . tumultuous."

"There's a word," Joe Hines said, and looked as if he wanted to spit.

Garfield looked at Ellis. "Any official changes since we met with Heinz?" he said.

Ellis forced a small smile. "None." He swallowed hard. "I—" he began, and stopped. All eyes in the room watched him. Ellis took a deep breath. "I have agonized over this," he said, "and I am prepared on my own authority to issue a general warning whenever you gentlemen"—he looked in turn at Garfield, Pete and Boggs— "give the word. I cannot in conscience do less."

Jimmy Silva broke into a smile. "Gutsy," he said. "I like that. You ever get a ticket in Encino Beach, chum, you bring it to me. I'll tear it up and kick the cop's ass up between his shoulder blades."

Garfield looked at Joe Hines. "We know of your plan to send certain large boats to sea in the care of . . . boys."

"Seamen, every one of them," Joe said, bristling. "The hell of a lot better than having the owners at the helm."

Garfield nodded. "I don't doubt it." His tone indicated no reservations. "Now what about the smaller craft?"

Joe hesitated, somewhat mollified, approving the question. "Some'll do fine even in"—he glanced at Boggs—"tumultuous seas. Others—" He shook his head. "They'd damn well better stay in harbor and hope for the best. I'll be out in the workboat, telling some owners to put to sea and telling others to carry ashore what they can, and hope. This ain't going to be like a nice, easy run over to the island. They capsize or founder outside, there won't be nobody to give them a hand."

Garfield looked then at Boggs. "That nuclear power plant at San Onofre. It's almost at sea level." His voice asked a question.

Pete said, "I've talked with Jim Forrest down there. It even begins to get bad, they'll shut down. It'll take time to bring down the heat level, but Jim says they can do it." He shook his head almost sadly. "If we do catch it bad, and any structure at all is left standing, it'll probably be those reactor domes the way they're built, but they won't take the chance."

Boggs said, "We are going to set up cameras on high ground beyond the coast highway with a good view of the peninsula and the channel as well as the harbor and Encino Beach itself. We—"

"You'll play hell keeping people out of the way of your cameras up there," Jimmy Silva said. He produced a notebook and pencil. "I'll give you some police protection, keep the crowds away. We'll all want a record of . . . what was."

Suddenly he shook his head, anger plain. "Goddamn it, why? Answer me that? Kids on Fourth of July setting a forest fire accidentally with cherry bombs, you can understand that. But these are supposed to be grown people, aren't they? Aren't they?"

He looked around at them all, the anger spent. "Okay. I know. And grown people started the war you and I fought in, too, didn't they, Joe? So what the hell am I asking silly questions for?" He shook his head again and looked at Boggs. "Set up your cameras. We'll see you get your pictures. Then you and me, Joe, we can look at them— and go out and get drunk, maybe find a fight to get into." He snapped the notebook shut. "Anything else?"

Boggs looked around the room. He said quietly, "I think that about covers it. Thank you, gentlemen. I will see that you are informed of any change in Hurricane Bob's status. Pete and Mr. Garfield, if you will stay for a few minutes?"

Jimmy Silva, Joe Hines and Ellis filed out with faint smiles and nods and hand gestures wishing luck.

Boggs said to Garfield and Pete, "You have plans, gentlemen?"

Pete said, "I want to watch the seismograph. My guess is it's going to jump off the paper. So I'll be here in the morning."

Garfield said, "What's the time zone for the test shot?"

"Good thought," Pete said. "One hour later than we are." He grinned suddenly. "So I won't have to get up before dawn. They won't shoot it off in the dark."

Garfield said, "I don't know my plans yet. I'll have to let you know."

He and Pete walked together out to Pete's car. Pete said, "You're thinking of what? Clara and Tom?"

"They're at sea. Maybe back today, maybe not until tomorrow."

"Tom's a good sailor," Pete said. "He'll keep his scanner on, and he'll be monitoring Bob's progress on all frequencies. If there's a threat, he'll run for home pronto." He was studying Garfield's face. "The point is, will we want him to come in or stay at sea, right?"

"Exactly."

"Clara," Pete said, "will want to be with the princess, and that means coming ashore. You can take that as read. The trouble is that with what we're expecting, they'll be safer out there. *Westerly*'s a good, stout boat. I've sailed aboard her. Wherever they are, if they head west, out of Bob's probable path, stay out and see what happens, they should be all right." He was watching Garfield's face carefully. "That's your thinking, too?"

"Precisely."

Pete sighed. "I know them pretty well. But you've known them a lot longer. Comes to that, think you can persuade them to stay at sea? Clara especially, with the princess ashore?"

"I can try."

"It would mean that somebody—you—would be taking responsibility for the girl. You realize that?"

He had already thought of it and, reluctantly, accepted it. "Yes."

"Then we wait and see if they come back in today?"

"I don't see an alternative."

Pete turned away and got into the car, closed the door. There he just sat for a few moments, his hands on the wheel, his face thoughtful while Garfield got in, too, and closed his door. Pete turned then to look at him, suddenly smiling now.

"Did you have any idea what you were letting yourself in for when you came down here for—what? A rest? Change? Vacation?"

Garfield managed a smile, too. It was a rueful effort. "All of the above," he said. "And the answer is no, I didn't have any idea."

"Well," Pete said, reaching for the ignition key. "All I got to say is that you really walked into it, didn't you?"

The rueful smile remained. "Nice understatement," Garfield said.

❧

The pilot of the Weather Service hurricane-hunter aircraft let his breath out in a long sigh of relief after they broke free into lighter air turbulence. Into his mike he said, "Bob plays rough." He could not resist glancing left and right at his wingtips to see if they were still there. "Wind shear like you wouldn't believe inside. He turned us every way but loose. Times I felt we were going at least three directions at once and wondering if this flying machine was going to hold together. But we're out of it now, and we'll have lots of poop for you when we come in. Over."

❀

At dinner with Betsy Barnes that night Maude Anderson was quiet.

"What's bothering you, hon?" Betsy said. "Something certainly seems to have gotten to you."

"I ran into Dan Garfield."

"And?"

Maude managed a faint smile. "We walked and we talked."

"I'm fascinated." She shook her head gently. "You don't open up very easily, do you?"

Maude wondered just how one could possibly express the confusion that was in her mind. There were too many factors. Dan, for one, and a changed Dan at that, a warmer, more sensitive man, as she had said. Did that change her own feelings toward him? No, damn it; the memory of her unhappy marriage was still too vivid. She was not prepared to give up the protection her freedom gave her.

And then there was Jack Barnes and his apparent lack of scruples, along with the threat of what Dan Garfield had described, and that, too, was all mixed up in her mind as if all of the factors had been thrown together into some kind of mental Cuisinart. How did one make sense out of all that? She said lamely, "I'm sorry."

"Men," Betsy said, "are the damnedest. I will endorse that. The trouble is that we can't get along without them. I know some who try." She shook her head. "And believe me, it doesn't work. Do I sound like the little mother of all living?"

Maude's smile was better this time, easier. "More or less."

Betsy was silent for a few moments. "Are you going to see him again?"

"I don't know. We didn't talk about that." And it was then, the impulse triggered by she knew not what stimulus, that Maude reached her decision. "I'm going back to town tomorrow, Betsy. I . . . think it's best."

"Let him come to you?" Betsy thought about it. "Maybe you're right. Sometimes running away until you finally catch him is the best system."

"I'm not looking at it like that."

"Maybe you'd better, hon. Maybe you'd better. Anyway"— Betsy's tone changed abruptly, and she reached across the table to pat Maude's hand—"don't think I don't appreciate your coming down to . . . let me cry on your shoulder. I don't know what I'd have done without you. I mean that."

Just before sleep came that night, Maude thought back to that remark and felt as if she had betrayed a friend.

ॐ

Lucy put two plates on the table. "It's chicken Marengo," she said, and studied Garfield's face. "You know about that?"

"Somewhat. Napoleon's chef using what he could find after the battle." He smiled. "Both the French and the Italians claim the recipe."

"Hey! I didn't know that! How come you do?"

Garfield made a small, deprecating gesture. "One of those little things that stick in your mind." He tasted the dish. "Good! That's understatement—it's delicious!" Her pleased smile was warming. "You're going to make some lucky guy some kind of wife, honey. Or am I being too male chauvinistic?"

Lucy was silent, the smile suddenly gone. "Todd and I had a fight this afternoon."

"I'm sorry."

"Why do guys think they have to pat you on the head and tell you it's only a movie, everything's going to be okay?"

"I don't know about that, honey."

"You don't do it. At least you haven't done it so far."

"I'll try to be careful." Garfield glanced at the kitchen clock. "Do you think your folks are coming in tonight?"

"No. It's almost dark, and if he can avoid it, Dad doesn't like

to have Mom try to pick up our mooring in the dark." She smiled
and shook her head. "I guess he's afraid she might fall overboard.
Silly, but that's the way he is."

"I find that rather . . . admirable. As well as considerate."

"Looking out for her, you mean? I guess." Unsmiling now. "But
sometimes we don't want to be looked after, you know?" A small,
puzzled frown appeared. "Or maybe you don't know. Maybe guys
never do."

"You may be right." Garfield had another taste of his meal.
"Napoleon should have had you as his chef, honey. I'll bet what he
got to eat after the battle that night wasn't as good as this."

Lucy looked at him carefully. "You're . . . smooth," she said.
"You know that? It's neat the way you can switch subjects, like a
guy who knows what he's doing using a stick shift in traffic." She
shook her head admiringly. "No wonder Mom trusts you so much.
I don't know anybody else she'd—well—leave me with like this,
except it was maybe—" She stopped, and color appeared in her
cheeks. "Well, maybe she just wanted real bad to be alone with Dad
for a little while."

"I think that was probably it," Garfield said. "So let's not let
her down, okay?"

It was well after dinner, the dishes done, when the phone call
came. "I've got it!" Lucy called into the living room, and there was
long, scarcely audible conversation in the kitchen. Then Lucy appeared.

"I'm going out," she said. "With Todd."

Despite himself, Garfield could not contain his surprise.

"So, okay," Lucy said, "we had a fight this afternoon. But that
was then. Okay?" The single word bristled with challenge.

"It's fine with me," Garfield said, and hid his smile.

"I . . . didn't want you to worry," Lucy said. "I'll be back early."

Garfield thought back to the dinner scene and this last episode
just before he went off to sleep that night. No, he told himself, what
he had said to Pete was whole and simple truth: He had had no idea
what he was letting himself in for when he allowed Tom to talk him
into coming down to Encino Beach.

Wednesday, July 30

Lucy seemed subdued at breakfast. "Bad dreams, honey?" Garfield said. "Sometimes even when you can't remember what they were, they leave you dejected. You've noticed that?"

"I suppose," Lucy said, and then added vaguely, "I don't know. Do you want more coffee? Mom says you've always drunk a lot."

Garfield smiled at the girl. "Bad habit, I'll admit. I used to smoke, too." The smile spread. "And I grew a sort of beard once."

Lucy's smile was wan, unappreciative.

Garfield said as casually as he could, "Your father has a radio transmitter here, doesn't he? Ship-to-shore?" He had a vague memory of Tom's asking his advice for a recommendation on radio equipment, but he had paid little heed at the time beyond asking a few questions concerning broadcast range and price limitations.

"In his study," Lucy said. "In the cabinet. Why?"

"Just wondered."

Lucy put down her cereal spoon, propped both elbows on the table and rested her chin in her hands. Her eyes searched his face. "You aren't telling me something," she said. "What is it?"

"We don't *know* anything yet, honey."

"But you have a good idea. What is it?"

Garfield tried evasion. "You heard the weather report."

Lucy nodded. "Is the hurricane coming up here? Is that it?" She shook her head, but her eyes did not leave his. "Dad's a good sailor. And he's not stupid."

"Of course not. He's—"

"He'll be monitoring the radio, all frequencies on his what you ma call it."

"Scanner."

"He keeps it on when he's at sea. So if it looks like trouble, he'll run for home. That—" She stopped, and her eyes grew large and round. "You're not talking about the hurricane, are you? Is it those big waves again? Is that what it is? Is it?"

"It's only possible, honey. We can't . . . know yet."

Suddenly the girl's eyes were filled with angry tears. She ignored them. "You guys are all alike!" Her voice was overloud. "You and Todd and . . . everybody! Last night—" She stopped, breathing hard, and tears unnoticed ran down the sides of her nose.

"What happened last night, honey?" Garfield's voice was gentle.

"It's none of your—" Again she stopped. "We had another fight! He won't . . . talk to me, tell me anything! Just like you! What gives you guys the right to think you can make all the decisions? I have feelings, too!"

"Honey—" Garfield began. It was too late.

Lucy jumped up from the table, and her chair overturned with a crash. She was unaware, her attention, her anger focused sharply on him. "I'm sick and tired of being patted on the head and being treated like a baby! By Todd! And now by you! And I won't sit here and take it any longer!" She was gone, almost running.

Garfield heard the outer door slam and sat, quiet, wondering just what he was supposed to do now. He was still there, at the table, breakfast unfinished in front of him, when Pete walked in, as usual without knocking.

Pete surveyed the scene. Wordlessly he bent and righted the overturned chair and sat down on it. "Little problem with the princess?" he said. His voice was mild.

"Probably my fault."

Pete nodded solemnly. "Probably. Whatever it was." He stood up. "Your coffee looks cold. I'll heat some for both of us." He busied himself in silence at the stove.

At the table again, fresh coffee in front of them, "I don't know much about girls," Pete said conversationally. "Maybe Daphne does. She was one once." He paused and produced a faint, wondering smile. "At least I guess she was, although sometimes it seems she was probably already grown-up when she was born. The British ever strike you that way?"

"I know the feeling," Garfield said. "Or used to." He had a sip of coffee and set the cup down thoughtfully. "Tom and Clara didn't come in last night."

"I know. I looked at the empty mooring. So what now? You can probably raise them on the ship-to-shore."

"Yes."

"Try to persuade them to stay outside, head west. Bob's still coming this way. And he's picked up more speed."

"I know."

"Tell Clara you'll take care of the princess. Where is she anyway?"

Garfield spread both hands and shook his head. "I don't know."

"Well," Pete said, "I guess we can find her." He looked at his watch and stood up. "The transceiver's in the cupboard in Tom's study. You'll know more about it than I do."

"Probably." Garfield was smiling, a wry smile, mocking himself, his situation. "For a change I'll be dealing with something inside my own field."

"I'm going to the institute, the seismograph. Have you taken a look at the surf this morning?"

Garfield shook his head.

"High, and getting higher. We're already catching Bob's fringe force. If he keeps coming—" Pete shook his head and looked at his watch. "High tide's in a little over three hours. It could be timed just right—or wrong—to coincide with . . . what we're expecting."

Garfield watched him quietly.

"Oh, yes," Pete said, "it's coming, worst possible scenario. I know it. You know it. I feel it right here." He patted his flat belly. "I don't believe in premonitions. Or I didn't—"

"I know," Garfield said, and stood up. "I had one once. All morning. Then in the middle of a class—integral calculus, I remember—they called me to the dean's office to tell me my father'd been killed in Vietnam." He made an odd, quick gesture of dismissal. "I'll call Tom and Clara."

"See you," Pete said. "After Murphy's Law goes into operation." He turned away and went out the back door. It closed gently after him.

Garfield went into the doctor's study. The transceiver was there in its handsome cabinet. Garfield's eyes swept the dials, gauges and knobs all as familiar to him as tools to a good mechanic. He flipped on the power switch, watched the red signal light appear, the dial needle react and the faint hum of the awakened circuitry commence. He left the selector dial at the frequency at which it was set, adjusted volume automatically and then picked up the hand microphone, depressed the button and spoke into it. "Calling yacht *Westerly.* Repeat, calling yacht *Westerly.*" He released the microphone button and waited.

There was no immediate response. He had expected none. He raised the hand microphone, repeated the call and again waited.

Tom Winslow's voice, distorted in transmission but nonetheless recognizable, said, "Yacht *Westerly* here. Come in. Over."

"Home base," Garfield said, confident that his own voice would also be recognized. "What is your location? In harbor? At sea? Over."

"In harbor hoisting anchor."

"You are following weather reports?"

"Affirmative. Weather looks bad. We're coming in."

"How much sailing time?"

"Depending on wind, four, five hours."

Exactly the wrong timing, Garfield thought. About three hours to high tide, Pete had said, and if the test shot took place soon, as Pete, citing Murphy's Law, seemed to anticipate—"Negative," he said into the mike. "We can't *know* yet what's going to happen, but—"

The telephone on the desk rang, its sound loud and unexpected. Garfield stared at it as he spoke again into the microphone. "Stand by. Phone call." He put down the microphone, reached the desk in two long steps, snatched up the phone and spoke his name.

Harry Saunder's voice said, "They've fired it." His tone was grave. "And it was a big one, bigger, I'm sure, than they expected; at least that seems to be the indication. That's all I can tell you now."

"Bless you," Garfield said, hung up and jumped back to the transceiver. "You're there, *Westerly?* Over."

"Right here. What's doing? Why—"

"I can't explain. You'll get radio warnings soon, I'm sure. Put to sea. Head north and west, and stay out. There won't be any shelter here. Acknowledge."

"Dan!" This was Clara's voice, suddenly shrill with excitement. "Dan! What is happening?"

"What we feared. It's all but certain now. It's—"

"Is Lucy with you? Is she, Dan?"

Garfield took a deep breath. "Not at the moment."

"Then where is she?"

"I'll find her. You can count on that."

"Dan!"

Tom's voice again. "We're coming in, Dan."

"Damn it! Believe me! It's—" Again the ringing phone interrupted. "Stand by once more! Phone!" He dropped the microphone and jumped to the desk to snatch up the phone.

Pete's voice, unnaturally calm, said, "It's coming. As promised. Boggs is calling Ellis now. It's—"

The sudden sound of a siren filled the study. It rose and fell, a banshee shriek of warning, reminiscent, Garfield thought fleetingly, of air-raid alerts on a war film's sound track. "I hear it," he said. "Thanks." He hung up and jumped back to the microphone. "It's sure now," he said into the mike. "It's all coming together. Clara knows what I'm talking about—those big waves. Three hours, if we're lucky. Can you hear the sirens?"

"Affirmative." Tom's voice was calm, appraising. "Stand by." The sound of the radio carrier wave ceased.

Garfield sat where he was, eyes closed, waiting. He could almost visualize the scene: Clara distraught; Tom no less upset, but by training and experience accustomed to facing crises, matters of life or death, irrevocable decisions that had to be made on the spot. The tension in the small cabin of the boat, Garfield thought, would be almost unbearable.

The carrier wave sound again filled the speaker, and Tom's voice, still calm, still appraising, said, "You are sure, Dan? There will be no shelter inside? It *is* that bad?"

"No shelter! Devastation!" He could accept it now. The die was cast. "Sorry, but that's it."

Tom's voice, in weary resignation, said, "Roger. We will put to sea, head northwest. Wish us—"

Clara's voice interrupted. "Dan! Promise me you will find Lucy! Take care of her! Promise!"

"Promise." Garfield closed his eyes. "Good luck."

"Thanks." Tom's voice again. "Over and out." The carrier wave was silent.

Garfield's hand moved slowly, reluctantly to switch off the transmitter. He watched the ready light fade and grow dark. Outside the sirens wailed on.

Interlude

At an elevation of thirty-eight thousand feet, miles distant from the scene, swinging in a great circle at steady cruising speed in the cloudless sky, the aircraft commanded a clear view for its cameras, their lenses covered with heavy, dark filters.

The crew of the aircraft, too, wore protective goggles, and before they left base, their instructions had been definite and decisive. "Do not, repeat, do *not,* look directly at the blast. Its light will be more intense than that of the sun, and the retinas of your eyes, even though these lenses, can be permanently damaged."

But with the first, sudden burst of light from the tiny atoll instantly triggering the cameras' power drives, and the immediate, sure knowledge that the test shot *had* been fired, the temptation to look directly at the scene was almost irresistible.

It was the scientific observer's voice that said quickly, harshly into the intercom, "Eyes away unless you want to walk with a white cane the rest of your life!" And that message did get through.

But micromoments later, as the fireball began to develop to its eventual gigantic size, rising swiftly in the clear air, brilliant flashes of light within it, they did look and then stare in wonder as the stupendous power of the blast began to display its awesome might.

Even the scientific observer, veteran of the U.S. hydrogen bomb tests, blew his cheeks out in awe as he watched. "Jesus H. Jumping Christ!" he said into his mike, automatically transmitting to shore listening stations. "They've got a real one going!"

❧

From sea level the scene was even more awe-inspiring. The seas surrounding the tiny atoll boiled and churned, throwing spray high into the air and completely blotting out all view of the atoll.

An enormous mushroom-shaped cloud rose and spread with unbelievable speed, and within the gigantic fireball that was its center, ignited gases roiled in a furnace of changing colors of which one witness later wrote: "For one irrational moment, I fancied that we had unleashed forces that were turning the earth itself into a miniature sun that would incinerate us all."

Great seas rocked the witnessing ships, and the thunder of the explosion, the same witness wrote, "defied description, not a bang, nor yet the boom of heavy artillery, but, rather, a deafening, earth-shaking, bellowing roar of rage that assaulted the senses and stunned even those wearing protective ear pads. For what must have been minutes, not seconds, speech was impossible, not only because of the thunderous sound, but because of the devastating effect of the entire scene upon one's consciousness. And when at last the seas around us began to subside, but while the gigantic fireball still hung above us like the threat of doom, we looked around and could see nothing but the limitless waters still tossing restlessly. The structure upon which the device had been mounted, indeed, the entire solid atoll itself, had been disintegrated by the blast and now hung in the air as dust."

❦

Sound shock waves spread instantly in all directions, but with greater speed through water than through air. The atomic submarine *Thrasher,* proceeding at cruising speed at a depth of twenty fathoms miles from the scene, shivered from the impact of the first shock wave, seemed to shake itself as a stunned boxer does, recovered its equilibrium and continued on its way.

The duty officer said, "What the hell was that?" And then immediately added: "Ask sonar what he made it out to be."

But the sonar operator was sitting almost frozen, a stunned expression on his face, unable to react to the question. Slowly he raised both hands and took off his headset, dropped it in his lap and pressed his hands to his ears, moaning softly as he rocked back and forth in his chair.

❦

Along the ledge Pete Williamson had studied from the minisub, fresh, minor cracks appeared in the rock, and small pieces broke free to drift down into the abyss in the leisurely manner of large snow-flakes falling in gray winter murk.

Gradually more fractures appeared in the rock structure, more small pieces broke free and drifted downward; had one seen it, a picture without sound. Here and there a larger rock piece dislodged itself and joined the falling debris, and cracks already in existence along the ledge began to widen almost imperceptibly.

Suddenly, massively along the entire structure, like an enormous building slowly absorbing the effect of dynamite charges exploded at its foundations, the ledge shuddered gently, hung poised against the sheer face of the submarine trench for long moments and then, with ponderous decision, separated from the parent rock to plunge into the depths.

Along almost one hundred miles of this gigantic submarine earth fracture, hundreds of millions of tons of rock, behaving like dominoes toppling in swift succession, began their fall, accelerating as they dropped, suddenly and forcefully displacing the water in the depths and, on contact, by their bulk and weight altering the shape and contours of the sea bottom itself.

On the surface, the ocean boiled and heaved as the energy from the disturbance beneath was transmitted upward, and from the surface area directly above this enormous underwater avalanche, directed outward in all directions as ripples spread in a pool, visible waves came into being, their crests scores of miles apart, their surface height, determined by the depth of water, no more than two or three feet, but their speed well in excess of 400 mph, and their energy almost incalculable.

The inexorable process had begun.

❦

Within minutes seismograph stations at Tahiti, Suva, Guam, Hong Kong, Shemya, Sitka, Pasadena, Santiago, and others, were receiving in order the P(rimary), S(econdary) and L(ong) waves emanating from the submarine source of the seismic disturbance caused by the underwater avalanche.

The difference between the arrival times of the different types of waves pinpointed the distance each receiving seismograph was from the focus of disturbance.

At the quadripartite array of seismic detectors located on the island of Oahu, Hawaii, and linked to the Honolulu Observatory, automatic calculations were immediately set in train to fix the epicenter of the quake, its magnitude and something about its tsunami-generating potential. A tsunami watch was issued immediately to the fourteen Pacific coastal and island nations and territories of the warning network.

The tsunami watch was followed shortly by a tsunami warning, and estimated times of arrival were quickly calculated and broadcast to each vulnerable Pacific locality.

"With an eight-point-seven Richter-scale reading for a seismic disturbance on the sea bottom," one official was quoted later, "there was no doubt what was going to happen. All that was left was to find out how much damage was going to be done. And where."

15

10:30 A.M.–11:40 A.M. Pacific Daylight Time

In his Office of Disaster Preparedness in Encino Beach, Wilbert Ellis took the call from Howard Boggs himself. He listened quietly, said, "Thank you," in as calm a voice as he could manage, and hung up the phone to stare at the far wall for one of the longest moments of his life. Then he roused himself, took a deep breath and, as promised, issued his orders.

"A county-wide alert on LIFE," he told his assistant. "At once." LIFE was an acronym for *L*ifesaving *I*nformation *F*or *E*mergencies, copied after the system first established in California's San Diego County.

Special LIFE receivers around the county were immediately notified by Touch-Tone telephone signals, Tone No. 1 alerting police and fire dispatch; Tone No. 2 alerting TV, AM, FM and CATV radio and television stations; Tone No. 3 alerting key county officials and

Tone No. 4 alerting hospitals and schools. These signals were followed by voice messages giving particulars.

❧

Olaf Hansen heard the first siren and went immediately, but
without undue haste, to the radio, which he turned on and tuned to
a local station.

". . . has issued a tsunami—that is, tidal wave—warning," the
announcer's breathless voice said. "Repeat, the National Weather
Service has issued a tsunami, tidal wave, warning for Encino Beach.
This is *not* a drill. Repeat, this is *not* a drill. Residents in low-lying
areas are urged to move to higher ground. Boats in harbor—"

"I believe we already know what boats in harbor ought to do,"
Olaf said as he switched off the radio. "Pete and Dan Garfield would
appear to have called their shots with accuracy." To Lydia: "I think
we should pack at once, as planned." His voice was calm, unhurried.
He looked at Daphne. "Are you still of the same mind, to remain
ashore?" It was as if he were asking if she had changed her mind
about not going shopping.

"No change." Daphne was smiling. "But there is ample time,
I should think, for me to make myself useful helping you transfer
supplies to the boat. I can row the dinghy, you know. It has also
occurred to me that I could see that your car, loaded with whatever
memorabilia you wish, should come to no harm."

Lydia said, "You *are* a dear."

"Please." Daphne made a small gesture of dismissal. "I am
already deeply in your debt, you know, for bringing me into an
entirely new and wonderful life."

Joe Hines heard the sirens and paid them no heed. They were
for folks who dwelt onshore; water was his element. When the telephone on his desk rang, he picked it up immediately and spoke his
name, never taking his eyes from the open door of his office and the
view of the harbor, where activity was just beginning.

"Thought you might like to know, Joe," the familiar Weather
Service voice said, "that Hurricane Bob has picked up speed and is

heading our way at a fairly good clip. We're already getting storm seas, and that's just the beginning, I'm afraid."

"Right," Joe said. "Thanks."

He got up from his desk and walked to the doorway to stand there and survey the scene. Directly across the narrow neck of the bay from his office was the expensive, sprawling house of J. Rex Anthony, vice commodore of the Encino Beach Yacht Club, and riding serenely in its slip in front of the house was *Circe,* the vice commodore's twin-screw diesel-power yacht, sixty-four feet of gleaming magnificence, constantly fueled and ready for sea. She had been designed and built for, and was quite capable of, cruising in any waters, equipped with every navigational and communications device available, sometimes referred to at the Yacht Club, and not always out of the vice commodore's hearing, as the "VC's big stink-pot with the solid gold keel."

The yacht had never been more than thirty nautical miles from her home port of Encino Beach, where she was built.

The vice commodore was an avid sailor—when the day was bright and pleasant, and the sea dead flat calm. He had ventured outside once as a guest aboard a fellow member's ocean-racing yawl when small-craft warnings were flying, and the experience had terrified him. While all others aboard, soaked to the skin, were jumping from task to task, wearing perpetual, happy grins as the yawl leaned into her work, rail down, tearing the seas to shreds, throwing spray high, shouldering the water aside almost with contempt and sending it hissing and gurgling along her sleek sides, the vice commodore had huddled on the cockpit seat against the cabin trunk, wishing he were dead. Mercilessly, he did not even have the comforting agony of seasickness.

He had heard the sirens now and immediately switched on the radio. What he heard from it brought nausea to his throat. As he could see from his window, already flying at the harbormaster's mast was a single square red flag, black centered, indicating full storm outside.

And the radio was saying that small craft which were capable should put to sea? Insane!

The vice commodore was watching Joe Hines walk back into the harbormaster's office when his wife came into the study. "Jason, dear," she said, using the first name he detested, "what are all the sirens and noises about?"

"The authorities seem to fancy that we are threatened," the vice commodore said.

"Threatened? By what?"

"Another tidal wave—tsunami, I believe they call it."

"But," his wife said, "that is ridiculous. We just had one." She thought about it briefly. "Anyway, what are you going to do about it, dear?"

The vice commodore improvised quickly. "I have a meeting in town."

"I didn't remember that."

"I don't bother you with every detail." The vice commodore stood up from his leather chair. "I think you might come up with me. We can have dinner at—"

"Jason, dear." His wife studying him carefully. "What are you trying not to tell me?"

It was the vice commodore's opinion, based on long observation, that some women were capable of second sight. It was an uncomfortable concept, but inescapable. "It seems that there may be something to it this time," he said. "They are talking about . . . inundation."

"Of what?"

"The entire bay."

His wife was frowning now. "The houses? The club? And what about *Circe*?"

It was the one question the vice commodore did not at this moment want even to try to answer, and he searched his mind for a credible means of dissembling his feelings in the matter. He was saved by the telephone bell which rang softly on his desk. He picked it up and spoke his name.

"Joe Hines here, Commodore. You've heard the warnings, I guess, and I expect you're taking *Circe* to sea." Luckily there was no pause here, no need for the vice commodore to reply. "What

I was wondering," Joe Hines went on, "was whether you could use a good hand to go along with you. That's a lot of boat to handle alone."

The vice commodore blinked, but that was the only reaction his wife could see. "Do you have someone, Joe?" the vice commodore said.

"I can lay hands on one or two who'd be happy to help out."

There *was* a compassionate deity looking on, after all, the vice commodore thought. He said, "As it happens, Joe, I have an engagement in town that *is* rather important. I would skip it, of course, if there were no other way, but . . ." He left the sentence dangling.

"Sure thing, Commodore. I'll send somebody around you can trust *Circe* to. He'll take her outside, where she'll be safe."

"I appreciate this, Joe," the vice commodore said, and added silently, you'll never know how much.

"Not to worry a bit." Joe hung up and looked across the office to the muscular nineteen-year-old boy watching him and waiting. "Goddamn fair-weather sailor," Joe said. "He'd be scared pissless to take that wonderful goddamn boat even as far as the jetties." He watched the grin on the boy's face. "But don't you make any cracks," Joe said. "You hear? Play it straight and take good care of that boat, or I'll have your hide."

The grin held, but there was respect in the boy's voice. "You got it, Joe."

In the vice commodore's study the wife said, "Do you know what I think, Jason?"

The vice commodore was quite sure he did not want to hear any part of what she thought, but answer was impossible to avoid. "No," he said, "what?"

"I think you planned the whole thing, you crafty old darling."

❧

Sixteen-year-old Tommy Parks heard the sirens, too, and switched on the radio in his room to listen to the warning. When he had heard enough, he switched the radio off and sat, indecisive, for long moments. In the end, as he had known all along he would, he told himself with scorn, he roused himself and went about his preparations.

With a change of shirt and trousers, a heavy sweater and foul-weather gear stuffed into a duffel bag, he let himself out of the big beach house and carefully locked the door behind him. His folks were in town, and he thought fleetingly of leaving a note for them, but in the emotional turmoil of the situation, he forgot. He drove his little sports car down to the yacht club, where he parked and hailed the shore boat to take him out to the sixty-five foot twin-screw gasoline-powered yacht *Lubelle,* tugging insistently at her mooring.

Once aboard, using the keys Joe Hines had given him, he unlocked the engine ignition switches, started up the blowers and let them run while he unlocked the cabin and went below to stow his gear and check supplies.

Back on deck and satisfied that the bilges were by now clear of any gasoline fumes, he fired up the big engines and let them idle, their underwater exhausts bubbling quietly, while he checked fuel tank levels, broke out the club burgee and yacht ensign, made sure that the dinghy and anchor lashings were secure and had one last look around the harbor before he went forward to cast loose the mooring.

He had grown up accustomed to boats, both power and sail, and he had crewed aboard *Lubelle* a number of times in the predicted-log races the club conducted outside the breakwaters, but being aboard alone in a crisis situation was an experience totally new, and frightening.

There were, as he well knew, all manner of ways to screw up under even the most favorable circumstances when you were handling a boat *Lubelle*'s size. Now, with that storm flag flying outside Joe Hines's office, indicating real wind and seas outside, merely to venture out was not something you undertook lightly. But he had given his word, and there simply was no way of backing out.

With one engine ahead and the other in reverse, he skillfully spun the big boat in little more than her own length, came ahead with both engines at near-idling speed, rudder amidships, and headed down-channel.

As *Lubelle* passed the harbormaster's office, Joe appeared in the doorway, bullhorn in hand, and waved approvingly, thumb and forefinger held in a circle, as he headed for the workboat in its slip.

Tommy swallowed hard and gestured vaguely in reply. The boat traffic was getting heavy down at the end of the bay, and he slipped into it with reluctance as they entered the narrow gut.

He watched both left and right warily, Joe's long-ago admonitions still ringing in memory. "Just because you may be the biggest thing afloat in the area," Joe had said over and over again, "don't mean you can crowd the others. You got another vessel approaching anywhere from dead ahead to two points abaft your starboard beam, you're the burdened vessel, and you give way and stay clear. You got that?"

Rules of the road, Tommy thought, and found some comfort in the orderliness they implied. When another boat crowded him from his port side, he blew a peremptory blast on *Lubelle*'s horn, and the intruding boat gave way. Tommy felt a little better.

He cleared the jetties and was immediately into deeper water. Ahead, the bell buoy rolled to the swells and clanged their number, and *Lubelle*'s motions changed; where before, in the sheltered water of the bay, the big boat had rolled only gently, seeming to thrust the small swells aside as unimportant, now, with the bell buoy falling astern, and the bottom beginning to drop off more sharply, *Lubelle* gave the impression of settling into her work, coping with the forces of the open ocean as she had been designed and built to do, pitching and rolling as if slipping punches, yawing only a few degrees with each swell and bringing her heavy hull obediently back on course without hesitation to face the next sea.

Tommy advanced both throttles a notch and felt the sudden surge of power as the tachometer needles climbed and then settled at a steady speed. The rolling, pitching, yawing motions diminished but did not cease entirely, and the V-shaped wake trailing astern took on a different, churning appearance.

The boats around him spread out as they left the constrictions of the channel, and all at once it seemed that Tommy and *Lubelle* were all alone. Tommy stifled the impulse to come about and head back into the bay, where at least he would have company.

He switched on the radio scanner and listened for a moment as it tuned from frequency to frequency, pausing briefly when a station was active, giving him a chance to hold on that frequency if he chose, before it continued its ceaseless searching of the full width of the broadcast band. At least he would miss no message of importance, Tommy thought, and turned his full attention to his helmsmanship.

"Stay well out beyond the ten-fathom line," Joe had said. "You may have seas to contend with, but you can handle them. *Lubelle*'s built for any weather."

Tommy switched on the fathometer and watched the changing depths appear on the screen: forty-five feet, forty-seven, forty-six, fifty . . . Ten fathoms was sixty feet. Coming soon. Tommy took a deep breath. So far, so good.

God, how he hoped he wouldn't screw up!

ॐ

Jimmy Silva had a captain of the California Highway Patrol in his office, and the door closed. "Most times you and me, we get along fine," Jimmy was saying, "and no reason we can't here, too. But like you know your freeways like the back of your hand, I know Encino Beach and its roads and its people, the kind you can trust and the kind you'd as soon kick their ass right back to where they come from, both. Way I see it, you got two big problems, and you handle them and I'll handle my end down here. Okay?"

The captain disliked being talked to like this by a beach civilian even if he was a mayor, but he had his orders to cooperate, and he said merely, "What do you see as my two problems?"

"Okay." Jimmy perched on the edge of his desk. "First," he said, "there are going to be a lot of goddamn fools, ghouls, who'll head for the beaches, especially here to watch the fun. According to the eggheads and their computers, we may get the worst of the damage right here in Encino Beach. Has to do with the way the water shoals between the headlands. Don't raise your eyebrows, goddamn it! In fifteen, twenty minutes, a half hour, you'll see I'm right. It always happens. A big storm, they come down to watch the waves, for Christ's sake! Park all the way out to the jetties! They do that this time, and the starfish and the spiny lobsters, those that are left, are going to have a lot of dead meat to feed on!"

The captain thought about it. "Maybe," he said. Then, although even the question was painful: "What do you suggest?"

"Shut off all roads coming down here except for folks who got business, a house, a boat, folks to get out, that kind of thing." Jimmy shook his head sympathetically. "The hell of a job, I know," he said, "but goddamn it, it's got to be done!"

The captain said without assent or disagreement, "And my second problem?"

"Coast highway's a goddamn deathtrap," Jimmy said promptly. "It runs only fifteen, twenty feet above mean high water— you know what that means? I seen pictures, and I heard somebody who knows, and them—whatever the hell they're called—soonami come in thirty, forty, fifty feet high with half the Pacific Ocean behind them, and they'll wipe out anything they hit! I mean, wipe it out, cars, houses, office buildings, people—you get the picture?"

He was beginning to, the captain thought—if, that was, this beach town clown had any idea what he was talking about, and against his inclinations the captain was beginning to believe that he did. There was that about Jimmy Silva in his aloha shirt, with his heavy, hairy forearms and an intensity in his voice and in his manner, that just about made you believe him. The captain said nothing.

"I grew up here," Jimmy said. "I know every waterway and path and old road there is, not just the paved ones we use now, but some of the others, too, that kids ride in beach buggies today but that still lead uphill to the heights—and that, goddamn it, is where we got to get folks just as fast as we can. I'll give you a couple local cops know the area as well as I do. They'll show you roads that can be opened and kept one-way—up! Like up where the ground is safe!" He took a deep breath. "Screw the coast highway! All it's good for is to get folks to a road heading uphill!"

He slid down from his desk and hitched up his trousers. "Like I said," he said in a new, different tone, "we get along fine most times." He faced the captain squarely. "How about it? We going to get along now, or are you and me going to have to go around and around like a couple tomcats in a cage?"

The captain took his time, pride of position struggling with what to his surprise had suddenly become conviction. Slowly he nodded and held out his hand. "We'll get along, Mr. Mayor," he said. "And I appreciate your explanations."

Part III

16

At Angelo's market there was discussion. Most who had been at C. Ward Struthers's open house were there, and a few more.

Helen DuBois, the watercolor painting teacher, who lived above Tillie Burke's garage, was openly scornful of the warnings. "Same like last time," she said, "pure crap. They do it to get everybody all uptight, and make themselves feel important." There was a big-city eastern seaboard defensive snarl in Helen's voice.

Tillie Burke, espouser of *Causes,* was hesitant as usual about making a definite statement. "There *have* been such things," she said meekly. "I remember a fund that was raised to help the poor residents of Anchorage after the 1964 earthquake and tidal wave."

C. Ward Struthers, his shopping bag stuffed with newly purchased liters of vodka and bottles of cranberry juice, said judiciously, "I've done some research on tsunami in my work. But we have three hours of warning, the radio says, and I intend to await further reports." He raised the shopping bag and smiled. "In the meantime, 'forewarned, forearmed.' That's from the Latin."

Helen DuBois snorted but said nothing, resenting Ward's show of erudition but afraid to challenge it.

Angelo himself said, "Who the hell knows? We all heard Jerry Diggs about those crab boats and that crazy wave up in Alaska." He shook his head. "Me, I figure it's better to be safe than sorry. I'm closing up shop in an hour, packing the family in the car and heading for the hills. So I lose the market, I lose the market. It's insured."

The Knit Shoppe lady said, "Oh, dear! I don't know what to believe! I've just received a shipment of alpaca. And some very special New Zealand wool is due any day—" She stopped, obviously close to tears.

Helen DuBois snorted again. "Like I said, pure crap! Was I you, I wouldn't even change the window display."

૨૭

Dan Garfield telephoned Pete at the institute. "You're busy, I know," Garfield said, "but have you any idea where Lucy may have gone? She was in a . . . huff. No, that's not even close. She was angry, furious."

"Try the Wilsons," Pete said. "They'll know if anybody does. Aside from that—" There was a pause. "She'll probably hear the sirens and come home. She—" Another pause. "You reached Tom and Clara?"

"They're putting out to sea—northwest."

"And you're left holding the baby? Okay. I understand, but, Jesus, I don't have a clue! She could be anywhere, and we've got"— another pause while Pete glanced at the clock—"about two hours and twenty-five minutes, is all." One more pause. "If you see Daphne, tell her I want her here."

"The Wilsons," Garfield said. "Thanks, Pete." He hung up and walked into the kitchen. The Wilson phone number, he remembered, was prominently displayed on the list beside the refrigerator.

Mrs. Wilson answered. "No," she said, "Lucy isn't here. Todd has gone up to town, and she isn't with him. Have you heard the sirens? And the radio? Have you—"

"Yes," Garfield said. "Tom and Clara are off in the boat. Lucy's my responsibility." And how in the world did I ever get myself into this position? he asked himself. Never mind. "She—"

"She is a very responsible child, Mr. Garfield. She'll probably be back in a few minutes. She couldn't miss all the . . . commotion in the streets, the sirens and all!" Mrs. Wilson's voice took on a shriller note. "Do you really believe what the radio is saying? I mean, last time it all came to . . . nothing!"

"This time," Garfield said, "believe it. All of it."

He hung up the wall phone and stood indecisively staring at the refrigerator. "All right, know-it-all," he said softly aloud, "what do you do now?"

11:45 A.M.–12:01 P.M. PDT

In the South Pacific 140°W and 9°S there is a tiny volcanic island rising abruptly from the sea to an elevation of 2,213 feet. In these moist tropical waters it wears during daylight hours a perpetual cumulus cloud parasol which can be seen for miles and for centuries has been used as a steering checkpoint for natives in their sailing canoes. The islet is uninhabited except by seabirds, which during nesting season occupy its south-facing cliffs.

The first tsunami struck here one hour and twelve minutes after the test explosion, the wave having traveled a little over 550 miles at an average speed of 460 miles per hour. The wave's arrival was witnessed only by the crew of a circling navy aircraft equipped with video cameras and dispatched to the scene for that specific purpose.

Unedited, and with sound track intact, the tape was shown in the secretary's office thousands of miles away only minutes after the event. Present were the secretary; Harry Saunders, the scientific adviser; an assistant secretary and a handful of high-ranking uniformed personnel.

"Calm sea," an admiral said as the tape began, "typical in those waters. "They're probably wondering what they're looking for."

The crew of the aircraft *was* wondering. "I don't see a damn thing," an unidentified voice on the tape said. "Those swells are only maybe eighteen inches high."

"One minute to ETA," a second voice said. "Look sharp. Its course is predicted to be about twenty-two degrees, northeast by north. Forty-five seconds. Thirty. Fif—"

"There it is! Migod, look at it go! And it's building!"

In the secretary's office they watched in sudden silence as the three-foot swell racing suddenly into view slowed perceptibly and began to rear itself high above the surrounding water, its front impossibly steep and its trailing mass piling ever higher, sleek and shining in the tropical sun.

In the silence, "The water shoals fast," Harry Saunders said. "That's what's causing the sudden buildup."

Higher the wave rose, and higher, ever steep, now foaming at its top as if in rage as it hurled its mass against the islet's cliff face in an explosion of solid water and blinding spray.

On either side of the islet the three-foot swell raced on, unimpeded and almost insignificant, while against the cliff face the crashing water piled higher and higher from the power of the following and suddenly obstructed wave energy.

"God!" one of the admirals said softly. "In forty years at sea I've never seen anything like this!"

As quickly as it had come, the climax was past, and at the foot of the cliff face there remained only a confusion of water, momentarily resembling rapids in a fast-rushing stream. Then that, too, was finished, and all that showed on the screen was the succession of miniature swells marching in parallel lines and swirling gently again as they met the rock face.

Harry Saunder's voice, unemotional, almost uninflected, the voice of a teacher lecturing, said, "That cliff face is approximately three hundred and twenty-five feet high. I measured it. The top of the wave—you can still see the watermarks—I estimate to have reached on the order of two-thirds of the cliff's height, or perhaps two hundred fifteen to two hundred twenty feet. That, gentlemen, is a tsunami. Under optimum conditions, of course, a steeply shoaling bottom and a sheer cliff face, but clearly demonstrating its power, I think, and its capacity for damage."

Someone turned the lights on in the office, and someone else switched off the picture. The secretary looked around the room. "Comments?"

"I think we might say, sir," a senior admiral said, "that we have met the enemy"—his faint smile was almost apologetic—"and I am not sure what we can do about him except hope and maybe pray." He paused for a moment. "All ships around the Pacific that are seaworthy are already ordered to sea. All aircraft on ground that could be considered at hazard have been ordered flown to safer airfields. All shore installations in areas at risk are already taking what precautions and making what moves they can."

"Quite," the secretary said.

"I will admit, sir," the admiral said, "that I for one was skeptical when Dr. Saunders made his recommendations. But he is amply vindicated by what we have just seen, and I apologize for my doubts."

"Generous of you, Admiral," Saunders said, "but the credit belongs with a stubborn oceanographer and an exceptional man both of them way out in California, rather than with me." He was unsmiling. "What's important now is what may be coming out there." He glanced at his watch. "In about two hours or a little less." He made a quick gesture correcting himself. "And elsewhere, of course, where there are buildings that cannot be moved and people who may not be able, or inclined, to move fast enough."

❦

It seemed to Jack Barnes that just about every state highway patrol officer in California was out and active and determined to keep him from reaching Encino Beach. The freeway had suddenly turned one-way, in places eight lanes of traffic heading inland, a rush hour such as no one had ever seen, so Jack took the lesser streets and roads, weaving and dodging, avoiding or sometimes ignoring automatic traffic signals as he slowly but steadily worked his way south.

He had long since switched off the car radio with its almost hysterical warnings and switched on the cassette player. Any kind of music was preferable to what he considered melodramatic radio acting. He let the orchestral sounds flow over him almost unnoticed while he weighed the various factors he had to consider.

The Encino Beach house was already in escrow, so presumably whatever might happen to it was no longer a concern of his, but the matter was academic anyway because at this point there was no longer anything he could do one way or the other that would make any difference. So forget the house. Jack had the gambler's ability to put aside his losses and go on to the next game.

He disliked driving his BMW into a danger zone. He was fond of the car, but the boat, being by far the more valuable, made that choice: He would leave the car at the yacht club and take the boat out to sea. If he lost the car, that was tough, but it was the only logical choice, and logic, practicality, played a large part in Jack's thinking.

Betsy. He could take her with him aboard the boat, but that had two major drawbacks: It would mean leaving *her* BMW where it, too, could be lost. He remembered seeing pictures taken at some place in Alaska—Anchorage? Seward? Kodiak?—after the tsunami waves of the 1964 earthquake had done their damage, and a car caught in such a predicament would end up as a pile of junk. That was the first drawback.

The second was that Betsy was decorative and pleasant company; but, face it, she was not worth a damn aboard the boat, and Jack would not put it past her to turn hysterical if they had to get into the kind of rough seas the radio had been talking about before the tsunami warning took over center stage. And so that choice, too, was made reasonably clear.

He reached the coast highway at last and found it blocked off by signs, which he ignored, and, dodging them, worked his way to the entrance to Encino Beach itself, where a local cop blocked his way.

"You're going the wrong way, buddy," the cop said. "We're evacuating this beach area. There's a tidal wave coming."

Jack nodded. "So the radio's been saying. I've got a house down here and a boat on a mooring. There's nothing I can do about the house, but I can take the boat outside where it's safe."

"Rough out there." The cop was an ex-fisherman. "Storm warning's up. And maybe worse to come."

Jack nodded and said nothing.

"Okay," the cop said, following orders. "It's your skin." He stepped back from the car and waved it through. "Luck."

Betsy was at the Onyx Street house and almost distraught. "What's happening? Answer me that? Is this for real? An honest-to-God tidal wave, or is it just another false alarm? You told me to stay here, and you don't even look worried!"

"Nothing to worry about," Jack said, and pulled up his cuff for a glance at his watch, "for about two hours, maybe a little less. By then you'll be back in Brentwood."

"And where will you be? Here? In this house? What's going to become of it? It and all our things! If we'd known this was going to—" She stopped in mid-sentence, and her eyes grew round. "Is that why we're selling? Because you knew this would happen? Is it?"

"Never mind." Jack's tone was easy, and his smile urged calm. "Let's just take it as it comes. We'll pack what valuables we can in your car, and you head for Brent—"

"I will not! Not until you tell me what you're going to do! The radio says—"

"I know what it says." Jack's voice was no longer soothing. "You're going to do just what I say, pack what valuables you can, get in your car and haul ass for Brentwood. I'm taking the boat out to sea."

"That's crazy! There's a storm out there! The radio says that, too!" Betsy stamped her foot in frustration. "Oh, damn, damn, damn! I wish Maude hadn't left! She'd help me talk some sense into you!"

Jack took Betsy's shoulders in both hands. He shook her hard. He was a big man, and strong, and Betsy's head jerked forward and back, and her hair came down over her eyes. He stopped shaking and held her still. "Now listen to me." His tone was low-pitched, commanding. "We're going to pack what valuables we can and load them in your car, and you're heading for Brentwood. Have you got that? Have you?"

Betsy brushed her hair back with both hands. Her frightened eyes did not leave his face. Slowly she nodded.

"That's my girl." His tone was softer. "And I'm taking *Spindrift* out to sea, where she'll be safe. I won't have her caught in harbor in the kind of mess we're going to get, any more than I'll have you caught here in this house. Is that clear?"

Betsy swallowed hard and nodded again.

"Then get humping," Jack said, and turned her around to slap her buttocks playfully. "Whatever you think we most want to save that you can carry. Move it!"

Still, she hesitated, half turned back to face him. "You—" She stopped and caught her lower lip between her teeth. "Outside in that storm they're talking about—"

"*Spindrift* and I'll be fine, just fine. She's been in rough weather before. She loves it."

⍟

Maude had left the freeway and was driving east on Sunset toward Westwood and her apartment when she heard the first announcement on her car radio.

"We interrupt this program," the announcer's voice said, "to broadcast an emergency bulletin. The National Weather Service has issued a tsunami warning—repeat, *warning,* not merely alert—to California seaside residents.

"An underwater earthquake registering eight-point-seven on the Richter scale, the most severe quake in recent memory, has occurred in the Pacific depths. It has been determined that tsunami waves, sometimes called tidal waves, have been generated and are threatening coastal areas of California from the Mexican border to the Oregon line.

"The first of the series of potentially destructive waves is expected by approximately one-thirty this afternoon, Pacific daylight time, and well before then, seaside residents are urged to move inland to higher ground. In the past, tsunami, or tidal waves, from such earthquakes as that of Alaska in 1964 and that which occurred on the coast of Chile in 1960 have caused extensive property damage as well as unfortunate loss of life when residents in low-lying communities did not heed warnings.

"Repeat: A tsunami, or tidal wave, warning is now in effect. . . ."

There was more, but Maude heard none of it. She was unaware that she had slowed the car until drivers behind her began to honk their horns, and it was with reluctance that she sped up again to conform to traffic flow.

At the entrance to UCLA she turned south off Sunset and at the first opportunity made a U-turn back to the boulevard, where she turned left and once again headed for the southbound freeway, which was not yet closed to southbound traffic.

She did not try to sort out her thoughts, or even to isolate her motivation, and was vaguely ashamed that she was allowing emotion almost total control.

Paramount in her mind was the thought, rapidly becoming conviction, that she had been both premature and foolish to leave Encino Beach in the first place. The decision had been pure vanity, no more than a reflexive retreat from possible humiliation had she stayed on. And what did that mere possibility amount to in the face of this . . . threat of real and total disaster? Betsy Barnes had been quite right: She, Maude, could play an active role or sit forever on the sidelines; there were no other choices.

Driving faster than she usually did, alert to the sudden intricacies of freeway traffic, the abrupt lane changes, the inexplicable speeding up or slowing down of cars ahead or alongside, the intrusion of additional traffic from each on-ramp and the inevitable jockeying for position that followed, aware of all this, and yet in her mind removed from it, all at once she realized with something of a shock that she felt lighter and easier, yes, and *freer* than she had in a long, long time. It did not even occur to her to wonder why.

By the time she approached the junction with the Harbor Freeway, a roadblock had been set up, and she was shunted off to lesser roads, which she negotiated more or less by dead reckoning, heading ever south and a trifle east.

As Jack Barnes had found, the coast highway was also blocked off, and Maude's determined reaction was the same as Jack's: She ignored the signs and worked her tortuous way to the entrance to Encino Beach. By the time the same cop who had stopped Jack flagged her down, her mood was almost ebullient. "Yes, Officer?" she said.

"We've closed off this area, lady. There's a tidal wave warning—"

"I know. That is why I must go in."

"Lady—"

"Officer." Maude looked straight up at him, her eyes holding his. "Have you ever been in love?" The words seemed to come out of their own accord and, once spoken, immediately took on a life and a conviction of their own.

"I got a wife and three kids, lady—"

"That," Maude said, the conviction having suddenly become certainty, "was not what I asked."

The cop scratched his chin. Maude watched him steadily. He began to smile. "Okay," he said. "I guess I see what you mean." He stepped back from the car. "Good luck."

Maude, too, was smiling as she drove into Encino Beach.

❦

Joe Hines, his bullhorn handy, took the workboat slowly through the moored yacht fleet. At one boat, a small sloop with only a cuddy for shelter and an outboard kicker mounted on the transom, he drew alongside to talk to the owner, who was busy taking off his sail cover.

"Stow it," Joe said in as kindly a voice as he could manage. "Outside with what's already there and worse coming, you won't stand a chance."

"I've worked on this boat," the owner said, "weekends, vacations, damn it, she's mine and she's sound and—"

"She's all of that," Joe said, "but she's just not enough boat. I know how you feel, but the only sensible thing to do is load what you can in the dinghy and take it ashore to high ground. I wouldn't fool you."

"You can't stop me. You—"

"I hope I can," Joe said, his voice still mild, "because if I can't, you're going to lose your boat anyway, and yourself along with it."

He raised the bullhorn suddenly to hail a power cruiser headed down-channel. "Slow down!" he roared. "You got plenty time to get outside without churning up the whole goddamn anchorage!" He watched until the cruiser slowed and then turned again to the owner of the small sloop. "It's tough," he said. "I know that." He shook his head gently in sympathy. "But that's how she goes. Believe me." He took the workboat on through the anchorage.

In front of the yacht club he drew alongside a large yawl, three men aboard, busy hoisting sail. "I'd take in that overlapping jib," he said, "and run up a working sail instead to balance your jigger. And reefing your main before you even get outside wouldn't be a bad idea, Captain. Word we get is you'll have your hands full no matter. You fueled up for your auxiliary?"

The owner said, "Thanks, Joe. I think we're all set."

"Northwest's your best course," Joe said, "out of harm's way. Luck."

So little he could do, Joe thought as he pulled away, so goddamn little.

He advanced the workboat's throttle and headed down the bay toward a nautical traffic jam that was developing. Through the bull-horn, "Now hear this!" he roared. "You in that Grand Banks cruiser, shear off and wait your turn! And all of you, slow down before you jam up that channel! You in the blue hull, belay that! You're no better than anybody else no matter who you are!"

❦

In the Winslow house the phone rang suddenly, and Garfield jumped to answer it. It was Pete. "We're getting transmission by satellite from Hawaii," Pete said. "ETA there is in about twenty minutes. Saunders called. They'd watched videotape of the first wave hitting a flyspeck island below the equator." Pete's voice was unnaturally solemn. "Big! Damn big! Over two hundred feet, Saunders estimated. We'd like you here to watch Hawaii, but . . ." His voice trailed off.

"Yes," Garfield said, "but—" His anxiety had turned to anger now. Damned silly girl behavior, he was thinking. She—

"No word?" Pete said.

"None."

"Why hasn't she heard the sirens, all the commotion? Where could she be and not hear?"

"Quite," Garfield said. And why hadn't he thought of that himself? Because he wasn't thinking, that was why, and the anger faded into insignificance. "I haven't seen Daphne either. She—"

"She's helping Olaf and Lydia. She's all right. She'll come along here now that they've sailed. Look." Pete's voice altered. "You can leave a note for the princess, damn it! She can read! She—"

"No. I have to find her."

"Great! Just how do you go about it?"

"I don't know. Yet."

"Okay." Pete's voice was resigned. "But keep an eye on the time. ETA here, thirteen thirty-two. That's confirmed. And that . . . there won't be any appeal for leniency. Or anything else. Remember that."

Garfield hung up. All right, so where could Lucy be that she would not have heard the sirens or some of the commotion? How about the beach? The wind and the surf making too much noise— how about that? Likely? How the hell do I know what goes on in a sixteen-year-old girl's mind? he asked himself angrily. And again the anger faded as quickly as it had arisen. So—

The telephone rang again, and he snatched it from its stand. "Garfield."

Maude's voice said, "I thought you'd be there. I hoped so." In her tone there was no undercurrent of doubt or even of hesitation, which had not been true before. "What are you going to do, Dan?"

The anger was entirely gone now, and not even annoyance remained. Somehow, too, there was more than a vague comfort in the sound of Maude's voice. "Lucy is gone. The Winslow daughter.

They . . . left her in my care. They're at sea. I don't know where she is, and I promised to find her." And then, quickly, a new worry beginning to set in: "Where are you? I thought, I hoped you were going up to town."

"I did." Was there amusement in the voice? "Then I came back. I'm at the Barnes house. Betsy is gone. So is her car. And I just saw Jack's boat, *Spindrift,* I think, is her name, going down the channel. Jack was at the wheel."

Garfield said, "You shouldn't have come back. Haven't you—"

"I have heard the radio, Dan. I have heard the warnings."

"Damn it, this is no joke! It is exactly what Pete Williamson has been predicting. The only sensible thing to do is leave."

"But you are staying."

"That's different! I have a reason!"

"So have I."

Garfield frowned at the wall. "I don't get it. What is your reason?"

The smile in Maude's voice this time was obvious. "You. I'm coming over, Dan. I'll be there in a few moments."

The line went dead.

Garfield hung up automatically and sat motionless, frowning no longer, still staring at the wall, trying to unscramble his thoughts and feelings.

No one emotion predominated; too many different emotions competed in a swirl of confusion that was anything but comprehensible. For one thing, he felt a vague sense of shame; why, he could not have said, but the effect was humbling, and he was not accustomed to humility.

He felt, too, a sense of anger; again, at what, he could not have said, because it had never been his way to rail at fate or the permutations of chance but, rather, to take results as they came and by his own capabilities to shape circumstances to more comfortable form.

He felt apprehension, not for himself, but rather for Lucy if he were unable to find her as he had promised he would, and for Clara if anything were to happen to the child.

He felt an almost belligerent sense of determination, even, although he had always despised heroics, a kind of Ajax-defying-the-lightning sense of defiance directed at the physical phenomena he had analyzed and he and Pete together had predicted. It could do its worst, but he, Dan Garfield, was not going to experience defeat of any kind. It was an attitude wholly unlike him, and he was subtly aware of the incongruity. He was also aware that an all-out no-hedging attitude of this kind would never have been possible for him before these last weeks of total refocusing of his interests.

It came to him now that during the process itself he had been entirely unaware of the depth and strength of the metamorphosis that had taken place within him. He wondered if others had, and found the speculation not only senseless but unimportant. Things were as they were, and examining effect and even cause in detail could accomplish nothing.

When the telephone rang again, he picked it up, wondering if Maude had changed her mind, and was astonished to find that he hoped she had not.

It was Todd Wilson, breathless. "What's doing? Mom said you called and asked if she knew where Lucy was. Where is she?"

"I don't know. She ran out at breakfast. She was . . . angry." Understatement.

There was a short silence. "Yeah," Todd said then, "I know what you mean. She's . . . been that way recently." Another silence. "Where are her folks?"

"At sea and not coming in. I persuaded them to stay outside."

"You—" Todd's voice stopped. "Oh, great!" he said. "I've got to help Mom and Tina. They're . . . packing. "I—" Another pause. "I don't know where she could be. Anywhere. If . . ." The voice ran down again.

"Right," Garfield said. "I understand." It did not even occur to him that he was speaking to the boy as an equal. All values had suddenly changed.

Todd said, "What are you going to do?"

"There's only one thing to do, wait here, unless somebody can think of someplace where she might be."

"Did she take a car?"

"No."

"Damn! Then that's out. I thought she might have driven up in the hills. She does sometimes to see the flowers and stuff. Or she could have gone down to Onofre." His voice altered completely. "Hey! Onofre! How about that atomic power plant there? It's right down almost at water level. Wouldn't it—?"

"Yes," Garfield said. "It's a problem. But let's stick to Lucy. Any other place you can think of?"

"No." The young voice was heavy with disappointment.

"Call me if you do."

"Sure. Hey!"

"Yes?"

"You call me, huh, if *you* find her? I mean—"

"I'll call you," Garfield said, and hung up.

From the doorway Maude said, "Tell me about the girl, Dan." She came in and sat down on a kitchen chair as if they were simply picking up a conversation where they had left it. "She is gone, you say, and you don't know where? Why is she gone? Do you know that?"

"My fault, I suppose." The words were automatic. He had never subscribed to the theory that confession was good for the psyche, but he did feel a sense of relief now in amplifying the statement. "I was . . . so damned adult, and male, and she thought I was treating her like a child—which I was."

Maude studied him quietly. "The change in you is even more apparent, Dan. Or maybe I'm just seeing things more clearly. Never mind that now. You have no idea where she might have gone?" She paused. "Do what you do best, Dan. Think!"

"She is probably somewhere where she wouldn't hear all the sirens, all the commotion." Pete's thought, which he ought to have seen for himself.

"Where would that be?"

"The beach, maybe. The surf will be high, booming and most likely deserted."

"That's easily checked. Anywhere else?"

Garfield shook his head. "I don't know."

"Have you ever walked out on the jetty?" Maude said. "It's all huge rocks piled there as a breakwater. When you walk out, you leave the land behind you. There is just you and the huge rocks and the sea on both sides of you. It's frightening. And beautiful. If a large wave comes, you get wet from the spray, and that makes you feel even more as if you are alone with the sea. Would she, the girl—"

Garfield shook his head again, more savagely this time. "I hope not. There are storm waves, and worse, coming. They'll break right over the jetty."

"Then you'd better go see, Dan."

"Somebody has to be here."

"I'll be here."

"Damn it, you—"

"I'll be here. I won't even argue about it. It is settled. Until you come back, I'll be here. That is final."

17

12:01 P.M.–12:31 P.M. PDT

Olaf and Lydia Hansen were gone in the motor sailer *Lydia,* and with them, Daphne thought, much of the atmosphere of the little house where she had lived—could it have been a whole year now?—so happily amid the Hansens' total lack of routine and openhanded hospitality; odd characters coming and going at uncharted intervals.

Occasionally, but with increasing rareness, she had thought of life in England and dismissed the memories with a smile. If one was lucky, one found one's niche. She considered that she had been lucky in the extreme to have stumbled on Olaf and Lydia in the first place. Now, with Peter in her life, she felt even luckier, if that was possible.

She closed the house carefully. She would have locked it, but as far as she knew there was no key. What was the line from *Porgy and Bess?* "I got no lock on my door/That's no way to be." George and Ira Gershwin ought to have known the Hansens.

She was smiling sadly and nostalgically as she walked out to the

Hansens' car. It was loaded, trunk and entire rear seat, with Hansen belongings precious to Olaf and Lydia beyond price—Eskimo soapstone carvings; two Navajo rugs; Olaf's small, select reference library and charts; photograph albums; a painting of the motor sailer *Lydia* in mountainous seas; Lydia the wife's scrapbooks; their collection of scrimshaw; a silver bowl wedding gift and assorted paintings, rubbings and sketches accumulated during their travels—a lifetime's gleanings.

The day had darkened, and the streets were almost deserted. Those were her first two impressions. And there was wind. She could feel it in the steering wheel when she drove into open intersections, but otherwise, with the total absence of trees to bend and sway, something she had noticed before and could never become quite used to, from inside the car she would not have known it.

Traffic signals were still working automatically, lending an odd, deserted air to the empty streets. Dutifully she obeyed each red light, and it was at one of those, near the center of town, that she was abruptly brought out of her nostalgic thoughts of life with the Hansens.

Quite suddenly, without warning, the right-hand front door was snatched open, and a man, a total stranger bent in to enter the car. He was smiling—a leer, really, was Daphne's immediate thought—and he said, "You need company, baby. You aren't safe alone."

Daphne did not hesitate. She swung her right hand in a backhanded power sweep, palm down, smashing its blade against the bridge of the man's nose with a satisfying crunch. At the same time, despite the red light, she floored the car's accelerator.

The car leaped forward, throwing the man to the pavement, where he lay, stunned. The door slammed shut from the car's momentum, and Daphne leaned across the seat to press down the lock button. "Careless of me," she murmured in self-criticism. "Bad show." She drove on without even a backward glance in the mirror.

At the main building of the oceanographic institute perched high on a bluff overlooking the now-turbulent sea, she parked, carefully locked the Hansen car and went inside and up the stairs to Peter's office.

Pete jumped up to greet her. "Just in time," he said. "Come on. We're about to watch Armageddon."

"Fanciful chap, aren't you?" Daphne said. She was smiling fondly as they walked down the hall toward the director's office, and she wondered idly if she should tell Peter about her little incident back at the traffic light. She decided not. It might worry him.

A console television set in Boggs's office was already turned on, and a color picture of superb clarity showed the city of Hilo, Hawaii, spread below, the harbor almost deserted and the city streets themselves totally devoid of life. A smiling Oriental face appeared on the screen, and the man's voice, also of splendid clarity, said, "Jerry Matsuo. I'll try to call the action. If Pete Williamson's watching, 'Hi.' 'Hi,' too, to Harry Saunders if he's in the audience. ETA—"Jerry Matsuo's voice paused—"is in about eight minutes."

"ETA, estimated time of arrival," Pete whispered to Daphne.

"Really, Peter, I do have that much knowledge." She squeezed his arm. "I *am* trying to master—or is it mistress?—your arcane studies."

Hobart Boggs said, "You know the Matsuo person, Pete?"

"I know him well. I've surfed with him. He's a cool head." Pete looked curiously at the TV console. "You're taping this on the VCR?"

"Naturally. We shall want to study it."

There were seven people in the large office, Daphne noted, and an air of expectancy hardly justified by the unexciting picture on the screen. She whispered as much in Pete's ear.

"That," Pete said, "is one of the . . . eerie aspects. Even if the camera were out at sea, there wouldn't be a thing to watch. A navy captain reported seeing a tsunami swell on radar when he was at sea, but that's not verified. In deep water they are merely low swells, hundreds of miles apart, moving at unbelievable speeds but not at all dangerous until they reach shallow water. Then—"

Jerry Matsuo's voice said, "It's beginning! See it? The harbor's draining!"

What he had watched so many times on his own film, impressive and even scary as it was, Pete was thinking, had affected only a small harbor in an obscure Aleutian fishing village. This was a major city, open, vulnerable, helpless, with millions of dollars of property and thousands of lives involved. He found that he was whispering to Daphne the same words he had said to Dan Garfield: "Textbook stuff. First the outflow. Then the . . . deluge!"

"*Après le déluge?*" Daphne whispered back. "But whoever said it was speaking of something else."

"But analogous. What they foresaw, and what we're waiting to watch is chaos. And devastation. Harry Saunder's report of that flyspeck island leaves no doubt what's going to happen."

On the screen Jerry Matsuo's voice, quite calm now, said, "Ewa Beach's time prediction is right on the money. It's due right now, and there it begins!"

In the perfect clarity of the picture, the water was rising now, swiftly, silently, its surface scarcely rippled by the enormous forces that were concentrating on this one area. Harbor bottom that had been exposed disappeared smoothly. A pier that only moments before had stood stark and gaunt on its pilings was now at water level and suddenly no longer visible. The pattern of the shoreline was hanging as they watched; what had been dry land simply sank out of sight, seeming illusion of what had been. Still, there was no sound but the faint whisper of Jerry Matsuo's breathing in his microphone. In the office there was only silence.

The camera's focus shifted suddenly, reaching out beyond the harbor's entrance, and Jerry Matsuo's voice came again. "There it comes! See it building?"

Only a faint line at first, but instantly recognizable as nothing anyone had ever seen before, the tsunami wave began to slow and grow, its outlines becoming plain, a swift swelling of water, growing as a bubble grows, but solid rather than empty, and moving at incredible speed directly toward the shifting camera focus. And with it came the first sound.

It was a low-pitched, rumbling, still-distant roar as if the earth itself and the waters it contained protested confinement and demanded release. And still the growing wave rushed on, relentless.

"That headland," Jerry Matsuo's voice said, no longer calm, no longer steady, "is thirty feet above mean high water! And look! It's going under!"

It was indeed going, and then entirely gone, all at once no longer visible. And the now-gigantic wave was rearing itself within the harbor confines, bearing down swiftly upon the city, its sound, still in low register, vibrating the TV console's speakers as mountain thunder vibrates the valley beneath it.

At its top, the wave was breaking, unable to contain itself, but its body rearing high above the harbor shore, remained intact, solid, a shimmering green mass hurtling down upon the land.

Daphne squeezed Pete's arm almost in desperation and was totally unaware of it. She was also holding her breath, her eyes wide open and fixed on the television screen. In the office there was no faintest whisper of sound.

The giant wave reached the shore and engulfed it. Its sound now a hoarse bellow of rage, it flung itself upon a row of buildings lining the waterfront. The buildings disappeared, and as the body of the wave passed, a single object, possibly a sealed drum, burst like a rocket from the water, flung high into the air by its own buoyancy— and disappeared again without a trace.

The wave swept on, unchecked, but meeting more solid opposition now in the form of masonry buildings which crumpled like matchboxes beneath the enormous weight and force of the water— and then they, too, were gone.

Jerry Matsuo's voice, shaking now, said, "Worse, far worse than 1960! Incredible! Stop it, damn it, stop it!" The words were smothered in the sounds of destruction.

Daphne whispered, "Peter! Peter!" and her hand closed even harder on his arm. She stared at the TV screen, unable to take her eyes away or to tune out the sounds that emanated from the speakers. "Is there no end? Is there?" Her voice was a desperate whisper that carried clearly across the room.

Gradually, its fury spent, the wave slowed, reached its farthest limit, visibly diminished and then began its retreat, exposing the tangled mass of destruction its swift and merciless onslaught had caused.

Here a reinforced concrete building was reduced to sodden rubble; there a pile of wreckage, twisted and nearly unrecognizable, was all that remained of some kind of automobile that had been smashed as from the wrecker's hydraulic press; a single wall of another building miraculously remained standing, empty windows gaping like eyeholes in a skull—and then suddenly it, too, collapsed into a heap of shattered masonry, filling what once had been a broad city street.

Someone in the office said in a hushed voice as if he were speaking in church, "I've seen this desolation before—in pictures of Hamburg and Dresden, Hiroshima and Nagasaki after the bombings! God! I wouldn't have believed it!"

Jerry Matsuo's unsteady voice said, "Show's over. For now. In about fifty-five minutes we'll probably have a replay."

"That long before the next tsunami wave arrives," Pete whispered to Daphne. "And all there is to do is wait." He raised his voice to address them all. "So now we know," he said. "And in a little over one hour we'll have a closer look. Right here." He stood up, drawing Daphne with him. "I'll be in my office," he told Boggs, "if you should want me."

The huge map of the Pacific hung upon the wall, dominating the small room. Pete stared at it, finding it incredible that the map itself was unchanged—sheer fancy, of course, but real nonetheless. His eyes went automatically to the tiny cross which marked the location of the trench and the submarine wall that, collapsing, had caused the catastrophe.

Daphne, standing alone, was staring at a different, more southern locale also on the map. "Those lovely, peaceful names," she said. "Atafu, Starbuck, Vostok, they read like a directory of the world. Do you know those waters, Peter?" She turned to face him, smiling.

"I'm sorry to say no." It was good to think of other things than the scene they had just witnessed. And Daphne herself was a warm presence that seemed to light the entire room. Pete was suddenly aware that he was grinning inanely like a schoolboy.

"Perhaps you would care to take me there one day?"

"Love to. But an oceanographer's salary does have its limitations."

Daphne's green eyes studied him carefully. "There is one matter we are absolutely not going to quarrel about," she said, "and that is that I am not exactly . . . penniless. I did utterly nothing to earn it; but there it is, and after what we have just seen, we are going to enjoy it. Agreed?"

Pete's grin faded. He hesitated. "We'll talk about that later," he said.

"No." Daphne's voice was definite. "There is nothing to discuss. I come as a package—all or nothing. You will just have to get used to it."

Pete walked to his desk and sat down at the phone. "Right now," he said, "what I'm concerned about is letting Garfield know what we've seen." He picked up the phone and began to dial.

✿

From the rocky point to the jetties, the beach was deserted. Garfield turned up the collar of his wind jacket for warmth as he walked, head bent, leaning slightly into the wind.

The waves were pounding now, and the sky had darkened almost as at evening. Within its depths formless cloud masses swirled, and here and there a rainsquall, darker than the rest, roiled the tossing waters even further.

Garfield could see boats well out beyond the bell buoy, most under power alone, but here and there a sail showed, reefed against the driving wind but providing a steadying force against the mounting confusion of the seas.

A bleak, almost frightening scene, Garfield thought, and obviously the girl was not here, and yet somehow he sensed that in her adolescent anger this could be precisely the kind of atmosphere she might choose to match her mood.

He made his way back to his car he had left on the beachfront road, got in and relaxed comfortably as he closed the door and the sounds and the chill of the wind were shut out.

He had never been out to the jetties; but they were plain to see, and he drove toward them through deserted streets. Most houses were dark, he noticed; but here and there a light showed, and he wondered if there were people inside who had ignored the warning of the sirens and the sound trucks.

He drove to the end of the road, parked and got out to walk again, collar up, bent against the wind. Here, only feet above the water, the wind's force seemed greater, and he picked his way carefully along the faint path that wound among the giant stone blocks that had been dumped in place for the breakwater. A hundred yards ahead a rainsquall swept across the jetty, instantly turning the dull gray rock a glistening, metallic color streaming with water.

Maude had been right. It was both beautiful and frightening. Underfoot he seemed to feel the thundering power of the waves as they dashed themselves against the piled blocks, throwing spray high in the air to be wind-driven almost like rain in shifting curtains of heavy mist. As on the beach, the wind and water sounds drowned out the still-wailing sirens.

Lucy was nowhere to be seen, and Garfield retraced his steps to the car to climb into its welcome warmth and shelter again.

He sat for a time, watching the threatening scene and trying to think wherever else Lucy might be, but in the end, defeated, he started the engine and drove slowly back along the peninsula to the Winslow house.

He found Maude on the porch, largely sheltered by the house itself from the wind sweeping in from the sea. She was studying the bay in its gray, tossing beauty, and she seemed to know that Garfield was there before he had spoken. "Come sit here with me, Dan," she said without turning, and seemed to take his acquiescence for granted. "Peter Williamson called."

Garfield sat down in the wicker chair. "And?"

"They would like you at the institute. Peter says that the director—is it Boggs?—seems to think you have second sight." Maude did turn then, smiling, to face him. "Have you?"

"Nonsense."

Her smile spread fondly, and her voice turned gentle. "Does it bother you, Dan, that so many people treat you with near reverence? You should be used to it by now."

"And what do I say to that?"

Maude watched him quietly for long moments. She said at last, "No sign of Lucy?"

"None."

"I've been sitting here thinking," Maude said. "How well do you know the girl?"

"We get along. Or, did."

"She is how old, sixteen? And you have been living here in the house for a matter of weeks?" Maude nodded. "You have talked, I'm sure. Before this last . . . disagreement, I mean. Isn't that so?"

Those times at San Onofre; sitting watching the ocean; here at mealtimes. "Yes, of course we've talked." Garfield was frowning. "What are you getting at?"

"Quite simple. A sensitive girl that age, with a much older man who is not family—it is easier to talk to someone like that, Dan, less embarrassing to talk about little, personal things than with your mother or father. Think about it. Did she ever tell you anything about . . . herself?"

"Absolutely inconsequential things."

"Are you sure? When you were young, didn't you ever . . . unburden yourself to someone who was handy at the moment, who maybe seemed very special?" Slowly she shook her head. "Maybe you wouldn't have."

"I don't see what this gets us—"

"Perhaps not. But think about it anyway. You possibly know more about her than you realize, more about what she might do. Now what about the institute?"

"They're the ones with the technical knowledge," Garfield said. "I'm not. I don't see what good I'd do there. And I can't go anyway until Lucy turns up. I gave my word."

Maude nodded. "Peter Williamson seemed to think that was how it would be. He also told me what they had watched on television—devastation in Hawaii, worse even than they feared."

"Which means that the place for you is in town."

"I am staying here with you, Dan." Her voice was definite, stating fact.

For long moments Garfield sat quiet and wordless. Admit it, he told himself, you take comfort in her mere presence; you want her near you for as long as she can safely remain. He glanced at his watch. "Thirteen thirty-two is the estimated time of arrival here," he said at last. "That is about one hour. If you stay, it is on one condition."

"That is?"

"That when I say you must go, you will." He hesitated, finding reluctance to say aloud what was in his mind, but strangely, the words finally emerged without effort. "Your safety is important to me."

"I think," Maude said slowly, "that is the . . . most wonderful thing anyone ever said to me. Thank you, Dan."

"It is agreed?"

She could smile then. "You must dot the *i*'s and cross the *t*'s, mustn't you? It is your way." Slowly she nodded, her eyes not leaving his. "I agree. I have no choice."

18

12:31 P.M.–1:00 P.M. PDT

Tom Winslow, with Clara at the wheel holding *Westerly* into the wind under power, had taken down the big jib and replaced it with a smaller one on a traveler, and roller-reefed the mainsail to about one-half its area. Now on course again—315°, northwest, as he had told Garfield—under reduced sail, he was back at the wheel, satisfied that the boat, on a broad reach, was snugged down and as ready as possible for whatever might come.

The wind had increased; the seas had lost their precise alignment and were beginning to break at their tops. Streaks of foam had appeared, spreading downwind, and spray was beginning to affect visibility.

Clara sat huddled on the leeward seat, her face and hair shiny with spray, her eyes fixed on the tossing waters. She showed no expression.

"Better go below and get into foul-weather gear," Tom said. In order to be heard, he had to raise his voice against the sounds of wind and sea. "No point sitting here in misery. That won't help anything."

"I can't help it." Clara's voice was scarcely audible. "We ought to be with Lucy, wherever she is."

"Damn it," Tom said, "go below and get into proper gear. Then come back up and relieve me, and I'll do the same. After that, we can talk."

Clara hesitated, then rose reluctantly and went below without a word.

Tom watched her. As a physician he was accustomed to talking out problems with patients, but he was not at all sure he could handle this one. His decision to put to sea had been logical, no doubt about that, and endorsed, no, urged by Dan Garfield. Still, how did one balance logic against parental affection? It was about as useful a question, he thought, as: How many angels could dance on the head of a pin?

The trouble was that he was suddenly beginning to realize he did not know his wife as well as he had assumed he did. She had always had unexpected depths, but over the years he had been confident that he had plumbed them all. Now he could only wonder—and wait.

Clara came up from below, wearing oilskins. In her hand she carried a large steaming mug which she held out to him. "Hot soup," she said. "You can use it. It's cold out here."

It was. It was also uncomfortable sailing. *Westerly* was a splendid sea boat, as Tom had found out many times before, but the corkscrew gyrations she was now forced into demanded the helmsman's full attention and skills lest she be allowed to broach to, or even, through sheer carelessness, unexpectedly jibe, putting the entire mast at risk.

"We're stuck on this course," Tom said after his first grateful mouthful of soup. "Uncomfortable as it is with the wind on our quarter in these seas, we still have to make some westing or we'll be closing on a lee shore."

"I understand." No mention of Lucy, but obviously the unhappy worry would still remain.

"Yes," Tom said, "of course, you do. I'm just talking to make sounds." Another scalding mouthful of soup. "Dan will see that she's all right," he said. "Damn it, he will! He promised!"

"I'll take the wheel," Clara said. "You go below and get into dry things the way you said. Go along now."

৪

Lucy was more frightened than she had ever been in her life. In her first anger with Garfield, she had given no real heed to possible danger in going to her own secret place where she could be alone and—face it, she told herself now—indulge her outrage and simply feel sorry for herself. Always before, making her way to or from this secluded spot had been easy enough considering he young agility.

But the rocks were wet now, soaked with heavy spray, and slippery, and one false step in the climb to safety could be her last. Staying here was fast becoming nonsensical; but the waiting had sapped her resolve, and she now lacked the courage to make the first hazardous move. It was clear that these were storm seas, nothing at all like the friendly breakers she and Todd rode on their boards down at Onofre. And—

She shrank back as she watched the largest wave of a sequence gather itself in reaction to the bottom drag. Its crest, windblown, rose higher and higher as the mass swept toward shore, and Lucy could only watch it in frightened fascination, a sick feeling growing in her stomach. As it prepared to break, she took a deep breath, the deepest, and closed her eyes against the imminent shock.

The wave crashed against the rocks with a booming sound that seemed to shake the earth. Its green water almost, but not quite, reached Lucy's cringing level; but the spray it flung into her shelter was heavier than before, and she emerged from it drenched, gasping with cold and increased terror.

She would die here, she was sure of it, and no one would ever know!

It had happened all at once, rather than gradually, and for the rest of his life, sixteen-year-old Tommy Parks thought, he would remember the sudden realization that he was doing everything right and was, in fact, enjoying himself immensely.

He had *Lubelle* headed into the mounting seas with just enough power in both big engines to maintain steady but almost imperceptible forward progress, which he measured constantly by beam sightings on the scarcely visible land contours.

The boat rose to meet each sea, and as soon as she had crashed her bow through the crest and the downward rush began, Tommy put the wheel over and took *Lubelle* into a course roughly parallel to the trough, again heading up as the next crest approached.

There was a rhythm to the exercise which he could feel and thrill to, and infinite minor adjustments within each maneuver which his hands on the wheel seemed to accomplish automatically almost as if they had decisive minds of their own.

This far out from land, he did not have the constant company of other boats; but from time to time he could sight another sail or power boat, and even though he could not recognize any boat itself, let alone those on board, he nonetheless felt a kinship with them and wished that they might all gather when this was over to exchange tales of their individual experiences. He was an imaginative boy, and out here, alone, master of his own fate, he felt himself all at once a full-fledged member of a bold fraternity of seafarers who were willing to dare the perils of the ocean while lesser folks cowered safely at home or fled to the hills.

When the radio scanner paused at one frequency long enough for him to hear, "Calling yacht *Lubelle*, calling yacht *Lubelle*. Come in," he pushed the button to hold on that wavelength, increased the volume as he picked up the microphone and, with his eyes never leaving the seas, said, "Yacht *Lubelle* here. Come in. Over." He was smiling.

"How you doing?" Joe Hines's voice. "Over."

Tommy wore a huge grin. "I'm having a blast. Over."

"Don't get cocky, younger. You got a big responsibility on your hands. Over."

The grin did not fade. "Aye, aye, sir. Over."

"Keep in touch on this frequency. Over."

"Roger. Over and out." Tommy hung up the microphone and, with both hands on the wheel, headed up to the next sea. His spirits soared with the rising bow.

ॐ

Todd Wilson said to his mother, "You and Tina take the car and head for home. I'll follow in my car."

Tina said, "He *won't* follow, Mom. He'll stay here, looking for Lucy. And we haven't even any idea where she could be."

Tina was two years younger than Todd, and from early childhood he had always loomed large in her life, a sturdy male pillar to lean on in times of stress, at need to fight her battles for her. "Don't let him. Lucy can look out for herself."

Jane Wilson said, "I don't think your father would want you to stay here at the beach, Todd. He—"

"He isn't here," Todd said. "And he wouldn't care about Lucy anyway. And the doctor and Aunt Clara are out somewhere aboard *Westerly*, and . . ." The words ran down. They sounded less than compelling even to his own ears.

"Mr. Garfield is there," Jane Wilson said. "He is—"

"Damn it, he doesn't know where Lucy is! He doesn't even know the places where she might be! He said so!"

"Do you?" This was Tina again.

"No. But I'll find out." He nodded abruptly to them both. "I'll see you in L.A." It was open revolt, and Todd felt guilty about it as he walked out to his car.

He had no real idea where he was going or what he was going to do, and he supposed he was being melodramatic, merely going through empty motions; but his affection for Lucy was suddenly stronger even than he had realized, and the prospect of never seeing her again expanded in his mind like a painful tumor. It was inevitable that having no real destination, he found himself in the alley behind the Winslow house. He stopped the car, switched off the engine and got out.

The kitchen door was unlocked, as always, and Todd went in. "Lucy! Hey! Anybody home?"

"In here." Garfield's voice from the doctor's study. Todd followed the sound. "Come in," Garfield said, and as if this were a cocktail party, he added, "Maude Anderson, Todd Wilson. Sit down, Todd. Do you know anything?" His voice was calm, but his eyes betrayed the strain he felt.

"No, sir." Todd sat down. Maude Anderson was something else to look at, Todd thought, and when she smiled at him, mere open friendliness, he was sure, the impact of the smile was nonetheless unnerving. "I guess you don't either?"

Maude said, "We've been trying to think. Perhaps you can help." There was that smile again that did things to Todd's breathing.

"Sure. I mean, if I can."

"You know her well," Garfield said. His tone had turned brisk, businesslike. "Has she disappeared like this before?"

A sudden wind gust rattled the windows, and the wailing sirens were plain. They ignored it all. For the present, what was outside this room was without importance.

Todd said, "She's funny sometimes. Girls are." He caught himself quickly. "I mean—"

Maude's smile was gentle, understanding. "We know what you mean," she said. "And they are. Even when they grow up to be women, they are funny sometimes." Her words seemed meant for Garfield, conveying a secret message. "It goes with the gender."

Garfield said, "She does go off by herself?" Something was tugging at his mind, and he could not put his finger on it. No matter; in time it would reveal itself. The trick was to dwell on the subject. "Where does she go?"

"She never tells me. Or Tina. That's my sister."

"Sometimes girls like to be alone," Maude said. "Doesn't your sister?"

Todd nodded agreement. "Well, yeah. That's so. I hadn't

thought about it." Something else for looks, body *and* brains, Todd thought, and warmed himself in her smile.

Garfield said, looking at Maude, "When you were a girl, you did?"

"Sometimes."

"Did you have a special place where you could be alone?"

"Up in the attic, where nobody ever went. Always. If I kept quiet, nobody knew where I was."

Garfield let his breath out in a long sigh. "Then I think we know where Lucy is. Her secret place. She told me about it once." He was looking at Todd now. "Out on the point, she told me, in a kind of cave where she couldn't be seen from above, only from below. Seals could see her, she told me." He looked at his watch. "One thirty-two is the expected arrival time of the first wave." He was remembering what Pete had once told him. "And their predictions are accurate to minutes. In less than forty minutes—"

Todd was already on his feet. "I've climbed around the rocks on the point. And I've dived for abalone there. There's that big moray eel Pete—I mean, Dr. Williamson—talks to. Never mind. I'll find her."

"I'll go with you," Garfield said. "You have a car? Good. You drive. You know the way." His voice held a tone of command, all doubts erased. "I'll be out in a moment."

Todd hesitated. Then, understanding, he nodded, smiled faintly at Maude and was gone. They heard the back door slam.

Garfield was standing. He held out both hands, and Maude rose to take them. "This," Garfield said, his smile mocking his words, himself, "as they say in films, 'is it.' I want you to—"

"You don't have to go, Dan. He, the boy, Todd knows the area, and you don't! He is young, strong—" The words ran down suddenly. She raised her hands and let them fall in a helpless gesture. "You will go," she said in a quiet, resigned voice. "Yes. You feel you have to. I understand. I will wait—"

"No." Garfield took her shoulders in both hands and shook them gently. "You will not wait. You will take your car now and drive up to the bluff. Pete Williamson will be there with the cameras they are setting up. Stay with him, and wait for me—us there."

"Dan—"

"You promised, remember? I had to dot the *i*'s, you said, and cross the *t*'s, and you agreed that when I told you, you would go. Unless you do—" He stopped at the sight of tears forming in her eyes, rolling unheeded down the sides of her nose. "Unless you do—" he began again.

"I will go, Dan." She brushed the tears away with the backs of her hands. A tremulous smile appeared. "I will go," she said again." She stood quiet, her eyes on his. "Kiss me, Dan." Her voice was soft, gentle.

It was not a long kiss, and when it was done, Garfield brushed her cheek gently with his fingertips. "There will be another," he said, "when I join you on the bluff. That is a promise, too." He turned away and hurried out to the car.

※

Olaf Hansen, in oilskins now, was at the wheel of the motor sailer, and the big diesel engine chugged on in a reassuring tempo. Olaf had hoisted a steadying sail, which decreased the rolling motions, although the pitching and yawing continued, inevitable in these confused seas. Lydia was below doing something at the galley stove.

Olaf felt no sense of panic or even of fear. The seas were large, and heavy streaks of foam from the windblown tops of the waves were spread downwind over the tossing waters. The shriek of the wind in the shrouds was a banshee sound out of a nightmare. But the boat *Lydia* was staunch, as splendidly strong in spirit as her namesake, and she had weathered storms before. To Olaf, the outcome was not even in doubt.

As for the discomfort of the driving spray that had forced him to take off his glasses and tuck them away, or the cold that seeped in even through a heavy sweater beneath the oilskins, to Olaf these were matters of complete indifference. It would have been lunacy to *choose* to put to sea under these conditions, but once the decision was forced by circumstance, there was even an amount of perverse pleasure to be had from facing the elements and conquering them. Far, far better this than a landlocked college campus with its creature comforts and its unimportant little squabblings and jealousies over inconsequential matters.

Olaf supposed he was a romantic at heart, a ridiculous anomaly in an old man who had spent his life at intellectual pursuits, and the concept amused him. Lydia, he knew, shared his amusement, although neither had ever spoken of it aloud. But between longtime married persons, when the marriage was *right,* there grew a vast reservoir of shared knowledge which did not need open expression to be understood and felt by both partners. Olaf doubted if most people ever comprehended this basic truth, let alone were ever in a position in which they might encounter it. The world, Olaf had long felt in company with Thoreau, was filled with men and women living lives of quiet desperation. He was lucky. He could sit now at *Lydia*'s wheel, holding the boat into the seas, and smile happily at the cold spray and the threatening waters.

&

Betsy Barnes pulled into the driveway of their Brentwood house and then just sat for long minutes, her hands resting on the wheel and her mind still almost numb as if the emotional discharge during that scene in Encino Beach had exhausted its capacity to think.

Jack would be safe. He had said that, and Betsy clung to his words. Until these last hours she had not fully realized how dependent she was on her husband, and the sudden knowledge was shattering. What if he was *not* safe out in what the radio called heavy storm seas?

What then? The concept was too dreadful to think about.

She had known widows, both real and merely divorced. Some had taken their single status in stride, even reveled in the sudden freedom. Some had launched an immediate hunt for a new mate with a singleness of purpose that was frightening. But some had simply come apart at the seams, finding themselves unable to make decisions; lost and bewildered, they had sometimes too quickly formed new attachments, or reached out to friends with pitiful yearning, to become instantly as dependent on them as they had been upon their husbands. Somehow, Betsy could see herself in the last category.

She roused herself at last and with difficulty concentrated on carrying into the house the things she and Jack had packed into the car. Inside, she made no attempt to put the things away but left them almost in a heap on the dining-room table. It was, she thought suddenly, a pitifully small and unimportant collection of items to represent her and Jack's life together: a picture of the two of them taken during an Acapulco vacation; her wedding sterling flatware scarcely ever used since the time of the sudden inflation of the price of silver; Jack's gold Rolex wristwatch, which he had given her for safekeeping when he put on his much less valuable scuba-diving chronograph to wear aboard *Spindrift* (Why? Because he was afraid he wouldn't come back? Oh, God!), the cup they had won at mixed doubles the year before at the yacht club; expensive clothes by the armful; Jack's 35mm SLR camera; half a dozen albums of recordings, mostly jazz; and a mixed case of Tanqueray gin, Noilly-Prat vermouth, Jack Daniel's bourbon and Chivas Regal scotch.

Tears were very close as she turned away and walked out to the large, immaculate kitchen.

Jack's wet bar tempted her. She stood indecisively before it, eyeing the row of bottles for long moments before at last she turned away and made herself a cup of instant coffee, which she carried in both hands to Jack's study. There she seated herself at Jack's desk and reached automatically for the telephone.

She dialed Maude's number and listened in near despair as the fruitless ringing went on and on far beyond the possibility of any answer. She hung up at last and just sat, alone and miserable, the cup of coffee forgotten. The growing feeling of emptiness in her stomach was perilously close to nausea.

1:00 P.M.–1:32 P.M. PDT

It was 4:00 P.M. EDT in Washington; but the day was still bright, and it was necessary to keep the blinds drawn in order best to watch the large screen that had been set up in the secretary's office.

They had already watched the inundation and destruction at Hilo, and distant cameras had just now finished surveying and projecting via satellite detailed pictures of Pearl Harbor and surrounding shore installations.

As the picture faded, the senior admiral let his breath out in a long sigh. "Damage minimal," he said, and added, "thanks to the warning. The fleet's at sea, sir, and Bert Henry, in command, in his last message asked if we were sure of our facts. Where they were, he said, the sea was like a millpond." The admiral was smiling. "Admiral Henry, sir," he said, "is an old friend and Naval Academy classmate."

"That is the sneaky part," Harry Saunders said. "In deep water tsunami swells are almost undetectable because they are too small, they move at speeds you cannot believe and they are hundreds of miles apart. But when they come ashore, as we have seen—" He left the sentence unfinished.

The secretary said, "But you are still concerned about the West Coast?"

"That," Saunders said, "is a different matter entirely. They are already experiencing heavy storm seas coupled with spring tides. The hurricane is fewer than two hundred miles from the coast of Southern California, and its effect is already being felt in very unpleasant ways. When the first tsunami swell arrives under those conditions, there is going to be 'hell to pay'—I am quoting Pete Williamson, who has been dead right in everything he has said so far. I believe him this time as well."

The admiral said, "San Diego is alerted, sir, as is San Pedro, and all ships have put to sea. Their reports do not indicate anything like the millpond they seem to have out in the Islands." He shook his head, unsmiling now. "We have also alerted all installations in the San Francisco Bay area, Mare Island in particular, and on up the coast in Washington, although the threat there does not appear to be as great."

The assistant secretary said, "What is the estimated time of arrival of the first tsunami wave in the Southern California area you are most concerned about, Dr. Saunders?"

"One thirty-two P.M. their time"—Saunders glanced at his watch—"which will be in about twenty-eight minutes, four thirty-two P.M. here. Facilities are being put in place for filming and transmitting the . . . action. I am expecting a phone call—"

As if on cue, one of the phones on the secretary's desk buzzed softly. The secretary picked it up, listened briefly and held the phone out.

Accepting the phone, "Saunders," the scientific adviser said.

"Pete Williamson. Cameras are set up, and I understand that transmission facilities are in place. You'll have your pictures. Maybe not quite as good as the Hilo coverage was because we've got storm conditions, rainsqualls, flying spray, but you'll be able to watch the fun nonetheless."

"Good work." Saunders nodded approbation. "Is Garfield with you?"

There was a slight pause. "Negative," Pete said. "There's a . . . lost girl, and he—" His voice stopped. "That's the situation," he said. "We'll try to stay in touch."

Saunders hung up slowly. "We will have transmission," he said, and walked back to his chair in silence, thinking of Dan Garfield.

ಜ

Jimmy Silva, still in his short-sleeved aloha shirt, impervious to the growing cold, sat in the right-hand seat of the black-and-white patrol car, window down and bullhorn in hand, as they drove slowly up one empty residential street and down the next. "We keep our eyes open for a sixteen-year-old girl," Jimmy was saying, "and for anybody else is damn fool enough to hang around."

The cop driving was named Connors, and he was as large as His Honor and as burly, but becoming increasingly nervous now as he kept glancing surreptitiously at his wristwatch.

"Forget the time," Jimmy Silva told him. "We got plenty. The eggheads say one thirty-two, and they been right all along, so one thirty-two it is. At one twenty-two we start for the bluff, not before. Stop here!" He pointed at a lighted house window and raised the bullhorn. "Hello, the house!" he roared. "Anybody there?"

The light promptly went out, a door opened and a man appeared. "Who's asking?"

"Me! Jimmy Silva." Jimmy squinted in the gloom. "That you, Hornby? Then what in hell are you still doing here? You deaf? Can't you hear the sirens?"

"I heard them. I heard them last time, too. And nothing happened. So this time I'm not walking off and leaving my house open to any mother who wants to come in and take what he wants. By God—"

"I'm going to tell you once," Jimmy said, "and after that, if I have to, I'm going to get out of this car and knock you flat on your ass and throw you in the back seat—in handcuffs, if I have to. You got that? You haul ass for the bluff right now. You hear?"

"Now, look, Jimmy—"

His Honor threw open his door and started to get out. Hornby threw up his hands and backed away hastily. "Okay. Okay. You say so—"

"Goddamn it, you heard me say so!" Jimmy said. "Get into your car and haul ass out of here! We'll wait to see you do!"

At the wheel Connors looked nervously at his watch again. It was eight minutes past the hour. Suppose the eggheads, like Jimmy called them, were wrong by maybe only ten, fifteen minutes, he thought, what then?

"Okay," Jimmy said as they heard a car engine start up. "Let's move on. We still got plenty time."

❦

Joe Hines released the button on his microphone but left the transmitter power on as he looked around his office and through the doorway at the partially empty anchorage.

He had called, one by one, all of the boys he had sent to sea in large power cruisers, and to a man they were enjoying themselves, as he had privately guessed they would—each one in sole command of a magnificent power yacht, outside in heavy seas that to their young tastes were more fun by far than even moderate conditions. The experience beat surfing at Onofre by a mile, one said, or even crewing up in the midwinter regatta on the one day of good wind the regatta always seemed to have. Hey! next to this, another of the boys had told Joe, the downhill spinnaker run in the Honolulu race was tame! This was, as young Tommy Parks had said, a real blast!

Joe guessed he had done just about all that he could do—which was, he told himself for he didn't know the how-manyeth time, very damned little. He glanced at the nude on the wall. "You may not be here, honey, the next time I come back," he said. Smiling faintly, he guessed that was pretty much the story of his life—a woman here, a woman there, rarely the same one twice.

The wall clock said ten minutes past the hour. Another ten minutes just to see if anybody called with a problem. Then he'd shut her down and head for high ground—when he'd the hell of a lot rather have been at sea himself.

ʊ

Leery of the sand that extended from the road out to the rocks of the point, Todd parked the car as close as he dared, shut off the engine and turned to Garfield.

"I've been thinking while I was driving," he said, "and I don't remember any place big enough for even someone Lucy's size to hide in. There're a lot of indentations and crevices, like, but what I've seen from the water—" He shook his head.

"It's there," Garfield said. His voice held conviction. He had already opened his door, and the howling wind made his words hard to follow. "It's got to be!" he said in a louder voice as he stepped out. "Come on!"

Together, bent against the wind, they trotted out to the rocky extremity.

To Todd, the scene was like nothing he had seen before with seas far more monstrous and savage than any he could recall shattering themselves against the solid promontory, throwing up heavy spray that filled the air. Remembering the rock remnants he had taken Pete Williamson to see, he shivered as he tried to imagine what gigantic waves must have been responsible for shattering the rock and then carrying that much weight that far inland to higher ground.

Between surges of the seas as wave after wave crashed against the point, Todd led the way almost to the edge. Down there, as nearly as he could figure, was where the big moray eel made his home—a spot to be avoided by all skin divers but Pete Williamson, who seemed oblivious of the animal's razor teeth backed by intense, innate and belligerent ferocity.

Todd peered over the edge and saw only sheer rock with occasional shallow indentations and crevices, as he had said, nothing large enough to hide even someone Lucy's size. He looked at Garfield.

Garfield pointed left and right, sharp, commanding gestures, indicating that they were to separate. Todd nodded and started off in his direction shouting as he went. "Lucy!" he roared into the wind. "Damn it, girl, where the hell are you?"

Wherever she was, he thought as he made his way as fast as he dared along the top of the sheer face, she would be cold and soaked and scared—as she damn well deserved to be if she had indeed come out here, as Garfield seemed so sure she had.

That was the thing, one of the things, about this Garfield character, Todd found himself thinking: He *always* seemed so damned sure of himself. And even Pete—Dr. Williamson—seemed to accept the man's self-confidence as normal and natural. Well, he, Todd Wilson, walking with difficulty along the top of this cliff was not at all sure that he would go along with that judgment because he was beginning to doubt if even a birdbrain as any girl, Lucy included, sometimes seemed to be would have come out here at a time like this. She had to be somewhere else, damn it! But despite his doubts, he continued to hurry along and look and shout. "Lucy! You little fool, where in hell are you?"

He reached the end of possibility, where the rocky point turned inland, away from the crashing seas, and there he stopped, turned and began to retrace his steps. Damn it, girl, he thought, we're running out of time! We're—

He looked up then and saw Garfield, a hundred yards distant, staring down at the waves. And then he looked in Todd's direction and made imperative beckoning gestures, and Todd burst into a careful trot.

He reached Garfield and looked down at the water, following Garfield's pointing finger.

A seal had poked his head up through the turbulence and seemed to whuffle through extended whiskers as he looked around. A huge wave threatened, and only microseconds before it crashed against the rocks, the seal's head disappeared without seeming haste, to reappear only moments later again, looking around with casual interest after the wave had shattered itself against the rocks.

"Oh, hell!" Todd shouted into the wind. "They do it all the time! They seem to think it's fun playing like that, and the rougher it is, the better they like it!"

But Garfield was shaking his head and gesturing down the rock face, sure of himself as always, and all at once Todd understood. "Omigod!" he shouted. "Of course! This is where they always play, and if she said they could see her . . ."

Garfield nodded and, turning to face inland, began to let himself down the rock face, searching for footholds and handholds, his face set in concentration.

Todd followed, hastily, but with care. A slip and a fall here and, unlike the seal, either man would be finished, helpless against the smashing waves. And again, as he clambered down, Todd raised his voice: "Lucy! You little fool! Come out! Come out!"

Her head appeared first, looking around timidly, questioningly. Then slowly her shoulders emerged from an opening in the rocks Todd could not even see.

She had caught her lower lip between her teeth, and it was obvious that she was terrified. And wet; her hair was plastered to her head, and rivulets of water streamed down her cheeks. Her eyes stared imploringly at Todd. "Come on!" Todd shouted. "Come out of there! Damn it, move!"

But there was Garfield again, shaking his head, glancing at his watch, his face set and almost angry as he pointed toward Lucy and motioned for her to retreat into her shelter. "Go back!" Garfield shouted. And he looked at Todd and beckoned peremptorily.

The girl hesitated, obviously uncertain, but there was that in Garfield's face and manner that made her obey. She disappeared from Todd's view, and Garfield followed. Todd went after them.

It was a small cave, as Lucy had told Garfield. But it seemed to have no rear wall, and as Todd's eyes accustomed themselves to the near darkness, he could see that the cave went back into the rock, how far he could not tell, but what difference did it make?

"We can't stay here!" Todd said. "Damn it—"

"Look at your watch," Garfield said. "We have less time than it took us to get here from the house, and we'd still have to get through town, run the causeway, get to an uphill road and climb the bluff! We wouldn't have a chance! We stay here! There's no other course!"

Lucy, shivering, looked from one to the other.

"We'll drown in here," Todd said, "like—rats."

"That depends how deep this cave is and whether it narrows as it goes back in! Move it! Both of you!"

The cave made a bend, and another, as Garfield had guessed, narrowing as it went. They reached its end at last, in the total darkness crowded together, feeling a solid rear face. Garfield's voice in the darkness seemed to echo. "When the tsunami wave hits," he was saying, "it will compress the air in here. The air pressure may— it just may be enough to save us by keeping the water out, the same principle as air trapped inside a sunken submarine." His tone changed, seemed to lighten. "Anyway," he said, "it's our only chance. Sorry about that."

Lucy made a small, whimpering sound. In the blackness Todd found her slim shoulders with his arm and drew her close. "Easy," he said. "Easy. Let's hope he's right." He shook his head vaguely, suddenly finding strange comfort in the new thought. "He seems to have a habit of being right," he said into the girl's ear. "Let's hope for that."

Garfield was speaking again, slowly, distinctly, as if he wanted no mistake in understanding. "The pressure," he said, "is going to be intense. There isn't anything we can do about that except one thing. Keep your mouths open when the pressure starts to build. That will help to equalize the pressure inside and outside your head." He was silent for a long moment. "Now," he said, "we just wait."

⊗

On the bluff the TV cameras were in place and manned, and the transmitting equipment, including the dish aimed at the satellite, was ready. Maude had joined Pete and Daphne standing near the edge of the bluff with as good a view of the bay, the channel and the peninsula as possible in the rainsqualls and blowing spray. To their right in the far background was the point; to their left were the jetties and the sand beach that had been built up south and east of them by the prevailing coastwise current.

Pete said, his voice raised above the sounds of the wind, "We're three hundred feet and a bit above mean high water here. That will be plenty, although I expect we'll catch some heavy spray when the first tsunami wave hits."

Howard Boggs, the institute director, had moved over to join them. "You are still confident?" he asked Pete. "That, despite the broad continental shelf, the tsunami waves will come ashore?"

"You saw Hilo," Pete said, "and you can see what the breakers are doing to the shore outside right now—what do you think?"

Boggs produced one of his rare smiles. The expression seemed almost painful. "I am afraid I am convinced," he said. "Your predictions have been right all along, and I have no reason to doubt the accuracy of this one." He was silent for a few moments, surveying the scene. "I do not believe that anyone has ever been able to watch this kind of . . . event this well. And live to tell of it, that is. We are fortunate indeed."

"That," Daphne said, "is the proper, dispassionate, scientific viewpoint, I'm sure. I just don't happen to share it." She glanced at Maude, who was staring fixedly in the direction of the distant point. "I doubt if you do either," Daphne said, and impulsively put her arm around Maude's shoulders. "I am sorry," she said. "I truly am. He ought to be with us here now."

"He and Todd and the girl," Maude said, her eyes not leaving the distant point and the automobile parked on it—Todd's? Whose else? "Oh, please!" she said. "Please!"

Pete said gently, "Don't wish for them to show now. It's too late. They'd be caught in the open."

Maude caught her lower lip between her teeth. She released it with effort. "Then where? How can they be safe?"

"I don't know," Pete said. "But if there is a place or a way, he'll find it if anybody can. You can count on that."

One of the technicians standing nearby, binoculars raised, said, "I see a line—a swell. It's growing! Beyond the bell buoy! See it?"

Pete glanced at his watch. "On time to the minute," he said.

A cameraman said, "I've got it, but migod! it's moving toward us so fast I can hardly keep it in focus!"

Within only a brief moment the line that was becoming a fast-growing swell was clearly visible even without binoculars or long-focal-length camera lens.

To Pete, the scene was familiar both from his own film and from the transmitted pictures they had seen of Hilo. And the swell was curving to conform with the bottom contours as the incoming swells curved at San Onofre—inward, concentrating its energy, precisely as he had predicted. It would reach the point first, Pete decided, and wondered where at that moment Garfield was. He closed his eyes and hoped.

&

Within the dark cave they could hear it: a deep, distant, low-pitched, angry, rumbling sound that echoed and reverberated within their small rock chamber and seemed to shake the earth itself.

"Here it comes," Garfield said. He kept his voice determinedly calm. "Remember, keep your mouths open. It might even help to shout." And with only a momentary pause, he added, "Luck. To us all."

Lucy, still shivering, stood within the protective circle of Todd's arm, pressed tight against his strength, his solidity, trying to draw courage from his presence. "Last night—" she began in an unsteady voice.

"Forget last night," Todd said. His voice was sharp. "Just keep your mouth open. And when it comes, shout, like the man said." His arm tightened powerfully around her slim shoulders. "Damn it, it's going to be all right! You hear?"

"I . . . hear." And Lucy closed her eyes as if by the action she could shut out the terror she felt.

The pressure came first, with unbelievable speed and force, a blast of damp sea air heated faintly by compression. It seemed to explode against the rear wall of the small chamber and continued to build, stifling, throttling, overpowering the senses. The cave was filled with a roaring sound that defied belief.

Garfield's mouth was open wide, and he was shouting as hard as he could trying by the effort to keep nasal passages and eustachian tubes open to equalize the pressure that threatened to burst his eardrums. His mind felt dizzy, and he was aware that he was blacking out. The roaring sound grew in intensity around him, and heavy salt spray drenched him from head to toe. Or was it solid water? No matter. It was the end. He tried to breathe and could not.

The last thing he remembered was that at least Maude was safe.

20

On the top of the bluff Jimmy Silva had appeared, and with him Joe Hines. They stood silent, looking seaward, watching the growing swell as the cameras whirred on. Because of the sheer dropoff on the ocean side of the point, they were unable to see the now-enormous swell as it met the rocks, but the solid sheet of water flung skyward at impact high above the top of the rocks told the story all too well.

They watched in near disbelief as that sheet of water, now reinforced from behind, crashed down upon the top of the point. It caught up the parked car, threw it high into the air, as if it were a toy, caught it again and by some quirk of mechanics carried it forward, born high on the swell's crest across the land to slam it finally down into the waters of the bay, where it immediately disappeared.

Pete said, "Look at the channel! That incoming wave is thirty feet high and still building!"

"More like forty," Joe Hines said. "Houses on that mainland bluff are sixty feet above high water." He was remembering the chief's tales of the China Station and typhoons and worse, and himself, then only a boy, not knowing whether to believe or not. Well, he believed them now, he told himself.

Jimmy Silva said, "There go the first houses! See there, middle of the peninsula! And the wave isn't even slowing!"

It was not. The huge mass of solid water was sweeping across the peninsula, burying houses within its monstrous body, bringing the sea itself across the land until the ocean and the bay were one, the peninsula no longer visible.

Still the wave swept on, its top a dirty whitish gray color now, frothing as a breaker froths, neither slowing nor collapsing in the manner of surf but, rather, continuing its relentless surge across the bay, the island and the causeway.

It reached and engulfed the coast highway and slammed itself at last against the solid mass of the high bluff with a crash and a shock that could be both heard and felt by those above as if they had witnessed a massive underground explosion.

Solid water and spray flew high and fell like a cloudburst on the onlookers, leaving them drenched and cold and partially stunned.

One of the cameramen spat, wiped his mouth with the back of one hand and spat again. "We ought to get underwater pay," he said. No one even smiled.

Unbelievably, almost as rapidly as it had come, the water began to recede, seeming to flow downhill like a gigantic stretch of river rapids. The backwash uncovered the bay, the scattered, battered and smashed boats, helpless and pitiful, torn from their moorings and cast about as jetsam. It uncovered the peninsula, displaying wreckage of the cheek-by-jowl houses, some shattered, some still partially standing in drunken attitudes as if the slightest push would bring them, too, crashing to the ground.

What remained of the beach on the ocean side of the peninsula was gradually visible again, but what had been smooth, plump contours were now scoured into gaunt, jagged stretches of rock, with wreckage of shattered houses carried seaward by the backwash strewn along the littoral as far as one could see.

The entire process had taken only a matter of a minute or so. And now all was again changed.

The seas retained their storm character, the wind still gusting in howling fury, still snatching spray from wave tops, still driving streaks of foam downwind in the roiling seas. But the monster wave was suddenly gone, retreated back into its watery lair, its fury spent, and the scene, instead of turbulently chaotic, seemed by comparison almost peaceful.

Pete said, in a voice that was not quite steady, "Curtain. End of Act One." He looked at Daphne. "Stay here!" He turned away.

Daphne said, "Where are you going? Unless you tell me—"

"I'm going looking." Pete's voice was low-pitched, angry. "I don't know what I'm going to find, but I'm going to be alone when I find it. Is that clear?" He turned away again and trotted down the wet and muddy road toward what was left of the coast highway, a small, lonely figure.

Daphne moved to follow, but Maude stopped her. "Stay with me," Maude said. "Please!" There was that in her voice that was difficult to refuse.

Daphne hesitated. Boggs said, "I believe he will be all right. He has been right in his thinking all along, and now—" He produced again that apparently painful smile. It was somehow reassuring.

"I'll try to keep an eye on him," Jimmy Silva said, and lumbered off down the muddy road.

❦

In the secretary's Washington office, a navy captain moved quietly across the deep carpet to the chair where the senior admiral sat. He bent to whisper in the admiral's ear.

"Right," the admiral said after listening quietly for a few moments. "Carry on." To the secretary he said, "Reports from San Diego and San Pedro, sir, indicate only minor damage from a seiche condition in the harbors."

"Seiche?" the secretary said.

"Oscillation of the water within the harbor," Harry Saunders said, "undoubtedly caused by what was happening outside. The water sloshes in a manner analogous to that of coffee sloshing in a cup. At the node, the center of movement, the effect is minimal, but at the edges the movements may be severe. I would imagine that slips and docks and wharves and any craft near them would have sustained the most damage."

"That is correct," the admiral said.

"I would say," the secretary said, "that unlike the city of Hilo and now this community of—Encino Beach? we have been lucky." He was looking at Saunders and frowning faintly. "Is this kind of . . . haphazard destruction usual?"

"There is no way of predicting it." Saunders shook his head faintly and corrected himself. "At least until now there have been no reliable predictions. Williamson and Garfield seem to have called the shots with astonishing accuracy." He smiled. "Even in the face of conventional skepticism."

"I believe we owe them thanks," the secretary said.

Saunders nodded, smiling no longer. "Yes," he said. "I just hope Garfield is still around to receive it."

§

Pete, still trotting as at his morning workouts along the beach, had reached the causeway now, and he paused briefly to study it. It was a low concrete-and-steel structure leading from the mainland across a broad inlet and mud flat to the island and then to the base of the peninsula. It was designed to carry two lanes of automobile traffic in each direction, and it seemed solid enough, but as Pete watched, one eight-foot section of two lanes of roadway without warning collapsed.

Behind Pete, panting from effort, Jimmy Silva said, "Better wait and see if the rest goes, too."

Pete shook his head, never taking his eyes from the causeway. "There's not that much time. The next wave—"

"You mean we get more of this?" His Honor's voice was incredulous.

"There'll be more waves," Pete said. "Maybe worse, maybe not. We'll just have to wait and see. They'll be a little less than an hour apart. So—" All at once he was running, not trotting, along the white line in the center of the two remaining lanes.

Jimmy watched him go.

Pete reached the area where the other two lanes had collapsed, and increased his pace to a sprint. The roadway held. Ten strides beyond the danger area Pete slowed to his steady, accustomed trot. In moments the still-standing wreckage of one of the boatyard buildings hid him from Jimmy's view.

Through the town's devastation, Pete jogged on, avoiding fallen debris, hurdling minor obstacles, through the edge of the town and as directly as the wreckage allowed toward the point, which was where Maude had said Garfield and Todd were headed.

Here he passed the body of a dog, and there a baby carriage smashed almost beyond recognition but, he saw as he went by, happily empty. He glanced only once in the general direction of his own small house, saw total destruction and did not look again but trotted on, his face set and determined.

He had little hope that he would find anyone alive; the havoc caused by the single, gigantic wave had been too complete. And maybe—the thought passed quickly through his mind, and he put it angrily aside—maybe, no, probably he was embarked on a fool's errand, a foolish act of juvenile braggadocio which could seem as if he were trying to make himself look heroic. So, okay. The hell with what anybody thought. He did not slow his steady pace.

Daphne had said that he, Pete, revered Garfield, and Pete had denied it. But he could not deny his admiration for the man, nor could he even question the affection he felt for him after all this time of their collaboration. He had never met anyone like Garfield, Pete had told Daphne, and that much was certainly true. But there was more, much more, none of which could fit into words.

And so he trotted on, out what was left of the road Todd had driven, to the place where Todd's car had been parked when the wave caught it, and there he paused to look around.

The top of the rocky point had been scoured clean of earth and vegetation. It was bare rock now, still wet, shining, in places showing small rivulets of water, tiny streams flowing down the slope.

A place where only the seals could see her, Maude had reported from Garfield's explanation of Lucy's secret place. Pete knew the point from the seaward side as intimately as he knew his own living room. That moray eel in particular had fascinated him, and at times he had even tried to cavort in calm water with some of the seals in their own special area, which was well away from that of the eel. Without hesitation he trotted toward the area where the seals cavorted.

He reached it and from the edge of the cliff looked down. Seals were there, apparently unharmed by even the tsunami's enormous turbulence, their agility and strength in the water unimaginable.

But of a cave he could see no trace. Nor was there anything else but rock and crashing water, howling wind until—

He saw a movement. A hand emerged from the rock. It seemed to grope almost blindly for support, a man's hand, muscled, strong, a young hand—

"Todd!" Pete shouted. "Todd, boy! Hang on!" And he let himself gingerly down the cliff's face, ignoring the spray and the waves that seemed to be trying to reach him, one foothold, one handhold at a time until, stretching to his utmost, he could reach the hand and grasp it. "Out!" he shouted. "I've got you!"

Todd's head appeared. He was blinking hard, and his eyes did not seem to be quite in focus, but there was strength in the fingers that grasped Pete's wrist as Pete was grasping his, a double grip, more secure than a mere handshake.

Pete pulled, pulled harder, but the boy's efforts resisted him. "The . . . others!" Todd said. "They're here! Lucy! Garfield!"

"Okay," Pete said, and could not resist a triumphant smile. It was hard not to shout aloud in relief. "You first. Find a secure position. Then pass the princess out. Then Garfield. Got it?"

❧

From the top of the bluff, Daphne, standing with her arm still around Maude, had watched Pete's progress across the causeway, into the town, where he had disappeared, and then watched him again as he reappeared and headed for the point.

With one hand she plucked the binoculars from a cameraman nearby with a "Thank you. There's a good chap," raised and focused the glasses and watched Pete bending over the edge of the bluff and then letting himself down to disappear again.

Daphne lowered the glasses. She took a deep breath and looked at Maude. "There has to be something, somebody, or he wouldn't be doing that." She paused. "I hope," she added.

Maude said, "Is it . . . possible?"

"I was not even thought of at the time of the blitz," Daphne said, "but I was raised on tales of miraculous rescues when all hope was long gone." She made herself smile. "That is all I can tell you. I am sorry. He—"

A distant movement caught her eye, and she raised the glasses again to see Lucy's head appear above the rock, then the rest of her body, and finally Pete's strong arm coming into view as he gave a final heave with his hand on Lucy's slim buttocks. The girl almost fell forward and then staggered upright, safe on the top.

"One up!" Daphne murmured in triumph. And she added, "Lecherous beast, clutching her young bottom like that." She was smiling, and the green eyes seemed to dance. "Have a look yourself," she told Maude, and held out the glasses. "I fancy there are more to come."

Next Garfield, finally, weakly reaching the top, standing, swaying faintly, breathing deep, his head turned in the direction of the bluff. Slowly he raised one hand and waved it, thumb and forefinger circled. Maude could see it through the glasses and was afraid that tears would come again. Miraculously they did not. Instead, she found that she could smile as she handed the glasses back to Daphne, who raised them again.

"There is the young man," Daphne said, "Todd, I believe. I have seen him around. And there comes Peter, herding his flock like a Highland Scots shepherd. All he lacks is a border collie." Smiling broadly, she lowered the glasses and handed them back to the cameraman with a nod of thanks. To Maude she said only, "There will be tales to tell. I shall enjoy hearing them."

Maude closed her eyes. She felt weak, empty, drained of all emotion except relief; but the smile that was on her lips and in her mind would not, could not be denied, and nothing else mattered. "So shall I," she said. "So shall I."

21

Sixteen-year-old Tommy Parks brought *Lubelle* into the Long Beach Harbor with confident caution, picked up and followed the harbormaster's pilot boat into a designated anchorage, brought *Lubelle* to a stop precisely where ordered and, nimble as a squirrel, left the wheel and scuttled forward to let go the anchor.

Both engines secured, cabin and wheelhouse locked, seabag over his shoulder, he dropped down into the shore boat for the short passage to the improvised welcome shed that had been set up.

To the coast guard officer keeping the log of arrivals, Tommy said, "Yacht *Lubelle,* Encino Beach Yacht Club, at anchor, safe and sound." It was difficult to keep pride out of his voice.

A large, bearded man, wearing a worn blue uniform coat with four stripes on the sleeves said, "Welcome ashore, Captain." He took Tommy's arm in one huge paw. "In here. There's a drink waiting. You deserve it."

Tommy opened his mouth to protest his age, closed it again in silence and nodded. "Much obliged, Captain," he said. It was hard not to laugh aloud with joy.

&

Motor sailer *Lydia,* Olaf at the wheel, and Lydia at lookout in the bow, came into the Encino Beach channel at slow speed past the devastation of the peninsula and into the open water of the bay. Olaf gave the floating hulk of a stoved-in cabin cruiser a wide berth, throttled his engine down even more and looked around.

"The ruins of Carthage must have looked something like this," he said, and smiled at Lydia. "No matter. We are home. Where we belong."

&

The yacht *Westerly* put into Long Beach, too. Tom Winslow at the wheel said, "Easy. They said on the radio that she's fine. She—"

Clara said, "There she is! See? On the float?"

"I see," Winslow said. He kept his voice carefully expressionless. "And she looks to be in one piece. Isn't that Todd with her?"

"You men," Clara said. There were tears in her eyes. "You have no feelings. None at all." She was smiling fondly, the tears unnoticed.

"That's us," Tom said. "No emotions at all." He, too, was smiling. "Let's get anchored and go ashore."

&

It was a coast guard cutter that located, towed to sea and destroyed what was left of the yacht *Spindrift,* owner Jack Barnes. "Didn't give himself enough sea room," the coast guard skipper said. "Or maybe his engine quit on him." He shrugged. "Could have been any one of a number of causes. Just log the boat's name and number."

"Somebody had to be aboard," the second-in-command said. "Maybe he was washed overboard."

"They'll probably never find him," the skipper said. "It's a big ocean. Let's proceed. There'll be others, how many, nobody can even guess. Our job is to find as many as we can."

The second-in-command said, "We may never know the count, you know that?" He had never thought of it before. "Maybe some just put to sea, nobody knew about it, so nobody misses them—how about that?"

"It's happened before," the skipper said. "No doubt it will happen again. Let's get under way."

Epitaph

Postscript

Five hours in time but, because of the international date line, also a day after the first tsunami wave had reached Hawaii, it rolled its might down upon the Japanese islands of Kyushu, Shikoku, Honshu and Hokkaido.

Of all the harbors on these four islands, Yokohama suffered the worst damage, which was duly recorded on videotape, a copy of which Harry Saunders obtained for the Encino Beach Oceanographic Institute.

Pete, Garfield and Howard Boggs watched in silence as the cassette picture on the console television screen in Boggs's office detailed the destruction.

"We fancy ourselves masters of our environment," Pete said when the film was done. "But what happened in Hilo, and here, in Cook Inlet and Juneau and in that village on the coast of Chile, as well as a hundred other places around the Pacific rim that suffered less damage—against that, we are totally helpless. Ironic, isn't it? We're just visitors on the skin of the planet, flies on a horse's back. Ironic, isn't it?" He was looking at Garfield. "You're thinking what?"

"Why greater damage some places than others?" Garfield said. "Configuration of the land, bottom contours, ocean currents or prevailing winds that cause deflection—what are the factors involved?"

Boggs raised his eyebrows faintly. "Mere idle curiosity, Mr. Garfield," he said, "or is it deeper than that?"

"If we knew more," Garfield said, "might we not be able to issue more precise warnings? Other, more specific predictions than time of arrival and approximate strength of the waves?"

Pete blew out his cheeks in a soundless whistle. "Sure we might. And more specific predictions would be valuable. No argument. But how do you gather the data on which to make the predictions?"

Boggs's eyes had not left Garfield's face. He was even smiling faintly, but he said nothing.

"What we've just gone through," Garfield said, "happens how often? Once in a hundred years? Five hundred? A thousand? But the experience is fresh right now. There are eyewitnesses, films, tidal gauge measurements, destruction that can be studied, analyzed—it's all available now, and in five, ten years, it won't be."

"So," Pete said, irony plain, "you're suggesting that somebody spends the next couple, three years visiting all the sites, gathering the data, and the next year or two trying to make sense out of it? Is that what you have in mind?"

Garfield was smiling. "Why not?" He looked at Boggs. "A worthy project?"

Boggs's smile had disappeared, carefully removed and hidden. "I would think so," he said. "But there is the matter of funding, of course—" He shook his head and left it there.

Garfield's nod was solemn, his face expressionless. "Yes. There is that." He looked again at Pete. "How about it? Care to do some traveling? The two of us?" He paused and the smile returned. "Or maybe four of us?"

Pete closed his eyes and thought of Daphne standing in front of the large wall map of the Pacific, reading the names of the islands and asking him if he would care to take her to them one day. He opened his eyes again. "What you're doing," he said, "is offering candy to a child, friend. If you're serious—" He shook his head slowly. "Are you?"

"I am. I'll fund the project."

"Then sign me on," Pete said. "For the whole cruise."

❦

Jimmy Silva and Joe Hines flew over the entire Encino Beach area in a chopper. "Bottom line," Jimmy reported later, "is that there ain't the whole hell of a lot left for me to be mayor of. And you"— he looked at Joe Hines —"are harbormaster without much of a harbor." Jimmy was resilient, and he had regained his sense of humor. "But we'll rebuild her," he said. "Bigger and better than before. You watch and see."

❦

Maude was at home in her Westwood apartment when Garfield arrived. "I've been waiting," she said.

"I've been busy. Sorry."

"I guessed that. And there have been telephone calls for you, people trying to reach you. The list is by the phone."

Garfield picked it up and read from it, "Walker Carmichael, Paul Case, Hawkins of Atlas—" He put the list down. He was smiling. "Names out of the past, out of another life. I'm finished with that."

"Are you sure, Dan?" She watched him steadily.

Garfield sat down. "I blacked out in that cave," he said. "I knew I was going to. I guess I was ready for it, or as ready as I could be. I was thinking of only one thing. Do you know what that was?"

She sat silent, waiting.

"You," Garfield said. "All the rest, including that past, is unim-

portant. I won't go back. Ever. I'm going forward into a new life."
He paused. "Will you come with me?"

She could relax then, savoring the moment, a growing smile
lighting her face, her eyes, bringing warmth into her mind. "I will
come with you," she said, "wherever you want to go."